ROCK THE

Rage and Rebellion

SMON & SCHUSTER
New York   London   Toronto   Sydney

CASBAH

across the Islamic World

Robin Wright

Simon & Schuster
1230 Avenue of the Americas
New York, NY 10020

First Simon & Schuster hardcover edition July 2011

SIMON & SCHUSTER and colophon are registered trademarks
of Simon & Schuster, Inc.

For information about special discounts for bulk purchases,
please contact Simon & Schuster Special Sales at
1-866-506-1949 or business@simonandschuster.com.

The Simon & Schuster Speakers Bureau can bring authors
to your live event. For more information or to book an event,
contact the Simon & Schuster Speakers Bureau at
1-866-248-3049 or visit our website at www.simonspeakers.com.

Designed by Renata Di Biase

Manufactured in the United States of America

10   9   8   7   6   5   4   3   2   1

Library of Congress Cataloging-in-Publication Data

Wright, Robin B., date.
   Rock the Casbah : rage and rebellion across the Islamic world /
by Robin Wright. —1st Simon & Schuster hardcover ed.
      p.   cm.
   1. Islamic countries—Politics and government—21st century.   2. Islam
and politics—Islamic countries.   3. Social movements—Islamic countries.
4. Muslims—Political activity—Islamic countries.   5. Radicalism—Islamic
countries—Public opinion.   6. Public opinion—Islamic countries.   I. Title.
   JQ1758.A58W75   2011
   322.40917'67—dc23   2011017355
ISBN 978-1-4391-0316-6
ISBN 978-1-4391-2306-5 (ebook)

For friends who have tolerated my lifelong writing deadlines,
for colleagues who have generously guided me,
and especially for the next generation—
Alexandra Hart Brown, Cameron Platter, and
Nonhlanhla Robin Sithole

CONTENTS

ROCK
THE
CASBAH

PROLOGUE

The Sandstorm

We are no longer afraid.

—Egyptian protester

The most important story of the early twenty-first century is the epic convulsion across the Islamic world. Rage against geriatric autocrats is only one part of it. Most of the region—stretching across three continents, from Morocco on the Atlantic to Indonesia on the Pacific—is also actively rebelling against radical ideologies. Muslim societies are now moving beyond jihadism, not only because of the dramatic death of Osama bin Laden on May 2, 2011.

I sometimes feel as if I've finally reached the climax—although not the end—of an epic book that has taken four decades to read. Since 1973, I've traveled most of the region's fifty-seven countries and covered its wars, military coups, revolutions, and terrorism spectaculars. I witnessed extremism's early outbursts, from Iran's 1979 revolution to the 1983 suicide bombing that killed 241 American peacekeepers in Lebanon. In the 1990s, as the trend took wider root, I drove the Khyber Pass to Afghanistan during the Taliban's rule. In Pakistan, I met members of the murderous Army of the Righteous at their training camp. Over four decades, I've interviewed many militant ideologues, from Hamas leaders in Syria and Gaza to the Hezbollah chief in Lebanon and Saudi fighters who fought with bin Laden at Tora Bora.

It's been one of the most tumultuous times since Islam was founded in the seventh century. But after a decade defined largely by the 9/11 attacks, the region is moving toward a different denouement. Two dynamic twists are changing the plotline.

First, from mighty Egypt to Islamic Iran, tiny Tunisia to quirky Libya, new players are shattering the old order. Uprisings in the Middle East—breathtaking in scope and speed, if unnerving in their uncertain futures—represent the greatest wave of empowerment worldwide in the early twenty-first century.

"I was one of the sleeping majority," said an excited Egyptian protester, as he made his way to Cairo's Liberation Square during the 2011 uprising against President Hosni Mubarak. "But now I've woken up."[1]

The awakening has involved hundreds of millions of people. And the political transformations—and tectonic changes—are only beginning.

Second, the far wider Muslim world is increasingly rejecting extremism. The many forms of militancy—from the venomous Sunni creed of al Qaeda to the punitive Shiite theocracy in Iran—have proven costly, unproductive, and ultimately unappealing.

On a balmy evening in 2009, I dined at an open-air restaurant along Jeddah's palm-fringed Corniche with a prominent Saudi editor, his wife, and some of their friends. Two of the men were smoking hubbly-bubbly water pipes. "The jihadis have lost their appeal," reflected Khaled al Maeena, the editor of *Arab News.*

"Every mother in Saudi Arabia or any other Gulf country wants her son or daughter to carry a laptop rather than a rifle or a dagger," he said. "The appeal of death and destruction doesn't carry much significance anymore because the jihadis have failed to provide anything constructive."

The transformation did not happen suddenly. Stirred by the young and stoked by new technology, rage against both autocrats and extremists has been building steadily within Muslim societies. I spent two years going back to key corners of the Islamic world to track the new trends; I talked to Muslims from dozens of countries to identify key trendsetters. The original goal was a book about what happened within the Islamic world in the pivotal decade since 9/11. When I started out, the project represented an intellectual risk in an environment not yet willing to embrace its counterintuitive themes. But the evidence since then—in bold acts of defiance as well as poignant personal stories—is now overwhelming. The rage and rebellions are visible for all to see.

Today, the Islamic world is in the midst of an extreme makeover politically. Its diverse societies are also moving to a different rhythm culturally. Together, they are now inspiring an array of imaginative rebellions.

Neither twist should have come as a surprise, even if they were little understood until raucous uprisings began to sweep across the region in 2011. For a decade, the outside world was so preoccupied with its "war on terrorism" that it gave little credence to efforts among Muslims to deal with the overlapping problems—autocratic regimes and extremist movements—that fed off each other. Extremism emerged largely to challenge autocrats in countries where the opposition was outlawed, exiled, under house arrest, or executed. And autocrats justified not opening up politically on grounds that extremists would take over.

As I traveled, I was struck by the disparate range of political rebellions. They fall into three broad categories. Each has its own characteristics. Specific catalysts have varied. So have the opposition movements. But the accumulative impact has produced a history-making phenomenon.

One category covers the Arab revolts, which have erupted in homogeneous societies as well as deeply sectarian countries, in military dictatorships as well as monarchies, in modern states as well as traditional tribal nations, in pitifully poor countries as well as oil-rich sheikhdoms. As of 2011, every one of the twenty-two Arab countries faced a serious political challenge. And every single one of them will come out different in some significant way, even in countries that forcibly tried to put down the uprisings.

The second category is the counter-jihad, which is unfolding in the wider Islamic bloc of fifty-seven countries as well as among Muslim minorities worldwide. The counter-jihad is the rejection of specific violent movements as well as the principle of violence to achieve political goals. It has been palpable since 2007, as Saudi and Egyptian clerics who were once bin Laden's ideological mentors began to publicly repudiate al Qaeda. Iraq's tribal leaders mobilized a militia of 90,000 people to push al Qaeda of Mesopotamia out of the most volatile province. Pakistanis turned on the local Taliban commanders. Indian Muslims marched against their militant brethren who engaged in terrorist attacks.

Every reliable poll since 2007 shows steadily declining support for the destructive and disruptive jihadis, even in communities where politics are partly shaped by the Arab-Israeli conflict. The counter-jihad has been especially evident among Sunni Muslims, who account for more than 80 percent of the Islamic world.

The third category is the rebellion against Islamic ideology, which is most typified by Iran. Its Shiite theocracy—in the first state to be ruled by clerics since the faith was founded fourteen centuries ago—had redefined the world's political spectrum after its 1979 revolution. It became the hub for movements that then altered the political landscape in countries with Shiite pluralities, such as large, oil-rich Iraq and little Lebanon, a longtime bridge between East and West. Shiites account for between 12 and 15 percent of the Muslim world's 1.57 billion people.

But in 2009, millions of outraged Iranians launched multifaceted civil disobedience against the regime after a disputed presidential election. The streets in several cities echoed with chants of "Where's my vote?" The peaceful protests evolved over the next six months into an outright rejection of rigid theocratic rule. They included economic boycotts and social media campaigns as well as street demonstrations. Tehran's theocrats used every ruthless tactic—mass arrests, prison rapes and torture, Stalinesque show trials, and executions—but the new opposition refused to submit. The Green Movement tried again in 2011. The theocrats got even tougher, persecuting men with stellar revolutionary credentials. But the Islamic Republic, the prickliest thorn for other Muslim nations as well as the West, only appeared more desperate—and more vulnerable than at any time since its revolution.

In each category, the rebellions are far from over. The process of change launched in late 2010 may ripple on—in diverse forms and bumpy phases—for years. Many of the new movements still face staggering obstacles; countries may face long periods of political uncertainty and economic instability along the way. Transformation is inevitably messy. In the Islamic world, it is complicated by the price of and access to oil, sectarian and ethnic divisions, the Arab-Israeli conflict, Iran's controversial nuclear program, Pakistan's nuclear capability, and border disputes, to name but a few issues. Then throw in poverty.

The bottom line: Uprisings produce a heady euphoria and sense of hope. The day after confronts raw realities, including the quest for credible leadership and solutions to wrenching problems. No country will get through its transition quickly or painlessly. Expectations will never be met fast enough. History is also replete with rebellions derailed.

Yet the drive to be part of the twenty-first century—rather than get stuck in the status quo of the twentieth century or revert to the ways of the seventh century—now consumes the Islamic world.

The profound political stirrings are supported by a strong culture of change. In the struggle to define their place in the twenty-first century,

Muslims have become quite creative in many other idioms as well. The social transformations are as pivotal as the political upheavals. Activists are not only adapting the technology of Facebook and Twitter to their causes. They are also experimenting with culture—from comedy to theater, poetry to song—as an idiom to communicate who they are and to end isolation caused by extremists within their ranks.

The message resonates in comedians' jokes and sermons from young satellite sheikhs, in playwrights' plots and poetry contests, in underground music clubs and women's self-empowerment sessions, in new comic book superheroes and hip-hop songs. They often reach an even wider audience than the political protests. Muslims in the West, especially the United States, are playing lead roles in creating a different public face for the Islamic world.

The themes are daring and defiant. The lyrics of Kiosk, an underground Iranian rap group, boldly challenged the fanaticism, repression, hypocrisy, and hidden depravity of Tehran's theocratic regime.

> *Immoral zealots, fanatic factions,*
> *Chinese-style economic expansions.*
> *Smuggling women to Dubai,*
> *Our noble men turning a blind eye.*
> *Foreign currencies are reserved,*
> *Border movements all observed.*
> *Oil-dependent economy is hooked,*
> *Incentive vacations overbooked.*
> *Counterfeit medication,*
> *Addiction as a recreation.*

During Iran's 2009 presidential election, the campaign of opposition candidate Mehdi Karroubi—a septuagenarian cleric—distributed one thousand CDs of hip-hop songs that rapped with pro-democracy messages.[2] As elsewhere in the Islamic world, both the medium and the message were changing.

AL QAEDA IS not dead, even with bin Laden's death ten years after 9/11. But it is increasingly passé. In the post-jihadist era, the movement is out of touch with both events and its audience.

The terror network issued a video communiqué after the Egyptian uprising that ousted Hosni Mubarak in February 2011. In a world timed more to warp-speed Twitter and cell phone texting, the thirty-four-minute videotape seemed from a bygone era.

The tape was made by Ayman al Zawahiri, an Egyptian physician who had been arrested with hundreds of militants after President Anwar Sadat's assassination in 1981. He served three years on weapons charges, then went into exile. He became leader of Egypt's Islamic Jihad, plotted against the Egyptian government, and later merged forces with bin Laden. He was widely considered the real brains behind al Qaeda. For more than a quarter century, he advocated violence to end Mubarak's rule.

But in the end, as Zawahiri began his tenth year in hiding on another continent, Mubarak was ousted by peaceful civil disobedience. The uprising took a mere eighteen days.

Al Qaeda took almost that long just to get its crude videotape posted. It was roughly dated in the Islamic lunar month of Safar between January 5 and February 3. The message indicated it was made in the early stages of Egypt's upheaval, which began on January 25. But it was not posted on a militant Islamist website until February 18—a full week after Mubarak resigned—and still made no mention of the transition of power. So it was at least two or three weeks out of date.[3]

The message also seemed antiquated. Al Qaeda's manifesto promoted creation of Islamist states. On the tape, Zawahiri rambled on for a half hour about Egyptian history since the eighteenth century, the country's disintegration since Ottoman rule, and the role of Western colonial powers in installing secular rule.

He opined that democracy "can only be nonreligious," as if that discredited freedom.[4] He was totally out of touch with the new Egyptian reality—and the growing demands for democracy elsewhere. Zawahiri's communiqué finally made it to the outside world on a weekend of demonstrations demanding liberty in Iran, Yemen, Libya, Bahrain, Morocco, Jordan, and Kuwait—events all posted on YouTube almost as fast as they happened.

In contrast, al Qaeda's tape combined a tedious audio over a still photo of Zawahiri, whose scraggly, untrimmed beard had grown white during his long battle in exile.

Al Qaeda is not finished. Its franchises will almost certainly try and try again. South Asia particularly offers volatile passions and deep problems to exploit. But the movement's remaining leaders and believers also have few options. They cannot simply acknowledge a new era and come in from the cold, as the Soviets did in suddenly becoming Russians when communism proved impractical and their empire collapsed. Al Qaeda's leaders are cornered, politically and physically. Or rather, they have cornered themselves.

More important, the movement has now lost the psychological edge, its most potent asset. Terrorism, in the end, can never win a war. It can only terrorize people enough to scare them into complying with extremists or making concessions.

The political uprisings and the broader culture of change have demonstrated how much al Qaeda has miscalculated, beginning with the 9/11 attacks that scared and alienated many Muslims too. A decade later, its strategic goal—of seizing a Muslim state and recreating the old caliphate—seemed almost silly. In a long treatise after 9/11, Zawahiri wrote,

> Liberating the Muslim nation, confronting the enemies of Islam, and launching jihad against them require a Muslim authority, established on a Muslim land that raises the banner of jihad and rallies the Muslims around it. Without achieving this goal, our actions will mean nothing more than mere and repeated disturbances that will not lead to the aspired goal.[5]

Al Qaeda has killed many, mostly its own brethren. But it has otherwise achieved nothing.

Even one of bin Laden's sons disowned the 9/11 attacks and condemned the movement. Omar bin Laden, who spent five years in Afghanistan and was there on 9/11, called the attacks acts of "craziness."

"Those guys are dummies. They have destroyed everything, and for nothing," he reportedly said. "What did we get from September 11?"[6]

A decade later, al Qaeda's goals seemed further away than ever. Compared with the vast number of democracy activists, cultural innovators, and new voices in the Islamic world, al Qaeda's extremists looked like pathetic thugs and losers.

* * *

After the Cold War ended in 1991, the notion of a "clash of civilizations" defined debates over the world's new ideological divide. It was always a somewhat arrogant concept. It was also simplistically summarized as a global split between Muslims and the rational rest.

"The crescent-shaped Islamic bloc, from the bulge of Africa to central Asia, has bloody borders," Samuel Huntington wrote in his controversial 1993 *Foreign Affairs* piece, as if countries with other religions had not initiated warfare or engaged in repression.[7] (Ten years later, the United States invaded Iraq on grounds that proved untrue. The US military presence has dragged on for almost a decade.)

Huntington concluded,

> The fundamental source of conflict in this new world will not be primarily ideological or primarily economic. The great divisions among humankind and the dominating source of conflict will be cultural . . . The conflicts of the future will occur along the cultural fault lines separating civilizations.[8]

The idea of a civilizational schism ignored an alternative truth: Even as the outside world tried to segregate Muslims as "others," particularly after 9/11, most Muslims were increasingly trying to integrate into, if not imitate, a globalizing world.

The Islamic world also no longer has identifiable borders. It now extends far beyond the fifty-seven predominantly Muslim countries on three continents, from Bosnia in Europe to Bangladesh in South Asia, from Iraq in the Gulf to Indonesia on the Pacific, from Tunisia on the Mediterranean to Turkmenistan on the Caspian. In the early twenty-first century, more than one out of every five individuals is Muslim, and they live on all six inhabited continents. Most do not speak Arabic, the language of the Koran.

The world's five largest Muslim populations—Indonesia, Pakistan, India, Bangladesh, and Turkey—have vastly different cultures, languages, races, and ethnic groups. None of them are Arab. And none are even in the Middle East, where the faith was founded in the seventh century.

India has the third-largest Muslim population—some 164 million people—even though it is a minority. China has more Muslims than Iraq. Russia, which has the largest Muslim population in Europe, has more Muslims than Jordan and Libya combined. Ethiopia has about as many Muslims as Afghanistan.[9] Islam is growing among Australia's Aborigines and on the tiny Caribbean islands of Trinidad and Tobago.[10] Argentina has the largest Muslim population in Latin America.[11] Only 15 percent of the 1.57 billion Muslims today are Arabs.

The Muslim world is also not over there, far away, somewhere. Islam is the fastest-growing religion in the United States. There are mosques in every corner of the country, from Arizona to Alaska, Minnesota to Maine, Washington state to Washington, DC. Even Salt Lake City, the home of America's Mormons, has a mosque.

A few American Muslims have indeed turned to terrorism. At the top of the list is Anwar al Awlaki, who was born in New Mexico, graduated from Colorado State University, and enrolled in a doctoral program at George Washington University in the nation's capital.[12] He fled to Yemen in 2004, where he has allegedly engaged in fund-raising, recruiting, training, and plotting attacks for al Qaeda in the Arabian Peninsula. His acolytes are linked to several recent plots to attack the United States. Both the United States and the United Nations have designated him a terrorist.

But the overwhelming majority of Muslim Americans have integrated in academia, the arts, business, government, the media, the law, medicine, sports, even space. Some have become quite famous in widely diverse ways.

Keith Ellison became the first Muslim member of Congress in 2007. The Minnesota lawmaker took the oath of office on a Koran once owned by Thomas Jefferson. Dr. Mehmet Oz, a cardiothoracic surgeon, became a popular talk-show doctor in 2009 after appearing on *Oprah;* six of his books on health were best sellers. Mohamed El-Erian is CEO of PIMCO, the world's largest bond investment company, with assets of over $1 trillion. He previously managed Harvard University's endowment fund, worth billions. Ahmed Zewail of the California Institute of Technology won the 1999 Nobel Prize in chemistry. (He returned to his native Egypt to help fledgling democratic forces after Mubarak was ousted.) Aasif Mandvi is among the comedic correspondents on Jon Stewart's *The Daily Show* on Comedy Central. And Shaquille O'Neal is one of dozens of famous Muslim athletes. In 2010, he gave an interview—posted on YouTube—noting his intention to perform the hajj pilgrimage.[13]

Among women, Anousheh Ansari, a Muslim engineer and businesswoman, was the first female space tourist. In 2006, she spent eight days at the International Space Station helping with experiments. In 2010, Rima Fakih became the first Muslim to be crowned Miss USA. In 2009, Bilqis Abdul Qaadir became the first high school basketball player—male or female—to score more than three thousand points in Massachusetts.[14] She went on to play point guard for the University of Memphis—with her arms, legs, and hair covered in keeping with modest Islamic dress.[15]

What was most striking in the early twenty-first century, especially as protests against tyranny erupted across the Middle East, was the commonality of civilizations.

During Egypt's uprising, Muslims and Coptic Christians—who have had deadly confrontations in the past—mobilized together. Ten percent of Egyptians are Christians. Several banners at Liberation Square blended Islam's crescent moon with a Christian cross. "One nation, one people," the banners declared.

In every country, the message of street movements was the same. "We want democracy. We want freedom," said a Libyan protester after security forces opened fire on the funeral procession of a slain demonstrator. "I want to go on the street feeling like nobody is looking after me, not looking over my shoulder."[16]

During a "Day of Dignity," Moroccans marched peacefully in more than one dozen cities to demand fewer powers for the king and more for the people. "Yes to a parliamentary democracy," read one sign.

"We no longer want to be subjects," said Abdelilah Ben Abdeslam, a leader of the Moroccan Association for Human Rights. "We want to be citizens."[17]

Symbolizing a new bridge between civilizations, Egyptian protester Jamal Ibrahim named his firstborn daughter "Facebook" shortly after Mubarak stepped down.[18]

As with other faiths, Islamic identity runs deep. The connection to religion may well deepen during difficult political transitions, for which many societies are poorly prepared. Religions have historically served both as a refuge during repression and a resource to define political alternatives.

"God who gave us life gave us liberty. Can the liberties of a nation be secure when we have removed a conviction that these liberties are the gift of God?" wrote Thomas Jefferson, a quote inscribed on the wall of his memorial in Washington, DC.

Globalization—or the traumatic transition to it—may also intensify personal affiliations with faith. Vast numbers from diverse faiths will want a local identity during change that redefines the patterns of governance and alliances, economics and trade, the media and culture. The church, the temple, the synagogue, and the mosque are all pillars to cling to during the transition's tornados.

Yet the uprisings are among the many signals that the Islamic world is no longer an exception to history's forces. A new generation is taking the helm. And the vast majority of Muslims are not attracted to the three major models that until recently defined political Islam's spectrum: al Qaeda's purist Salafism, Iran's Shiite theocracy, and Saudi Arabia's rigid Wahhabism. All three have a singular vision. All three are exclusive of anything else.

The new movements are about pluralism. The alternatives they create—over time, perhaps a great deal of time—may not be liberal in the Western mode. Alcohol and pornography are (sometimes hypocritically) not on the list of freedoms embraced even by liberal Muslims. But most Muslims do want to end political monopolies and open up space—to play whatever music they want as well as to have a genuine choice of political parties.

"The majority of Muslims today believe in Allah, the Koran, the prophets—all of them, dating back to Abraham, Moses, and Jesus," said Ghada Shahbender, an Egyptian poet who joined her children to protest against Mubarak's rule.

"They pray occasionally, pay alms when they can afford, although the majority can't afford it right now, and fast during Ramadan. That is as Islamic as their behavior becomes," she told me. "Extremism today is less attractive than it has ever been."

As hundreds of thousands took to the streets in Cairo, Egyptian protester Ali Bilal put it simply: "We've had enough time stolen." [19]

PART ONE

Extreme Makeover

1.

The Scent of Jasmine

**With our blood we will teach the world the
meaning of FREEDOM.**

—Egyptian protest sign

A revolution that rocked authoritarian rule across the Middle East was ignited by a seven-dollar bribe. The spark, literally, was a young Tunisian street vendor with black curls, deep brown eyes, and a wry smile.

On most days, Mohamed Bouazizi pushed a wooden cart loaded with seasonal fruits to the center of Sidi Bouzid, a forlorn town where almost one-third of the labor force was unemployed and rights were often decided by bribes rather than the law. At twenty-six, Bouazizi was the family's main breadwinner. His father had died when he was three; he had worked since the age of ten. His family—five siblings, mother, and ailing uncle—lived constantly on the edge in a three-room home off a dusty alley.

The political fate of an entire region turned on December 17, 2010, when Tunisia's corrupt autocracy pushed the young peddler too far. It started out as a minor incident. A city inspector, a middle-aged woman, hassled the lanky youth over his business permit. It was not the first time. Like other professions, street vendors often paid bribes to get or to keep permits. The standard bribe was ten dinars, about seven dollars, but it was also often a whole day's earnings. This time, however, Bouazizi protested. The two swore at each other, according to local reports.

"Should I become a thief?" Bouazizi shouted at the inspector, according to a friend. "Should I die?"[1]

The inspector then seized his winter apples and—details are disputed—may have slapped him. Two of her colleagues reportedly then knocked Bouazizi to the ground and walked off with his electronic scale.

Without his produce—often acquired by street vendors on credit—Bouazizi pushed his empty cart to the Sidi Bouzid town hall to appeal. He was rebuffed. He refused to capitulate. He next went to the local governor's office—Sidi Bouzid is the capital of one of Tunisia's twenty-three provinces—but was again turned back. Officials were otherwise engaged.[2]

The most popular picture of Bouazizi showed a young man with high cheekbones and fashionably unshaven facial stubble. He wore a blue-gray jacket and a white T-shirt in the candid photograph, captured as he clapped his hands. He looked happy.

But on a cold December day in 2010, Bouazizi was clearly desperate after his failed appeals. Around midday, according to local accounts, he hauled his cart back to the governor's office, this time with paint thinner. He stood in the middle of the street and shouted, "How do you expect me to earn a living?" He poured the highly flammable liquid over his body. Then he lit a match.

Flames burned through his clothes and then engulfed his body, even burning off his lips.

The young Tunisian actually survived, despite third-degree burns on 90 percent of his body. But the match he lit ignited other flames. Bouazizi's mother, family, and friends picked up where he left off. They gathered at the governor's office later that day.

"Here is your bribe," they shouted, throwing coins at the gate.[3]

Sidi Bouzid is a three-hour drive south of cosmopolitan Tunis. It is a rural area of unpaved roads and crumbling buildings largely ignored by the government. But cell phones are common, and the Internet is popular. Over one-third of Tunisians are Internet users. Some 20 percent use Facebook. Bouazizi's cousin posted a video of the family protest on YouTube. Al Jazeera picked it up and aired it within hours, as eventually did other independent satellite stations circumventing state-controlled television. A local lawyer who witnessed Bouazizi's self-immolation used Facebook, one of the few online video sites not censored, to mobilize the public for broader protests. Word spread quickly on Twitter.[4]

Within twenty-four hours, the world's first "virtual" revolution rumbled across Tunisia.

Enraged and then emboldened, Tunisians were increasingly sucked into the drama. Over the next ten days, turmoil traveled from the poor interior—Kasserine, Thala, and Menzel Bouzaiene—to the scenic capital. Protests signs became increasingly bold in an authoritarian state. One sign borrowed from Barack Obama's presidential campaign. "Yes we can, too!" it boasted.

As the protests swelled, so did the issues. Bouazizi's self-immolation resonated especially among youth, who suffered the highest unemployment and bleakest futures. Demonstrations of disgust grew to demands for jobs, justice, and then the regime's ouster.

"We were a volcano that was going to explode," reflected trade union leader Attia Athmouni. "And when Bouazizi burnt himself, we were ready. Protesters demanded payback for the blood of Bouazizi, and this developed into economic, social, and political demands." [5]

Tunisia's government fumbled its response from the beginning. President Zine al Abidine Ben Ali and the state-controlled media initially ignored the trouble.

Like many Arab countries, the little North African country was ruled by a ruthless autocrat. Ben Ali was only its second leader since Tunisia—which is slightly smaller than Wisconsin, and squished between Algeria and Libya—gained independence from France in 1956. Habib Bourguiba was its first leader; I first visited Tunisia in 1974 as he laid the groundwork to become president for life. Bourguiba ruled for thirty years. He was ousted by Ben Ali, then the prime minister, in 1987 on grounds of mental incompetence. By then, Bourguiba was eighty-four.

Ben Ali followed the same pattern. By 2010, he had been in power for almost a quarter century. According to widespread reports, his family, especially his wife, was notoriously corrupt.

Cables from American diplomats released by WikiLeaks in late 2010 chronicled their kleptocracy, which one classified cable called a quasi-mafia. A cable in 2008 was particularly disparaging. It was entitled "What's Yours Is Mine."

"Corruption in Tunisia is getting worse," it reported. "Whether it's cash, services, land, property, or yes, your yacht, President Ben Ali's family is rumored to covet it and reportedly gets what it wants." As an example, it noted reports that Ben Ali's nephews seized a French businessman's yacht in 2006. The family acquired control over everything from the most lucrative bank to a university.

Other cables detailed a dinner party given by the president's son-in-law—for the American ambassador—with desserts including ice cream flown in from St. Tropez on the French Riviera. The son-in-law's estate was replete with a large tiger—named Pasha—living on the grounds. It reminded the envoy of Uday Hussein, the son of former Iraqi President Saddam Hussein who had a personal zoo, including lions and cheetahs, at his Baghdad palace.

The Ben Ali family was widely reported to control banks, an airline, supermarket chains, television stations, vast real estate holdings both at home and abroad, and pricey foreign car dealerships. Some estimates claimed the extended family—especially through Ben Ali's second wife, a former hairdresser—controlled one-half of the Tunisian economy directly or indirectly.[6]

The US Embassy warned of the potential impact. "With Tunisians facing rising inflation and high unemployment, the conspicuous displays of wealth and persistent rumors of corruption have added fuel to the fire," it reported.

Ben Ali was finally forced to address the growing national turmoil on December 28, eleven days after the young street vendor had set himself alight. The president publicly reprimanded the protesters and threatened punishment. He warned of the economic consequences to a country heavily reliant on tourism. The whitewashed hamlets and Mediterranean beachfronts were particularly popular among Europeans. Ben Ali even equated the demonstrators with "terrorists."[7]

To quell dissent, the government deployed police who used tear gas and then live ammunition. But as protesters started to die, the opposition only got angrier. Many cell phone videos of the shootings and their bloodied victims ended up on Facebook, the only video-sharing platform beyond the government's control. The images shocked Tunisians.

As pressure increased, Ben Ali began to cede some ground. A cabinet minister raced to Sidi Bouzid and pledged millions of dinars for jobs and development. Ben Ali even went to Bouazizi's hospital bedside in the intensive care burn unit.

The visit was clearly a publicity gimmick. The government released a photograph of Ben Ali's entourage consulting with the doctors and "extending his thanks to the medical team who is exerting all efforts to provide the needed care to the patient."[8] Bouazizi was so totally swathed in thick bandages that he looked like a mummy. He could not see, hear, or speak. He was unaware of the president's visit.

Bouazizi died one week later, on January 4, 2011, barely three weeks after his confrontation over a seven-dollar bribe. He was buried outside Sidi Bouzid, among the cactus and olive trees, with a gray concrete slab as a marker.

By then, the uprising had evolved. Hundreds of thousands of Tunisians were turning out across the country to demand that the president step down. They started to call it the Jasmine Revolution. Jasmine is Tunisia's national flower.

Appearing increasingly desperate, Ben Ali imposed a state of emergency and a dusk-to-dawn curfew. He banned all public gatherings of more than two people, vowing that violators would be shot. His security forces, wielding machine guns, patrolled the streets. Gunfire echoed sporadically through Tunis, as tanks rumbled along the capital's streets. Even the airport was shut down.[9]

Ben Ali also took dramatic political steps to appease public anger. He fired his whole cabinet. He pledged to conduct parliamentary elections in six months. He vowed reforms, the release of political prisoners, and an investigation into the deaths of protesters. He then promised not to run again in 2014.

It was all too late. On January 13, Ben Ali's own military commanders turned against him. They refused to continue using army troops to put down the protests.

The next day, with tear gas still hanging over the capital, Ben Ali and his wife fled to Saudi Arabia. With dizzying speed, it was all over in a month. The Jasmine Revolution was the first popular uprising in an Arab country that forced an autocrat from power.

The impact of Bouazizi's desperate act of defiance was as profound as any of the region's legendary wars. It transformed politics—both who was empowered and how—in the last bloc of countries to hold out against change. It created a new model.

"We used to offer catastrophic models of 'Lebanonization,' 'Somalization,' and 'Iraqization.' We now have a model that is worthy of respect to offer the world: 'Tunisification,' " wrote Yasser abu Hilalah in Jordan's *Al Ghad* newspaper.

"Those who grew up in the shadow of systematic and destructive repression for twenty-three years have toppled the dictator without being implicated in violence, terrorism, or links to foreign powers. They did not need favors from anyone." [10]

But Tunisia's Jasmine Revolution did more than create a new model. It launched the fourth in a series of pivotal turning points for the Middle East over a century. The first was the collapse of the Ottoman Empire after World War I, which led to the formation of modern Turkey and the creation of new Arab states. The second was the creation of Israel after World War II, which reconfigured the region's borders and battle lines. And the third was Iran's Islamic revolution in 1979, which redefined the world's political spectrum and codified fundamentalist dogma.

The Jasmine Revolution also exposed the depth of desperation— economic need, political rage, and social despair—across the Arab world. Within days, at least sixteen men in five other countries emulated Bouazizi. Seven Algerians from widely diverse parts of the country set themselves ablaze amid growing pro-democracy protests. Most— including a father of six—were protesting unemployment or housing problems. In Egypt, six men reportedly set fire to themselves, one in front of parliament in central Cairo to protest the price of bread. A Mauritanian set himself alight—in his own car—in front of parliament to protest treatment of his tribe. A Moroccan doused himself with flammable fluid in Casablanca. [11]

Regimes tried to stem the trend. Cairo's Al Azhar University, the oldest center of Islamic learning, dating back more than a millennium, warned that suicide was against teachings of the Koran—even in the struggle for justice. In Saudi Arabia, the birthplace of Islam and site of its two holiest shrines, Grand Mufti Abdel Aziz al Sheikh issued a fatwa on January 20, 2011, condemning all forms of suicide and specifically suicide over harsh living conditions. But the fatwa did not prevent a Saudi from Jizan, an underdeveloped region near the Yemen border, from pouring gasoline over his body and setting himself on fire the next day. He died in the hospital. [12] The rage was not only from the young. The Saudi was in his sixties.

The numbers were striking, if small. Regimes insisted at least some of the men were mentally unfit.

But the tactic marked a turning point. In a region famed for suicide bombings as a favorite idiom of opposition, Bouazizi's self-immolation tried a different tack. He did not take anyone else's life to intimidate or terrorize. The young Tunisian instead killed himself to shame the state. And he succeeded far better than any suicide bomber.

Three weeks after Ben Ali fled, Tunisians organized a "Caravan of Thanks" to Sidi Bouzid. The caravan, protected by an army escort, began in Tunis and picked up cars, vans, and buses along the way. By the time it reached the town that Ben Ali's government had forgotten, some 10,000 Tunisians had joined in. The caravan was almost three miles long. Like the revolution, it had been mobilized through Facebook. The caravan ended at Bouazizi's grave.

The political lexicon changed after Tunisia's upheaval. In a region of radical ideologies—from al Qaeda's Sunni jihadism to Iran's rigid Shiite theocracy—civil disobedience suddenly caught on. And it was far more successful, even in confronting guns. The old men of decadent, self-indulgent regimes were suddenly on the run. The old Arab authoritarian order was cracking.

And the Jasmine Revolution was only the beginning.

I N EGYPT, THE turning point for President Hosni Mubarak was the battle for Lovers' Bridge. It happened on the fourth day of unprecedented protests across the country, from ancient Alexandria on the Mediterranean and teeming Cairo on the Nile to steamy Suez, the southern terminus of the legendary canal. The revolt in Egypt had been initiated just eleven days after Tunisia's president fled his country.

Challenging the old order suddenly seemed not only possible but necessary. Egyptians wanted to do it too.

The "Day of Rage" protest on January 28, 2011, was organized by a surprisingly small clique of young bloggers and activists. Most were under the age of thirty; they had limited—and largely unsuccessful—political experience. But anger over the regime's repression was so widespread that more than 50,000 people signed up on a Facebook page to support the rally. It was set for a Friday, the Muslim sabbath, when many Egyptians were off work. The protest marches began after midday prayers.

In Cairo, the plan called for demonstrators to gather at preselected mosques. They would then march through diverse parts of the sprawling, palm-fringed capital and converge on Tahrir Square, or Liberation Square. The landmark plaza was at a strategic juncture of Egypt's past and present—the Museum of Antiquities, the headquarters of the twenty-two-nation Arab League, and nearby, state television and offices of the ruling National Democratic Party.

The pivotal group started at Mustafa Mahmoud Mosque. As they marched down Cairo's dusty streets, they called to passersby and people watching from tiny balconies to join them. Hundreds grew to some 20,000 by the time they arrived at the bridge, formally known as Qasr al Nil—or Palace of the Nile.[13]

The overpass, which spans the world's longest river and is adorned with massive bronze lions at both ends, is popularly called Lovers' Bridge because young couples stroll its wide sidewalks in the evening. In a poor country—where 40 percent of 85 million people live on less than two dollars a day—the bridge offered a charming setting for an inexpensive date.

On a sunny winter day in 2011, however, lovers avoided the bridge. The marchers from Mustafa Mahmoud Mosque were greeted instead by riot police strategically deployed to cut them off just before Liberation Square. The notorious force, wearing protective helmets, stood shoulder to shoulder several rows deep in a human barricade. They were backed up by powerful water cannons and armored cars.

The battle for Lovers' Bridge should not have been a contest. But it was. Indeed, it went two rounds.

As the crowd surged onto the bridge, protesters were almost joyful in their defiance. Some chanted in loud rhythmic unison, "Throw out Mubarak." Others sang the Egyptian national anthem. A few took their turn singing the Tunisian national anthem in honor of the Jasmine Revolution.

Riot police quickly advanced on the crowd, simultaneously firing round after round of tear gas. Streams of white gas spiraled through the air like jet contrails, then exploded into thick noxious clouds. A protester with a bullhorn urged demonstrators to regroup as needed but not to retreat.

When the crowd resisted, police next unleashed water cannons. Protesters ducked or pulled back to avoid the punishing sprays. A few dozen protesters knelt, then touched their foreheads to the ground. Prostrating themselves in the Muslim prayer position offered greater resistance than standing up. Whenever the crowd regrouped to move forward, riot police pushed back, beating anyone who got close, with long black truncheons. Television cameras captured armored vehicles trying to run over protesters who refused to budge.[14]

Police won the first round in the battle for Lovers' Bridge. By late afternoon, reinforcements separated and then dispersed the crowd. The bridge cleared.

But it was only a temporary lull.

As the sun began to set over the Nile, demonstrators came back for a second round, this time pushing uprooted guard booths in front to shield themselves from water cannons. They were clearly better organized. Some had hospital masks to filter the tear gas. Others covered their faces with cloths or scarves soaked in vinegar. Many brought colas to wash their eyes. As tear gas landed at their feet, they threw the canisters into the Nile, where they popped and fizzed. Some even tossed the tear gas back at police.[15]

The new strategy worked. By evening prayers, protesters pushed through the security cordon. Police retreated, then gradually disappeared completely from Cairo's streets. As the muezzins wailed the call to prayer, many in the crowd again prostrated themselves on the bridge—this time in victory. Then they moved on to Liberation Square.

The balance of power in Egypt started to shift that afternoon. Brute force could no longer scare the public or contain its rage. In the conquest of Lovers' Bridge, quite ordinary Egyptians began to empower themselves. The writing was literally on the wall. A message to the regime was spray-painted across the pedestal of the bridge's huge lions. In large black letters, it read, "Game Over Mubarak."

As police lost control, the presidential palace announced Mubarak would soon speak to the nation. Egypt's octogenarian leader had been peculiarly silent since the unrest started. For years, Mubarak had been an absentee landlord, spending much of his time in Sharm el Sheikh, a sleepy resort town on the distant Sinai Peninsula. The catty Cairo grapevine was full of stories about Mubarak falling asleep in cabinet meetings; political gossip claimed he had serious memory slips. His crude hair dye—he had more gray hair when he became president in 1981 than he did thirty years later—was the butt of jokes even among his colleagues.

By 2011, Mubarak had ruled longer than all but three pharaohs and pashas in Egypt's six-thousand-year history. He seemed bored with politics yet also reluctant to stand aside, even as he groomed his son Gamal to succeed him. A favorite Egyptian joke recounted Mubarak being vis-ited on his deathbed by an aide.

"Mr. President, don't you want to say good-bye to the people?" the assistant asked.

"Why?" Mubarak responded. "Where are my people going?"

Mubarak had once told parliament that he would remain in power "as long as I draw breath and my heart beats in my chest."

Until the protests began, it looked like he meant it.

Finally, shortly after midnight, Mubarak appeared on state television. He seemed weary; he was heavily made up. He acknowledged public grievances, although he mentioned no specifics.

During Mubarak's rule, the gap between rich and poor had increased even as the economy started to grow. By 2011, about 40 percent of Egypt's 85 million people lived on less than two dollars a day. One of the handmade protest signs, a big yellow placard, put it simply, "I'm very, very hungry."

Over three decades, Mubarak had also become increasingly autocratic. His government outlawed many political parties. After the 2005 election, the leading opposition candidate—who got only 7 percent—was jailed for three years on flimsy charges of forged election petitions. Emergency rule, a form of martial law, had been in place since the 1981 assassination of President Anwar Sadat. Civil society was controlled by restrictive and hard-to-get permits. Police had a free hand in enforcing Mubarak's will.

But in his midnight speech on January 29, 2011, Mubarak blamed others for his problems. He angrily charged that the turmoil was a plot.

"What happened in these protests," he told the nation, "extends be-yond looting, chaos, and fire to a larger scheme aimed at shaking stabil-ity." He was equally contemptuous of his own colleagues. He announced that he had fired his entire government. He also issued a warning.

"I will not shy away," he insisted, "from taking any decision that maintains the security of every Egyptian."

Mubarak had always been a lumbering, even clumsy speaker. He had none of the charisma or political dynamism of his two predecessors, Sadat and Gamal Abdel Nasser. Although all three presidents emerged from Egypt's military, Mubarak had remained the villager, raw and un-sophisticated, even as he donned tailor-made suits. Interviews with him were difficult; he did not have a way with words, and he offered few new ideas. I had interviewed him many times, attended even more press conferences, and traveled with American presidents and secretaries of state to Middle East summits that usually began with visits to Mubarak. As the years passed, I developed a kind of dread of seeing him. The leader of the largest Arab population had increasingly little to say. In the most desperate moment of a sixty-year career, his midnight speech was also notably empty.

Mubarak's one concession, the next morning, was to appoint a vice president. For thirty years, the Egyptian president had been so politically paranoid that he had refused to appoint a second in command—the very position that had brought him to power. He named his long-standing intelligence chief, Omar Suleiman. *Foreign Policy* magazine once dubbed Suleiman the Middle East's most powerful spy chief, even more influential than his Mossad counterpart in Israel. Suleiman had made a career out of brokering among big powers as well as the region's bad boys and extremists.

Mubarak's ploy, however, was not enough.

After the battle for Lovers' Bridge, protesters set up permanent camp at Liberation Square. Flagrantly disobeying martial law as well as a new dusk-to-dawn curfew, they vowed not to leave until Mubarak stepped down. A middle-aged man excitedly explained his preparations to a television reporter. He pointed to a sack with a plastic sheet to protect against water cannons. He showed a scarf to ward off tear gas. Oh, he added almost gleefully, he had also written his will.[16] Several Egyptians brought tents to sleep in—one playfully dubbed "Hotel Freedom" in a handwritten sign—and burned fires for warmth against the cold January night. Volunteers took turns ferrying in food, picking up debris, and manning security checkpoints to prevent anyone with weapons from gaining entry.

The protest epicenter became a carnival. During the day, parents brought their children to experience both the unfolding history and the merriment. Several protesters painted their faces, like football fans, in variations of the red, white, and black Egyptian flag or wore tricolor ribbons tied around their foreheads. Others carried defaced official posters or mocking caricatures of their president. The crowd became quite creative in expressing disdain. When military helicopters hovered overhead, protesters formed a human chain to form the word *Go* in Arabic.[17]

The new public confidence was reflected in a flippancy unthinkable even one week earlier. "Go already," said one sign. "My arm's starting to hurt."[18]

"Egypt," another boasted, "is mine."

IN A COUNTRY politically stagnant for thirty years, Egypt's opposition coalesced with stunning speed. But the Little Uprising That Could did not erupt out of the blue. The challenge to Arab authoritarian order was inevitable, even if the exact catalyst was unpredictable. The rebellions in Egypt and Tunisia and the swelling unrest elsewhere were produced by a confluence of at least four factors: education, raised expectations, demographics, and communication technology.

In 2011, the Arab world was flooded with energetic youth; they were a decisive majority in all twenty-two Arab countries. The median age in Egypt was twenty-four. In Tunisia, it was twenty-nine. The median age was even younger elsewhere: twenty-one or younger in Iraq, Jordan, the Palestinian territories, Sudan, and Syria. It was eighteen in Gaza and Yemen.[19]

In all, 100 million people—roughly one-third of the entire Arab world—were between the ages of fifteen and twenty-nine.

The young particularly wanted to have a say in their own lives, and not just politically. They shared a common mission, although the demonstrators came from all walks of life. They were taxi drivers as well as teachers and techies, the jobless as well as young doctors, farmers as well as stockbrokers. They were secular and religious, devout young Muslim men in prayer caps rubbing shoulders with lawyers in suits. And women were everywhere, as equals, girls wearing Islamic headscarves as well as young women in tight jeans.

For the first time, the majority of Arabs also had some degree of education or literacy that moved them beyond ambitions of daily subsistence. Most were also well aware of conditions outside their villages or national borders. In 1996, Al Jazeera became the first regional satellite channel to broadcast news that circumvented the state's control. By 2011, more than five hundred independent satellite channels broadcast across the Middle East.

Knowledge and numbers were already a combustible combination. But the young were also restless. Arab countries had the highest proportion of unemployed youths in the world. As literacy standards increased, the sense of having no meaningful future became pervasive.

Egypt's government promised all university graduates a job. But the waiting list averaged three years even with a college degree. And jobs were often still menial, meaningless, and poorly paid. In Tunisia and elsewhere in North Africa, unemployment was so widespread—visible among young men leaning aimlessly against buildings—that the job-less had a nickname. The word for "wall" in Arabic is *hit*, so the unem-ployed became known as the *hittistes*, or "those who lean against the wall."[20]

The overwhelming majority of young Arabs also believed their lead-ers had failed them, according to a Gallup poll in Egypt taken on the eve of its uprising. More than 70 percent of Egyptians between the ages of fifteen and twenty-nine said the government was unsuccessful in tap-ping human potential, especially on three counts: providing jobs, helping new entrepreneurs, and generating a sense of opportunity and respect for the young.[21]

The decline was dramatic—down 10 percent in just one year between 2009 and 2010. Young Egyptians were among the most dissatisfied in the Arab world, but the young in Iraq and Lebanon were even angrier. Young Palestinians, Sudanese, Moroccans, Syrians, and Mauritanians were not far behind.

Finally, social media and technology offered a new means of commu-nicating and mobilizing beyond the state's iron-fist control. Facebook, launched in 2004, literally revolutionized communications in the Arab world. So did YouTube, created in 2005. And cell phones—60 million alone in Egypt, a country of 85 million—made texting a critical tool in communicating and mobilizing protests.

One of the crude cardboard placards at Liberation Square declared simply, "Thank you Facebook."

Despite Egypt's poverty, more than one in five people was an Internet user by 2010. More than 5 million Egyptians were signed up on Face-book. In Tunisia, more than one-third of its 10 million people used the Internet. In Bahrain, Iran, Kuwait, Oman, Qatar, Saudi Arabia, Turkey, and the United Arab Emirates, roughly 40 percent of the population was on the Internet.[22]

"If you want to free a society, just give people Internet access," said Wael Ghonim, a young Egyptian and Google executive who created a

Facebook page to mobilize protests. "This is definitely an Internet revolution. I call it Revolution 2.0." [23]

Yet the Arab uprisings were not just about ousting geriatric leaders like Hosni Mubarak. They were ultimately about shedding an oppressive past. Egypt had been ruled for some six thousand years by autocrats, military despots, kings, colonial masters, pashas, and pharaohs. Some rulers had been popular, but none had really empowered. Elites always prevailed; traditions dating back centuries still defined life.

Tunisians, Egyptians, Libyans, Yemenis, Bahrainis, Jordanians, Moroccans, and many others were part of a broader historical pattern. Over the previous three decades, communism had collapsed in the Soviet Union and Eastern Europe. Minority rule and apartheid had died in Africa. And military dictatorships had ended in Central and Latin America. It was not yet "the end of history" in the full acceptance and application of democracy. But the end of the twentieth century witnessed unparalleled political openings.

The Arab world, the last bloc of countries to hold out against the tide, was just playing catch-up in the early twenty-first century. The fears of confronting dictatorships had finally begun to fade.

"The people have discovered their collective power. They have discovered that their voices have power," said Khalid Abdalla, a noted young Egyptian actor who starred in the movie *The Kite Runner*, which was based on a best-selling book. He too joined the protest and pledged not to leave Liberation Square until Mubarak stepped down. [24]

"People are asking that the state be in their service," he added, "and that the state not be allowed to terrorize them." [25]

EGYPT'S YOUNG REBELS were hardly walk-ons, however. For many of them, the uprising did not happen overnight. Several pivotal players had been searching for up to five years for ways to ignite a popular outpouring. Many had turned to blogging. Ahmed Maher, a young engineer with close-cropped brown hair, a wide goatee, and thin, rectangular glasses, was a pioneer. His blog was The Unlucky Ghost.

Born in 1980, Maher experimented with civil society outlets like Kefaya, or "Enough," during the so-called Arab Spring, a burst of democratic activism in 2005. He joined the fledgling opposition party El Ghad, or the Tomorrow Party. Both fizzled, as did the Arab Spring, under the weight of Mubarak's secret police. In 2006, Maher turned out to support an unprecedented judges' strike—the judiciary was the one traditionally independent branch of government—but was detained by secret police. He was held for two months, although never formally charged or tried.

"I was stripped, beaten, and threatened with rape," he told me when we met at The Hideout, an outdoor café in Cairo. It was little more than an alley with a dirt floor, wobbly plastic chairs, and several hubbly-bubbly pipes. Maher ordered a pipe and a Pepsi.

In 2007, Maher supported labor strikes, which were repeatedly quashed by arrests, threats, and harassment. He then turned to the Internet for alternative ways of mobilizing dissent.

"When I left prison, I decided, 'Why not create a political group out of this Facebook?' " he told me. "Security was so tight by then that there was really no other way for us."

In 2008, Maher and a friend tested the waters with a Facebook group to support a workers' strike. The group—the April 6 Movement—took its name from the date of the strike. The reaction exceeded Maher's wildest expectations; more than 74,000 people signed up. By 2008, Facebook was the third-most-visited site on the Internet in Egypt.[26] Although he worked at a construction firm during the day, Maher became a Facebook fanatic at night—sometimes all night.

"I sent so many messages," he told me with a chuckle, "that Facebook suspended my account because it thought I was a spammer."

He also launched his blog to further boost the April 6 Movement. Egypt was then one of the ten worst countries in which to be a blogger, according to the Committee to Protect Journalists. (Tunisia was also among the top ten.) Yet the number of Egyptian bloggers—in Arabic, English, or a mix—soared from just 40 in 2004 to an estimated 160,000 by mid-2008.[27]

"Which has greater influence—Islam or the Internet?" Maher said. "Until April 6, no one was more organized than the Muslim Brotherhood. Since April 6, a new culture has developed, and now the Internet has a stronger value. The Internet also brought us together as youth."

April 6 became a hub for young activists who advocated civil disobedience. It plugged away at causes. It organized illegal demonstrations—often in pitifully small numbers, and always outnumbered by police—over rising food prices, political prisoners, even on Mubarak's eightieth birthday. April 6 turned to Myspace, Flickr, and Twitter to tell the young opposition when and where to gather, where police were deploying, and how to avoid arrest. After their small demonstrations, its members used YouTube and their blogs to chronicle events never reported by state media.

The movement's tactics sometimes seemed quixotic. April 6 called for silent protests—days when followers all stayed home from work or wore black T-shirts or hung flags on their doors. At one protest on an Alexandria beach, its members tried to fly a kite painted the red, white, and black of the Egyptian flag as they handed out flyers about democracy. They were stopped almost instantly by Egypt's Mukhabarat security police.

"Our main aim was to mobilize people, get them out of their passivity, and make them believe they should make peaceful change because the system didn't work," Maher told me, pulling smoke from his hubbly-bubbly.

The outside world, particularly the United States, never grasped the power of the restless young and their new tools. A US Embassy cable in 2009 described the April 6 Movement as "outside the mainstream of opposition politicians and activists." Its goals were "unrealistic," concluded the cable, which was later released by WikiLeaks.

But Mubarak's regime clearly saw the young bloggers as a threat. It increasingly harassed the emerging activists. During Maher's second detention, secret police beat him just to get a password for a Facebook page. He subsequently posted pictures of the cuts, welts, and bruises on his body.

The regime's brutality eventually backfired, however.

In 2010, Khaled Said, a twenty-eight-year-old businessman, was at an Internet café in historic Alexandria when two plainclothes police approached him. They reportedly suspected that he had a cell phone video—which he was about to post—of police with illegal drugs. They hauled the US-educated youth outside and beat him, literally, to a pulp. They banged his head against an iron door, marble stairs, and a concrete wall. Despite Said's pleas to stop—"I am dying," he cried, according to an eyewitness from the Internet café—the police continued until a yellow liquid oozed from his mouth. He did die. [28]

Police took Said's body away. They later told his family that he had died from suffocation when he tried to swallow a bag of drugs. But a picture of Said's deformed corpse—his skull fractured, jaw badly askew, nose broken, front teeth missing, blood spattered across his face and seeping from the back of his head—turned up on the Internet. It had been taken in the morgue. Most eerily, Said's eyes were still open.[29]

The picture horrified Egypt's cybergeneration. The young were further galvanized when a cell phone video of drug dealings among Egyptian police showed up on YouTube a few days later. Thousands of Egyptians posted responses. Among them was a message from a member of April 6. It said, simply, "We are Khaled. Each one of us can be Khaled."[30]

A few days later, a new page—"We are all Khaled Said"—appeared on Facebook. It quickly became the most popular dissident website in Egypt. Its anonymous creator then called on members to turn out in Alexandria and Cairo to protest Said's brutal murder by Mubarak's thugs.

It worked. Defying Egypt's martial law banning public gatherings, large numbers took to the streets. Many carried posters with two pictures—one of a gently smiling Khaled Said in a gray sweatshirt with a hood, the other of his battered corpse in the morgue. No words were necessary. The marches generated a momentum. They continued once every week during the summer of 2010 and sporadically during the fall.

Then, on December 17, thirteen hundred miles away, Mohamed Bouazizi set himself on fire in Tunisia.

The Jasmine Revolution's impact on Egypt was almost immediate. When President Ben Ali fled Tunis on January 14, Cairo's cybergeneration was already fired up. And Ahmed Maher's April 6 Movement had also already planned to hold one of its irregular rallies. January 25 was a holiday commemorating the failed Egyptian police revolt against British colonial rule. Inspired by Tunisia, the April 6 Movement and the anonymous creator of the "We are all Khaled Said" Facebook page pushed to get even more Egyptians out on the streets on January 25. At night, Maher and members of other groups plastered Cairo with posters.

The January 25 protest marked the beginning of Egypt's rebellion. This time, the turnout exceeded all expectations. Maher was among the young demonstrators who took Lovers' Bridge.

"We succeeded at what the traditional opposition failed at doing," Maher told me, "because we mastered the technology to organize ourselves."

* * *

Hosni Mubarak made one last stand. It dragged out for ten days. And he almost pulled it off.

In a country with six thousand years of history, Mubarak appealed to Egyptian nationalism in a second televised address on February 1. He announced—as if it had been the plan all along—that he would not run a sixth time for president when his term ended in eight months, and he dwelled on his own sacrifices on behalf of a great nation.

"I never wanted power or prestige," he said in a ten-minute speech, again close to midnight. "The Hosni Mubarak who speaks to you today is proud of his achievements over the years in serving Egypt and its people! This great country is my dear homeland, the same way it is every Egyptian's country. I lived in it. I fought for it and defended its soil, sovereignty, and interests.

"I am now absolutely determined to finish my work for the nation," he added, forcefully. "On its soil I will die. History will judge me and all of us."

The speech swayed many Egyptians. Dalia Ziada was one of the young female activists. "Mubarak played it right and now he is gaining control again," she messaged me. Her own mother, a barometer of the older generation, was quite moved and supported his decision.

"I think we are losing the momentum," Ziada emailed me.

The regime unleashed its goons the next day to make sure. On day nine of the protests, a herd of men on camels and horses swooped into Liberation Square. They swung whips and long sticks wildly as they galloped through the crowd, knocking over men, women, and children, leaving many abruptly bloodied. They were followed by men on foot armed with machetes, spears, chains, clubs with studs, and screwdrivers. It was a well-coordinated stampede. And it was brutally medieval.

After pledging compromise and a political transition, Mubarak had basically stiffed his own people.

The unarmed protesters were caught by surprise. They had relied on civil disobedience, basically their mere presence. In Egypt, which outlawed any meeting of more than five people, just showing up was a bold act of defiance. Some protesters initially tried to prevent violence, standing out in the square waving their arms, as the attackers swept through. But the showdown soon became an issue of survival. As Mubarak's backers attacked, protesters picked up stones from the ground to throw back. Hand-to-hand street fighting erupted.

Liberation Square became a combat zone.

Protesters improvised. They hastily assembled primitive barricades with tall pieces of blue corrugated tin and railing ripped from sidewalks. Others picked away at the street for stones to hurl. They had to constantly duck and weave, as Mubarak's thugs started lobbing hundreds of fiery Molotov cocktails or dropping firebombs from buildings. Big plumes of black smoke were visible even in the dark sky.

Then the shooting began. The night echoed with a cacophony of heavy automatic gunfire. And there was no exit. Mubarak's muscular thugs ringed the central plaza. The plaza was under siege.

Unlike the battle for Lovers' Bridge, the showdown at Liberation Square became deadly. A nearby mosque and a subway station were converted into trauma wards since Mubarak's supporters blocked ambulances from entering. Hunter Moore, an American teacher in Cairo, helped tend to the injured at a makeshift clinic. Wounded protesters arrived every three to five seconds for hours, he told CNN. Ninety percent had head wounds.[31]

The next day, secret police went after the media too, beating journalists, confiscating cameras, dragging reporters out of their vehicles, tracking them down in homes and hotels. The regime wanted to stop twenty-four-hour coverage of both the opposition's brave defiance and its own brutal response from being beamed around the world. Dozens of reporters and photographers, including Americans and Europeans, were detained.

Two *New York Times* journalists reported their own horrific detention, which included being blindfolded and interrogated at a secret police prison. The worst part was listening to torture heard through the prison's thin walls.[32]

> Our discomfort paled in comparison to the dull whacks and the screams of pain by Egyptian people that broke the stillness of the night ... For one day, we were trapped in the brutal maze where Egyptians are lost for months or even years. Our detainment threw into haunting relief the abuses of security services, the police, the secret police and the intelligence service, and explained why they were at the forefront of complaints made by the protesters.

Despite the odds, the opposition at Liberation Square held out. Soldiers near the Egyptian Museum of Antiquities reportedly played a role—whether on orders or on their own initiative was unclear—to limit the fighting. The army refused to intervene in domestic turmoil, but soldiers fired into the air to signal an unwillingness to tolerate more bloodshed.[33] With both the opposition and the army in their way, Mubarak's plainclothes thugs eventually retreated. Protesters regained control of Liberation Square by dawn on day eleven.

In the end, Mubarak's crackdown actually accelerated the tectonic shift in power from elites to the streets, from the old guard to a younger generation.

Faces of the regime started to defect. Nile Television correspondent Shahira Amin resigned her job and joined the protesters rather than "propagate lies." The spokesman for Al Azhar—a center of Islamic learning that dated back more than one thousand years and was government-controlled—announced he was resigning too. "My position is a position of support to the revolution all the way," said Mohamed Tahtawy. "I am part of it until the last drop of my blood."[34]

But it was Wael Ghonim, the thirty-year-old computer nerd, who most symbolized the generational shift. He was largely unknown in Egypt. He lived in Dubai, where he worked as the Google executive for Middle East marketing. He had flown home to join the protests. Then he disappeared.

Only a few friends knew Ghonim's secret: He was the anonymous creator of the "We are all Khaled Said" Facebook page. He had been outraged by the pictures of Said's battered corpse in June 2010. Already a Facebook and YouTube junkie, he used the pseudonym el Shahid, "the Martyr," to create the page to help spur protests over Said's death.

"My purpose," he told a friend, "is to increase the bond between the people and the group through my unknown personality. This way we create an army of volunteers."[35]

Ghonim—through the Facebook page—had been one of the two most important organizers of Egypt's uprising, along with Ahmed Maher's April 6 Movement. By January 25, seven months after it was created, the page had more than 350,000 followers. When Ghonim sent out word asking followers to protest, more than 50,000 clicked yes.

Egyptian intelligence figured out Ghonim's role. On day three of the protests, the young techie called a friend to say he thought he was being followed. He was going to ditch his phone because of its tracking device. It was too late. Four men rushed him on the street and forcibly handcuffed Ghonim as he shouted "Save me! Save me!" at no one in particular. For the next twelve days, he was blindfolded, interrogated, and kept awake for days at a stretch.

As word began to leak out about Ghonim's arrest and his secret role in the uprising, international pressure mounted on the regime. He was released after twelve days. A few hours later, he appeared on Dream TV, an independent satellite station in Cairo. His emotions were still raw; so was the interview.

"This abduction was a crime, and that's exactly what we're fighting. If you want to arrest me, there is a law," he said, brimming with passion. "I'm not a terrorist or a drug dealer. You can't force emergency laws on me."

He insisted the protest organizers were motivated only by love for Egypt. "We are not traitors," he said. They had thought through how to keep the demonstrations peaceful, he said, right down to cleaning the streets they occupied.

But Ghonim still knew little of what had transpired while he was imprisoned. The young interviewer began to air a slide show of young people killed in the protests. "What previous generations couldn't do," she said, "we can do."

Ghonim sucked in his breath and began to weep at the pictures.

"I want to tell every mother and every father, truthfully, about the people who died: I am so sorry," he said. "I swear to God, it's not our mistake. It's the mistake of those who are in charge of the country and don't want to leave their positions."

The young broadcaster tried to comfort him. "Don't cry, Wael," she said. "Don't cry." Unnerved, he unclipped the microphone and rushed off the set. She got up and followed him.

His emotional reaction riveted Egyptians, who love their soap operas but were used to tightly controlled coverage of news. "Ghonim's tears have moved millions and turned around the views of those who supported [Mubarak] staying," reported the website masrawy.com.[36]

Many in the older generation started to vocally side with their activist children. "Not only mama but everyone in the country was moved by this interview," Ziada, the young female activist, told me. "It was very real, and the guy was very honest and speaking from his heart.

"He revived the revolution," she said.

Ghonim showed up at Liberation Square the next day. "We will not abandon our demand, and that is the departure of the regime," he told the largest crowd yet assembled on the square.

By then, the protesters knew they had tangible power.

Three days after Ghonim's release, Mubarak gave a third address to the nation. The brief, prerecorded speech was confounding and obtuse. He dwelled on articles in the constitution that would be changed and, again, vowed to see the transition through to the finish.

But the speech was his last public act as president.

The next morning, Mubarak and his family snuck off to their vacation compound in Sharm el Sheikh. Vice President Suleiman, in office only two weeks, appeared unannounced on television with a terse statement.

"Taking into consideration the difficult circumstances the country is going through," said Suleiman, ashen-faced, "President Mohammed Hosni Mubarak has decided to leave the post of president of the republic and has tasked the Supreme Council of the Armed Forces to manage the state's affairs." Then Suleiman just as abruptly turned around and walked away.

The news broke as tens of thousands of Egyptians knelt in evening prayer at Liberation Square. Many leapt straight into the air with exhilaration. Even Egyptians who had supported Mubarak just a week earlier turned out for noisy, raucous celebrations that ran the length of the mighty Nile in Egypt.

In the end, Mubarak had no choice. The tide turned for three critical reasons: First, the regime could no longer isolate the movement. The opposition began to take its demonstrations beyond Liberation Square to parliament, with a pledge to encamp at other government sites too. Second, labor began to side with the opposition. Already crippled economically by the flight of 1 million tourists, Egypt could not afford to see strikes spread and the country completely paralyzed. Finally, the military became concerned about the costs of wider instability lasting for weeks or months. It acted in the end to preserve one of the region's oldest and proudest states, not Hosni Mubarak.

It took only eighteen days to unseat a long-standing leader with powerful international allies in a country considered the most stable in the Middle East. Egypt's uprising transformed the tools of opposition and even the major political actors. For the first time in six thousand years, elites were sidelined.

Egypt's uprising not only ousted Mubarak, however. It also discredited al Qaeda, whose chief ideologues were Egyptian. Ayman al Zawahiri, a physician, had led the Egyptian Islamic Jihad organization's violent campaign to overthrow the regime. In 1998, he merged his movement into Osama bin Laden's al Qaeda. He was often described as the brains behind al Qaeda, while bin Laden had been its public face and chief financier.

The anger that ousted one of the Middle East's most autocratic rulers came from the same well of grievances that al Qaeda exploited. Al Qaeda and the protesters shared common goals. Both sought to end the hoarding of political and economic power and the humiliation of the masses.

But to topple a tyrant, Egyptians rejected both al Qaeda's extremist ideology and its violent tactics.

During Egypt's uprising, the imagery of activism in the world's most volatile region also began to change. After the 9/11 attacks, haunting pictures of the World Trade Center's dusty collapse defined perceptions of Arabs for a decade. And however distorted the perception, Islam and extremism became synonymous. But after Egypt's uprising the imagery shifted to peaceful demonstrations and, eventually, celebratory crowds at Cairo's Liberation Square.

Over the next few days, dozens of Facebook pages were launched about Ghonim—backing him as a presidential candidate, nominating him for the Nobel Peace Prize, and calling him a gladiator. The most striking was the "We are all Wael Ghonim" page.

THE SCENT OF jasmine swiftly wafted across the Middle East. Street protests, small and large, erupted in half of the twenty-two Arab countries. Panicked regimes promised change at a breathtaking pace. A single week—between January 29 and February 4—set a record.

Hours after Mubarak announced that he would not run again, Jordan's King Abdullah II fired his government and pledged sweeping reforms. He too had faced weeks of simmering protests throughout his hybrid kingdom of Bedouin tribes, Palestinian refugees, Iraqi exiles, and others. A statement from the royal palace announced that a new prime minister would take "practical, swift and tangible steps to launch a real political reform process, in line with the king's version of comprehensive reform, modernization and development."

In Iraq, the prime minister abruptly announced that he would not seek a third term in office. He also called for a constitutional amendment to limit the prime minister to two terms.

"One of the characteristics of a lack of democracy is when a leader rules for thirty or forty years," Prime Minister Nouri al Maliki said in an interview with Agence France-Presse.[37] "It is a difficult issue for people. It is intolerable, and change is necessary."

Maliki's move would have been virtually unthinkable a year earlier. In March 2010, his party had come in second during national elections. But Maliki was so set on staying in power that he balked—for nine months—at any coalition that he did not lead. Iraq was paralyzed, at a critical juncture, as American troops began their pullout. Maliki won out. His new government took office December 21, 2010, just four days after Mohamed Bouazizi lit himself—and the region—on fire.

Seven weeks later, Maliki was suddenly willing to limit his time in office. He even seemed sympathetic to Egypt's protesters. "People have the right," he said, "to express what they want without being persecuted."

Maliki also cut his salary in half. In a country about twice the size of Idaho, he was estimated to make around $360,000—just under an American president's salary of $400,000—at a time when more than one-quarter of Iraq's labor force was unemployed and electricity ran as little as three hours a day.[38]

"That will help limit the differences in the social living standards," he said, "for different classes of the society."

His concessions came just hours after both Shiite and Sunni clerics warned the government that it faced unrest too if it failed to deal with Iraq's growing poverty, corruption, and desperation.

"All governments—even those which embraced democracy—have to study the essential reasons that have led to this overwhelming popular anger against the political regimes in those countries," said Sheikh Abdul-Mahdi al Karbalaie. "They have to learn the lessons from what is happening."[39]

After thousands took to the streets in Yemen, President Ali Abdullah Saleh—who had ruled since 1978—also announced that he would not stand for reelection. "I won't seek to extend my presidency for another term or have my son inherit it," Saleh told parliament. Like Mubarak, the Yemeni leader had been grooming his son as heir apparent.

"I make this compromise today for the sake of the country," he said. "Yemen's interests come before personal interests."

The shift was a total flip-flop. Just one month earlier, the Yemeni leader had asked parliament to amend the constitution so he could stay in power—for two additional terms of ten years. The request had not initially generated much opposition in a country already facing a rebellion in the north, secession in the south, and the world's most active al Qaeda faction. Yemen is also the poorest Arab state.

Saleh went even further. He slashed income taxes in half. He ordered price controls. He raised salaries for civil servants and the military up to 25 percent. He moved to create 60,000 jobs. And he exempted students from the rest of their tuition at state-run universities.

In Algeria, also plagued by sporadic protests, President Abdelaziz Bouteflika promised to lift emergency rule dating back two decades— just one day after insisting that martial law was still vital to contain extremism. The Palestinian Authority pledged long-delayed local elections "as soon as possible."

The sheikhdoms on the Arabian Peninsula used their oil wealth to try to preempt protests among restive populations. Kuwait, a city-state where the per capita income already exceeded $50,000, announced a "gift" of more than $3,500 to each of its citizens. It also pledged almost $1 billion for new food subsidies. On the eve of a Day of Rage protest, the emir of Bahrain promised $2,600 to every family in the little island nation.

Even Syria showed the political shakes. In an interview with the *Wall Street Journal*, Syrian President Bashar al Assad acknowledged that the Tunisian and Egyptian uprisings signaled a "new era" in the Middle East. Arab governments would have to do more to accommodate rising expectations, he said, especially among the young.

The Assad dynasty had governed Syria for more than four decades— Hafez al Assad for thirty years and his son Bashar for over ten—and brutally repressed the opposition throughout its rule. In 1982, Assad's father had unleashed his military to put down an uprising in Homa. An estimated 20,000 people were killed.

In 2011, Syria reluctantly lifted a long-standing ban on Facebook and YouTube. "If you did not see the need for reform before what happened in Egypt and in Tunisia," conceded Assad, a former ophthalmologist, "it is too late to do any reform."[40]

But none of steps taken by any of the Arab regimes was enough to stem the opposition. Murderous crackdowns no longer ensured that any regime, however brutal or brittle, could hold on to power.

The night Mubarak stepped down, CNN's Wolf Blitzer interviewed Wael Ghonim, the young Egyptian Google executive. Ghonim had been dancing around a room filled with young techies assembled to celebrate Mubarak's departure.

"First Tunisia, now Egypt," Blitzer said. "So what's next?"[41]

Ghonim smiled. "Ask Facebook," he said.

2.

The Counter-jihad

**Clearly 9/11 was a turning point for Americans.
But it was even more so for Muslims.**

—Parvez Sharma, Indian Muslim filmmaker

On November 23, 2008, ten members of Pakistan's Army of the Righteous hijacked an old fishing trawler in the Arabian Sea, killed four of the crew, and ordered the captain to sail toward India. It took three days. When the trawler neared Mumbai, the gunmen killed the captain and transferred to motorized rubber dinghies. They snuck into India's teeming port city just after 8:30 p.m. under cover of darkness. They then split up.[1]

Over the next three days, the ten extremists went on a killing spree. They attacked a railway station, two luxury hotels, a hospital, a cinema, a Jewish community center, a popular café, and several other sites along the way. More than 170 people, including many foreigners, were killed; more than 300 were injured in a terrorism drama relayed live by satellite television channels around the world. The siege finally ended when Indian security forces killed nine of the gunmen and captured the tenth on the morning of November 29.

The brutal violence reflected extremism's reach almost a decade after 9/11. But for the Islamic world, what happened next was even more striking.

Thousands of Indian Muslims—in the world's third-largest Muslim population—took to the streets to condemn the extremism of their brethren. They carried banners declaring "Killers of innocents are enemies of Islam."[2]

India's Muslim charities also refused to bury the assailants in Mumbai's sprawling Muslim cemetery.

The response signaled a wider turning point in the Islamic world: Men who once might have been deemed martyrs to a cause were now considered cold-blooded murderers. "People who committed this heinous crime cannot be called Muslim," Hanif Nalkhande, a spokesman for one charity, told the *New York Times*. "Terrorism has no place in Islamic doctrine."[3]

The government finally buried the Pakistani militants from Lashkhar-e-Taiba in a secret location in 2010—fourteen months after the deadly attack.[4]

A decade after the 9/11 terrorism spectaculars, the Islamic world is now in the throes of a counter-jihad. The new struggle pits Muslims against their brethren. Its goal is to rout extremism in its many forms, from the deviant doctrine launched by Osama bin Laden to the rigid rule of Iran's theocrats.

For the majority of Muslims today, the central issue is not a clash with other civilizations. It is instead a struggle within the faith itself to rescue Islam's central values from a small but virulent minority. The new confrontation is effectively a jihad against The Jihad. And it epitomizes the new phase in the Islamic resurgence.

"Muslims are now trying to reclaim space denied us—by our own people," Indian filmmaker Parvez Sharma told me after the release of his daring film *A Jihad for Love*. "We can no longer continuously talk about the most violent minority within Islam and allow them to dictate the tenets of a religion that is fourteen hundred years old."

The counter-jihad is reflected in the mundane and the remarkable, from central Asian girls named for the holy city of Medina to clerical summits to probe Islam's sacred texts for twenty-first-century application. Its new role models are portrayed by action figures, each endowed with one of God's ninety-nine attributes, in Kuwaiti comic books. Its messages are being conveyed by new televangelists in reality television programs. Its institutions include modern schools from Turkey to Pakistan that were built on Islamic principles but teach physics, economics, and modern literature. Its themes echo in Palestinian rap, Egyptian Facebook pages, and the flurry of Koranic verses text-messaged among students from Morocco to Indonesia.

The counter-jihad takes disparate forms. It is visible when men who were once Osama bin Laden's ideological mentors publicly repudiate al Qaeda and when Muslim comedians ridicule militancy altogether. It has been manifest in Tehran's street protests, the evolution of Turkey's ruling party, the resistance of Pakistani villagers to Taliban intrusions, and the debates among former jihadis in Egyptian prisons.

"I have declared a jihad against terrorism," pronounced Tahir ul Qadri, a senior Pakistani cleric. He issued a six-hundred-page fatwa in 2010 that condemned al Qaeda, outlawed suicide attacks, and warned bin Laden that he was leading Muslims into "hellfire."

"They're not going to have paradise, and they're not going to have seventy-two virgins in heaven. They're totally on the wrong side," ul Qadri pronounced. The detailed edict, which cited scriptures and Islamic traditions at length, is "a jihad against brutality, to bring them back towards normality," he said. "This is an intellectual jihad."[5]

The new counter-jihad has vastly different goals. For some it is about reforming the faith. For others it is about reforming political systems. But for many it is about achieving basic rights—on their own terms. The common denominator is the rejection of venomous ideologies and mass violence to achieve those ends.

"Only nations living in the past produce martyrs," Iraqi parliamentarian Iyad Jamal al Din told his brethren on an Al Jazeera news program. "They take more pride in their past than they look to the future."[6]

T HE COUNTER-JIHAD WILL define the next decade as thoroughly as the extremists dominated the last one—even as the al Qaeda franchises continue to plot ambitious terrorist attacks.

In the decade after 9/11, the United States thwarted more than two dozen major plots. Nine were in New York alone. Extremist schemes included destroying the Brooklyn Bridge, blowing up Wall Street financial institutions, igniting an airport fuel pipeline, releasing cyanide in the subway system, and attacking train tunnels between New York and New Jersey. Others envisioned attacking shopping malls in Ohio and New Jersey, blowing up refineries and pipelines in Wyoming and New Jersey, and bombing a Dallas skyscraper.[7]

Other threats ranged from the inane to the unthinkable.

The fringe website www.revolutionmuslim.com warned the creators of Comedy Central's cartoon satire *South Park* to stop portraying the Prophet Mohammed in a bear costume—or they would end up like Theo Van Gogh. The Dutch filmmaker, a relative of Vincent Van Gogh, produced a short film entitled *Submission* about violence against Muslim women. Van Gogh was shot eight times as he bicycled to work; a photo of his body sprawled on the pavement was included in the website posting.

"This is not a threat," the fringe website boasted, "but a warning of the reality of what will likely happen to them." [8]

As I started this book, three extremist plots against the United States were thwarted or uncovered in their final stages. In 2010, Pakistani-born Faisal Shahzad parked a bomb-laden van in Times Square that set off small plumes of smoke but failed to ignite the intended fireball explosion in the heart of New York's tourist district. The son of a Pakistani air force officer, Shahzad had just one year earlier received his American citizenship. He was nabbed moments before his plane departed JFK International Airport for Dubai.

Nigerian-born Umar Farouk Abdulmutallab was arrested after he set off a small bomb aboard a Northwest Airlines flight from Amsterdam to Detroit on Christmas day in 2009. The bomb, hidden in his underwear, sparked a small fire that was extinguished by passengers and crew.

And Afghan-born taxi driver Najibullah Zazi pled guilty to plotting to place several bombs in New York's subway system, following through on orders he had received during a trip to the Afghanistan-Pakistan border in 2008.

As I finished this book, a twenty-year-old Saudi student was arrested in Lubbock, Texas, for attempted use of weapons of mass destruction. Khalid Ali-M Aldawsari was charged with purchasing chemicals and other equipment to make explosives. He also allegedly bought a gas mask, a hazardous materials or "hazmat" suit, and a stun gun. In emails to himself entitled "nice targets," he listed twelve dams in California and Colorado, nuclear power stations, and the Dallas home of former President George W. Bush, which he referred to as the "tyrant's house." The FBI reported that the Saudi had done research about how to use baby dolls to contain the explosives.

In his blog, Aldawsari had allegedly written, "You who created mankind . . . grant me martyrdom for Your sake and make jihad easy for me only in Your path."

The dangers of terrorism at home will probably not diminish for a long time. In 2010, President Barack Obama held a summit of forty-seven world leaders to formulate a strategy to prevent terrorists from gaining access to nuclear technology. It was the largest gathering hosted by an American leader since the 1945 conference creating the United Nations.

"We are drifting towards a catastrophe beyond comparison," Obama said, quoting Einstein after development of the first bomb.

A decade after 9/11, the dangers to American interests abroad had actually grown. The wars in Iraq and Afghanistan generated new causes. Al Qaeda had spawned new franchises, all small but disproportionately deadly. In 2011, extremists in Pakistan's mountainous tribal regions posed a greater danger to American interests than militants in Afghanistan had in the 1990s.

US counterterrorism tactics, especially missile strikes from pilotless drones, eliminated senior leaders, vast arsenals, and major operation centers. But they also killed civilians, including children and families at wedding parties. The presence of foreign troops often fueled a backlash. In 2009, a Jordanian doctor turned double agent walked into a remote CIA station in Afghanistan, detonated himself, and wiped out most of the staff at a frontline intelligence post.

Given this reality, the counter-jihad is the most pivotal trend in the Islamic world. It is the only way that militancy—which has always been limited to a distinct but dedicated minority—will be eradicated as a tactic or an ideology.

Western armies can win only battles, especially on foreign turf. They will never be able to eradicate the ideas behind Islamic extremism with guns alone. With home-field credibility, only Muslims can defeat the most serious threat to global security. And many Muslims are pushing to do just that.

"It is time for the devout, silent, peace-loving Muslim majority to speak for Islam. Let us become louder than the radical voices that claim to represent us," said Sadia Dehlvi, an Indian Muslim and noted feminist. "Sincere moral outrage needs to be expressed at Taliban atrocities in Afghanistan and Pakistan, political kidnappings and assassinations, militancy in Kashmir, Shiite-Sunni killings in Iraq and Pakistan, fatwas that condone suicide bombings in the Israel-Palestine conflict, and all other such atrocities that affect innocent lives."[9]

* * *

YET THE COUNTER-JIHAD—in any of its many forms—is not suddenly embracing Western ways or aligning with the United States.
Nor is it about abandoning Islam for secular lifestyles or politics. Far
from it. The counter-jihad is more vibrantly Islamic than ever. Even as
Muslims reject Osama bin Laden's ideology, Islam is increasingly their
idiom of choice, albeit in different ways.

Politically, the counter-jihad craves changes compatible with a globalizing world and basic rights for the faithful. But it rejects strict
secularism and Westernization. The quest is more about "just values"—
equitable justice for all, political participation for all, free speech for all,
and rights of self-determination for all—adapted to Muslim societies.

"They want democracy to the extent it provides accountability, but
they don't want to be like us in a secular society. And they don't want a
theocracy but they don't see the inherent contradiction between religion
or religiosity and government," explained Richard Burkholder Jr., Gallup's director of several surveys of Muslim attitudes.

"They reject extremists, not just al Qaeda. But they also have reserva-
tions about the West," he told me. "Their attitude is: There's a plague on
both your houses."

Culturally, the counter-jihadis are deeply conservative in practices and
appearance, even as their goal is to adapt to the twenty-first century. As
in the Egyptian and Tunisian uprisings, they are synthesizing Koranic
values with ways of life spawned by the Internet, Facebook, and satellite
television. And they want to do it at a safe distance from the West.

"There's a growing sense that the West is not the only worldview
to look up to. Muslims today sense there are other ways of sharing the
world or negotiating our place in it," mused Ibrahim Kalin, founder of
Turkey's Foundation for Political, Economic and Social Research. "And
with it has come more confidence about dealing with issues of reason,
constitutionalism, science, and other aspects of modern society—but
without abandoning Islamic traditions."

A growing number of Muslims now want to use their faith as a
means to an end, rather than an end in itself—or as a way to find answers rather than being the answer itself. For them, Islam is often more
about identity than piety, about Muslim values rather than Islamic ideology. Islam is a comfortable space and a legitimate vehicle to search for

solutions compatible with global trends; it is no longer about creating an ideal Islamic state or even voting for Islamic parties.

But the shift does mean a wider embrace of Islam as the organizing principle of life, politics, education, social mores, and dress. It is about reform in a conservative package.

"There is a growing movement now in Islamic thought that is discussing and reclaiming the original *jihad al-nafs,* or the struggle within the self, and the greater jihad within Islam—not a jihad against outsiders," said Parvez Sharma, the Indian filmmaker.

The counter-jihad's goals and tactics will often confuse, and potentially alarm, an outside world that understands almost as little about Islam and Muslims as it did on September 11. The counter-jihad looks more Islamic, with more women wearing headscarves known as *hejab* to signal Islamic modesty. It also sounds more Islamic, since the counter-jihad has seriously altered street slang.

Young Arabs particularly often invoke the *shahada,* the Muslim declaration of faith, "There is no God but God," in greetings. Many also answer the telephone *Salaam alaikum*—"Peace be upon you"— instead of "Hello." And they often add the tagline *bi izn Allah*—"if God permits"—when discussing everything from the weather to politics.

"They think they're getting a bonus with God," mused Egyptian activist Dalia Ziada, a young Egyptian blogger.

Yet in contrast to Iran's turbulent upheaval in 1979, which marked the introduction of political Islam as a modern state ideology, the counter-jihad is more like a soft revolution. It is quieter, more personal, and in many ways more profound in its goals.

"It's a nonviolent revolution," explained Ziada, "that's trying to mix modernity and religion."

THE COUNTER-JIHAD IS the fourth phase of the Islamic revival and different from earlier waves in pivotal ways. The first three phases were largely reactive to one or more flashpoints: repressive regimes, regional conflicts, or foreign intervention. The weight and pace of modernization—in everything from ideology to fashion, commerce to entertainment—also eroded comfortable traditions, muddling what it was to be a modern Muslim.

Politicized Islam—Islamism—emerged in the midst of multiple crises as an alternative to the dominant ideologies of either East or West. Its leaders argued that the outside world was out to exploit, control, or destroy Muslim lands. The only way to defend the faith was to fight back, politically and physically.

Phase one had roots in the Muslim Brotherhood's birth in 1928. A twenty-two-year-old schoolteacher named Hassan al Banna mobilized six disgruntled workers from the Suez Canal Company in a grassroots religious and social reform movement. The new organization slowly gained momentum across the Islamic world. The revival was channeled into a popular mass movement after the colossal Arab defeat in the 1967 Middle East war. In a mere six days, tiny Israel overwhelmed the armies of Egypt, Syria, and Jordan, which were backed by men and arms from Iraq, Saudi Arabia, Morocco, Algeria, Sudan, and Tunisia.

In less than a week, the Arabs suffered the worst losses since Europe colonized the region. Egypt lost the massive Sinai Peninsula and the teeming Gaza Strip. Jordan lost the fertile West Bank and East Jerusalem, one of Islam's holiest sites. And Syria lost the strategic Golan Heights.

The biggest political losers, however, were the secular ideologies that had defined Arab politics since independence from colonial rule. Islam filled the vacuum, at first largely by default.

Phase one peaked during the 1970s. The formal turning point was the 1973 war. Arabs fought for the first time in the name of Islam. Egypt's surprise attack on Israel—during the simultaneous religious celebrations of Yom Kippur for Jews and Ramadan for Muslims—was code-named "Operation Badr" after the Prophet Mohammed's first victory in 623 as he began to build the Islamic empire. The rallying cry was *Allahu akbar,* or "God is great."

The Arabs again lost militarily. But they did win important political objectives, including the principle of land for peace. Islam suddenly became a winning way to mobilize the public and fight a regional war.

The revival's first political victory was the overthrow of Iran's monarchy in 1979. From exile, a spindly octogenarian named Ayatollah Ruhollah Khomeini managed to coalesce Iran's motley opposition factions—rival nationalists, communists, democrats, and ethnic groups—under the banner of Islam. In a mere fourteen months, the unlikely coalition forced Shah Mohammad Reza Pahlavi and his glamorous empress to abandon the Peacock Throne. Holding a small jar of Iranian soil in his hand, the shah flew out of Iran. He was the last king in a string of Persian dynasties dating back more than two thousand years.

Iran's 1979 revolution produced the world's only modern theocracy. It was the first time in Islam's fourteen centuries that clerics ruled a state.

By the end of the 1970s, political Islam was not only a viable opposition force. It had also redefined the world's ideological spectrum. Variations of democracy and communism had dominated much of the world since World War II. Islam suddenly offered an alternative.

P HASE TWO WAS marked by the rise of suicide extremism and mass violence in the 1980s. The shift was symbolized by the 1983 attack on the United States Embassy in Beirut. Shortly after 1 p.m. on April 18, a delivery van made a sharp left swing into the guarded cobblestone entry—and drove straight into the seven-story building. It was the first suicide bombing against an American target.

Eight months later, a yellow Mercedes truck circled the Beirut compound housing US Marine peacekeepers asleep inside on a balmy Sunday morning. A Marine guard later recalled seeing the driver's eerie smile as he turned and drove toward the four-story concrete building next to Beirut International Airport. The bomb was the largest nonnuclear explosion since World War II. It produced the largest loss of American military life—241 Marine and Navy personnel—in a single incident since the Battle of Iwo Jima in World War II. A decade after 9/11, it still held the record, despite heavy US losses in Iraq and Afghanistan.

Both attacks, and many that followed, were the work of Shiite militants in the embryonic cells of Hezbollah, the Lebanese Party of God. A few months later, in early 1984, the United States pulled its Marines out of Lebanon; their incomplete mission was widely considered a failure. A suicide bomber soon attacked the temporary American embassy in Lebanon—the third bombing against a US target in seventeen months.

The violent tactics by religious extremists began to redefine modern warfare. And it was only the beginning. The trend started among Shiite extremists, for whom martyrdom has been a central tenet for fourteen centuries. It soon spread to Sunni militants, for whom it was not a long-held belief.

During the 1980s, Osama bin Laden got his start alongside his Sunni brethren fighting the Soviet Union's occupation of Afghanistan. The Mujahadeen "holy warriors" fought Soviet troops for a decade. Bin Laden used his personal wealth to recruit and support foreign fighters helping the Afghans, a network that later became part of al Qaeda. He learned the arts of war along the way.

The Soviet withdrawal in 1989 was the last battle of the Cold War. It also marked the beginning of the end of the fifteen-nation Soviet empire.

Palestinian politics were also redefined by two militant Sunni movements. The Palestinian Islamic Jihad was launched in the early 1980s in Gaza. Its manifesto called for elimination of the "Zionist entity" and creation of a Palestinian state governed by Islamic law. It dispatched human bombs against Israeli soldiers as well as civilians at an outdoor café, a nightclub, an open-air market, a bakery, a pizza parlor, a shopping mall, and on several buses.

Hamas emerged in 1987 in Gaza during the grassroots uprising popularly known as the *intifada*, literally the "shaking off." It, too, soon started dispatching suicide warriors.

The common denominator among Shiites and Sunnis was cause: Lebanese, Afghans, and Palestinians took up arms to challenge what they viewed as occupation by outside armies or intervention by foreign powers.

PHASE THREE BEGAN with the rise of Islamist political parties in the 1990s. The emphasis began to shift from the bullet to the ballot—or a combination of the two.

Algeria was the trailblazer in the early 1990s, as the Islamic Salvation Front appeared on the verge of beating more than fifty other parties in the Arab world's first fully democratic election. The Front ran an impressive campaign, but it also worked the streets, literally, at a time the government appeared paralyzed. During a national strike by sanitation workers, the Front's followers rolled up their sleeves and picked up massive mounds of stinking garbage that had accumulated along the boulevards and winding alleys of Algiers.

The Islamists were perceived as doers, a stark contrast to the corrupt and lethargic party that had ruled since Algeria won independence from France three decades earlier. "Islam is the solution" was their campaign slogan and agenda. In the first round of parliamentary elections, the Front won the largest share of votes, by far.

But the Arab world's first experiment in democratically integrating a popular Islamist party was derailed before the final election runoff in 1992. The Algerian army seized power, ousted the president who had introduced reforms, and nullified the vote. With tanks rumbling through the streets of Algiers, the new junta outlawed the Islamic Salvation Front and imprisoned its leaders.

The Arab world's first democratic experiment was aborted. An underground militant faction, the Armed Islamic Group, soon began attacks on government targets. Over the next decade, more than 100,000 Algerians died in a civil war between the military regime and extremists.

Yet Islamic parties elsewhere continued an experiment that coincided with political openings—from South Africa to Chile, Russia to Romania—after the Cold War's end. In 1992, after a decade underground, Hezbollah's Hassan Nasrallah led the Shiite party into Lebanese elections. Egypt's Muslim Brotherhood ran more openly for parliament in 1995, after a decade of competing under the cover of other political parties. Jordan's Islamic Action Front became the largest opposition party in parliament.

From scenic Morocco and sleepy Kuwait to teeming Yemen, Islamist parties captured the imagination of many voters—and the wrath of all their regimes.

P HASE FOUR BEGAN after 9/11, which was as traumatic for many Muslims half a world away as for Americans who witnessed attacks on the World Trade Center or the Pentagon. The vast majority of Muslims rejected the mass killing of innocent civilians. But hundreds of millions of Muslims also suddenly found themselves tainted by a man and a movement they neither knew nor supported. Islam was increasingly associated with terrorist misadventures. And Muslims were increasingly unwelcome in the West, as cracks along a civilizational divide threatened to spawn a new cultural cold war.

Tensions only grew as two new hot wars were launched in predominantly Muslim Afghanistan and Iraq. During the first decade of the twenty-first century, many Muslims felt trapped between the furious West and the Islamist furies.

For many Muslims, the West's attempt to create new democracies in the Islamic world was unconvincing. American military victories over the Taliban in Afghanistan and Saddam Hussein in Iraq turned into quagmires. In both countries, new democratically elected governments proved inept and corrupt. Crime, unemployment, daily hardships, even the failure to provide electricity only grew worse.

Phase four produced a decisive disillusionment with the Western model, which failed to deliver.

Yet militant Islam failed to deliver too. Almost 3,000 people died on 9/11. But extremists also killed more than 10,000 of their brethren in suicide bombings and other attacks over the next decade. The costs to Muslims unleashed an angry backlash—and the counter-jihad.

By 2010, long before bin Laden was killed in a US raid, public opinion polls in major Muslim countries showed dramatic declines in support for al Qaeda. Support for bin Laden had dropped to 2 percent in Lebanon and 3 percent in Turkey.[10] In pivotal places like Egypt, Pakistan, and Indonesia—which are populated by vastly different ethnic groups thousands of miles apart—only around one in five Muslims had confidence in the al Qaeda leadership, according to the Pew Global Attitudes Project.[11]

Muslims' attitudes on modernization and fundamentalism also shifted. In a sampling of Muslim countries on three continents, the survey found far more people identified with modernizers—by two to six times—than with fundamentalists. Egypt and Jordan were the two exceptions; in both, the split was about even.[12]

During the first month of Egypt's uprising in 2011, another poll found that 52 percent of Egyptians disapproved of the Muslim Brotherhood. Only 4 percent strongly approved of Egypt's largest Islamic movement. Its leaders got barely 1 percent in a presidential straw vote. The survey, by the pro-Israeli Washington Institute for Near East Policy, found even higher disapproval of Iran. Almost six out of ten Egyptians disapproved of Tehran's Islamic government.

"This is not," the survey concluded, "an Islamic uprising."[13]

Yet after the uprisings in Egypt and Tunisia, many Arabs also told me that they wanted a new democratic political life that was compatible with their culture.

"Without Islam, we will not have any real progress," explained Diaa Rashwan of Cairo's Al-Ahram Center for Political and Strategic Studies. "If we go back to the European Renaissance, it was based on Greek and Roman philosophy and heritage. When Western countries built their own progress, they didn't go out of their epistemological or cultural history. Japan is still living in the culture of the Samurai, but in a modern way. The Chinese are still living the traditions created by Confucianism. Their version of communism is certainly not Russian.

"So why," he mused, "do we have to go out of our history?"

A S THEY REJECT extremism, Muslims have begun experimenting with alternatives. In 2010, Palestinians launched a passive resistance campaign against Israeli occupation. It was a strikingly different tactic after decades of war, suicide bombings, airplane hijackings, and two uprisings. Villagers along the 256-mile barrier dividing Israel and the West Bank launched peaceful marches every Friday, the Muslim Sabbath.

The model was not Islamic extremism but a pacifist Islam. Palestinian officials, including men once tied to militias, often joined the peaceful village marches.[14]

"We emulate the Prophet, peace be upon him, who was the first to practice passive resistance and peaceful jihad, and spent thirteen years without raising a weapon or ordering a violent response to the harm done to him and his companions," said Palestinian Social Affairs Minister Mahmoud Habash.

"Our people's interests today require choosing a means of resistance that minimizes losses and realizes achievements."[15]

In Bilin, which spearheaded the campaign, protesters dressed up each week in costumes from popular culture to draw international attention to the blockade that cut many villagers off from their farmlands. One week they all dressed as Santa Claus, another week as a chain gang in gray prison stripes. But the protesters generated the most attention when they chose the blockbuster movie *Avatar* as their theme. Villagers painted their bodies and faces sky blue, adding pointy ears, long braided wigs, tails, and loincloths to look like the oppressed Na'vi aliens.

"When people around the world who have watched the film see our demonstration and the conditions that provoked it, they will realize that the situations are identical," said Mohammed Khatib, one of the protest-ers.[16] Israel declared Bilin a closed area for the six months after news-papers and blogs worldwide ran pictures of the *Avatar*-esque villagers waving the Palestinian flag.

Yet the weekly protests persisted in other forms elsewhere.

In 2010, Palestinian Prime Minister Salam Fayyad confronted Israeli forces on Palestinian Land Day not by raising a gun but by putting his foot down against a rusty plow hitched to an old nag. In West Bank land under Israel's control, he dug a furrow to plant a tree—and then defi-antly declared the land would be part of a future Palestinian state.[17]

"We have to ask ourselves, each one of us," he said, "What is it I am going to do today to move this project forward an inch, a step?"[18]

Palestinians also launched an economic boycott of goods produced in Jewish settlements in the West Bank. The Israeli-Palestinian interim peace agreement prohibited boycotts of Israeli-made products and pro-duce. But it did not cover settlement products, worth about $200 million a year.[19]

Palestinian communities held bonfires to burn settlement goods. In 2010, more than $1 million worth of food, cosmetics, hardware, diapers, paint, soap, and other goods produced in nearby settlements were set alight in the small town of Salfit. The Palestinian prime minister, a for-mer World Bank economist, took the ceremonial lead, tossing a big yel-low box into the flames and setting off a spitting black plume.[20]

Big billboards declared, "Your conscience, your choice."[21] The Pales-tinian government imposed stiff fines on stores that violated the boy-cott. In one raid, officials seized from markets in Hebron eleven tons of watermelons that had been imported from nearby settlements.[22]

The civil disobedience campaign gained international attention. Mar-tin Luther King III traveled to the West Bank to lecture on nonviolent resistance at a West Bank conference.[23] The grandson of Mahatma Gan-dhi visited Bilin in the spring of 2010.

"What happens in this village," Rajmohan Gandhi told its residents, "is a model for contemporary nonviolent popular resistance."[24]

West Bankers increasingly started talking about a strategy of *sumud*—or steadfastness—instead of intifadas, or uprisings.

"Steadfastness must be translated from a slogan to acts and facts on the ground," Fayyad said, after plowing the field. "It is based on the peaceful daily expression, in a non-violent manner, of opposition to occupation and settlements, boycotting the products of the settlements and invigorating the popular movement against the wall.

"Resistance without blood," he said, "is also resistance." [25]

T HE NEW COUNTER-JIHADIS have rejected extremism for reasons ranging from the personal to the philosophical. But first and foremost is disillusionment. Causes vary: Idealistic zeal is eroded by harsh realities. Members split over ideology, tactics, or targets. Leaders are corrupted and followers fall off. Or the attraction simply fizzles. For young men, jihad often initially provided an exciting novelty, an independent identity, the feeling of fraternity, a source of employment, or a sense of purpose—all of which can wear with time.

In his videotaped farewell message, the Jordanian double agent who blew up the CIA station in Afghanistan chastised his brethren for treating jihad as little more than an adventure. "How long will love for jihad be just a dream, little more than a hobby which you do on your off time?" Humam Khalili Abu Mulal al Balawi scolded his fellow jihadists.[26]

In most cases, disillusionment is a gradual process; commitment unravels over years rather than months.

In 1989, Noman Benotman left Libya to join the armed jihad. He was twenty-two. He first went to Afghanistan to get military training and to fight the communist regime left behind after the Soviet Union's withdrawal. A picture of Benotman from that period showed a lean young man, sporting a short beard and dressed in the long, loose *shalwar kameez* shirt and baggy pants common in South Asia. His was light blue. He was cradling an AK-47 rifle as he picked fruit from a tree.

"I went originally for the sake of Islam, to do jihad, to defend the Muslim nation," he told me two decades later. "In the 1980s, communism was the antidote of humanity. And in the Islamic world, anyone supporting communism was not a Muslim anymore," he said. "So Afghanistan represented a real war. I spent a long time on the frontlines. And I was fully prepared to sacrifice my life."

Benotman was in Afghanistan for almost four years. He hoped to eventually return home and confront the regime of Colonel Moammar Qaddafi, which he viewed as corrupt and un-Islamic. With other Libyan dissidents, Benotman helped found the Libyan Islamic Fighting

Group. In the Libyan camps in Afghanistan, the young militants trained in guerrilla warfare tactics, simple arms such as mortars and machine guns, celestial navigation, coded communications, and basic first aid for war injuries. Their instructors were Afghan Mujahadeen trained by Pakistan and armed by the United States during the decade-long war against the Soviet occupation. They often used American and British training manuals.

As a young fighter, Benotman idealized bin Laden. He listened to the Saudi's taped messages, heard stories from fellow fighters, and read about him in the growing literature of militant Islam. The two men also overlapped in Sudan in the 1990s, where both were biding time in exile.

But as bin Laden was building a network of militants in the run-up to creating al Qaeda, Benotman was developing doubts.

"The big shock for me was the Algerian war," he explained, in a cadenced British accent. Sixteen of his colleagues had gone to fight with the Armed Islamic Group in the mid-1990s.

"I started to notice things—like how the Algerians were justifying violence against civilians with fatwas and how badly their leadership functioned," he said. "I had direct contact with some of them and, frankly, I thought they were idiots."

Algerian militants, who feuded among themselves, also engaged in brutal massacres of teachers, thinkers, journalists, and women that eventually sapped public support. "I came to the conclusion that this is risky business for jihadi groups to continue," Benotman said.

In 1998, when the Libyan movement held a meeting of its exiled members in Istanbul, he expressed his doubts about extremist tactics that were killing innocent Muslims. "I asked, Is it efficient? Will it bear fruit? Is it practical? Is it fair to sacrifice people?" Benotman recalled.

In 2000, he dared to take his concerns to the top. Benotman was among hundreds of jihadis invited by bin Laden to attend a five-day conference on strategy in Kandahar, the Taliban stronghold in southern Afghanistan.

"The leaders of most jihadist groups were there and, of course, all the leaders of al Qaeda," Benotman recalled. "When it came time for my presentation, I told them that after almost twenty years, the jihadist movement had failed, that we had gone from one disaster to another, like in Algeria, because we had not mobilized the people.

"I told them our message to the Muslim world only reinforces the idea of extremism. It's about destroying and not about building a state or a society," he continued. "That's why we have never mobilized a single society behind us.

"Look at the Egyptian experience," he added. "Out of seventy million, where is your support? Don't say it's because of the security services. We don't have the public behind us because there's something wrong with our message. And we need to stop and think about it."

Benotman also challenged al Qaeda's strategy. He told bin Laden bluntly that targeting the United States was a potentially fatal mistake.

"I warned him that if he did something stupid and kept testing the United States to the limit, the response was not simply going to be more cruise missiles," he recalled, referring to the 1998 cruise missile attacks on al Qaeda camps after the American embassies in Kenya and Tanzania were bombed. "I told him the Americans would occupy the whole region."

Benotman still remembers how Ayman al Zawahiri, al Qaeda's operations chief who also led Egypt's Islamic Jihad movement, initially laughed.

"Well, you can imagine," Benotman said. "They were shocked."

Bin Laden told Benotman that he had one attack already in place that he could not and would not recall. Benotman has always assumed that the al Qaeda chief was referring to the 9/11 operation.

"Nine eleven was considered the Achilles' heel for the whole jihadi tendency," Benotman said.

Disillusioned with the scope of violence, Benotman opted out in 2003. He quit the Libyan Islamic Fighting Group and eventually ended up in London. He took to wearing tailored suits and fashionable ties, replaced his beard with a designer mustache and small goatee, and began frequenting cafés that served a decent espresso. By 2007, he was sufficiently transformed that Qaddafi's son Saif approached him to help broker reconciliation between the imprisoned leadership of his former movement and the Libyan government. Benotman flew to Tripoli to test the interest and sincerity of both sides, then agreed.

The former jihadi spent the next three years secretly negotiating a package that basically called for the leaders of the Libyan Islamic Fighting Group to renounce violence and al Qaeda in exchange for the freedom of more than two hundred political prisoners.

The deal had far broader implications, however. The final document, which ran more than four hundred pages, also outlined a new code for jihad. It had credibility in jihadist circles because it was crafted by the Libyan Islamic Fighting Group's top leaders, including Abu Mundhir al Saadi, the movement's religious guide. Al Saadi was respected by bin Laden and Zawahiri and was reportedly a former confidant to Taliban leader Mullah Omar.[27]

"Jihad has ethics and morals because it is for God," the document pronounced. "That means it is forbidden to kill women, children, elderly people, priests, messengers, traders, and the like. Betrayal is prohibited and it is vital to keep promise and treat prisoners of war in a good way. Standing by those ethics is what distinguishes Muslims' jihad from the wars of other nations."

It amounted to a blunt rebuke of al Qaeda.

A decade after 9/11, I asked Benotman what jihad meant to him.

"The Koran is from the words of God, and jihad is part of Islam. We have forty verses talking about jihad and regulating it. It's nonnegotiable," he told me.

"But there's no connection with that and what's going on now," he said. "What we see now is the militarization of Islam, and that's not jihad."

Benotman was not unique. Extremist ideologies have always been vulnerable to defections and disaffection, even among the most committed. A decade after 9/11, its mythically omnipotent image was being shattered.

One of al Qaeda's original 9/11 operatives—Mushabib al Hamlan—dropped out in the final stages. After training in Afghanistan, he returned to Saudi Arabia to get a visa for the United States. But Hamlan opted to stay home after he learned that his mother was ill. He returned to college.

Ziad Jarrah, a second al Qaeda operative from Lebanon, reportedly almost dropped out because of his troubled relationship with 9/11 mastermind Mohamed Atta. In the end, differences were papered over. He went on to pilot United Flight 93, which crashed into a Pennsylvania field as passengers challenged the al Qaeda operatives.[28]

For all its ideological zeal, extremism can also be vulnerable to everyday disputes, human ego, and financial realities.

In his early twenties, Jamal al Fadl was recruited in a Brooklyn mosque to join the Afghan campaign against the Soviet Union in the

1980s. The Sudanese youth grew close to bin Laden and was in on the early planning to create al Qaeda. He eventually served as a business agent for bin Laden, buying equipment and reportedly even discussing acquisition of materiel to make chemical weapons.

But Fadl also became offended by al Qaeda's fluctuating pay scale. His salary was $500 a month, while Egyptian militants earned $1,200. So Fadl began embezzling from al Qaeda; he stashed away more than $100,000. When bin Laden discovered the scheme in 1996, Fadl defected. He ended up as a CIA informant, providing critical early evidence about bin Laden's plans to attack the United States.

Moroccan-born L'Houssaine Kherchtou went through training to become bin Laden's personal pilot. But he fell out with al Qaeda when it refused to give him $500 so his pregnant wife could have a cesarean section. He too turned against bin Laden and became an American informant.[29]

For all the family wealth he inherited, bin Laden had a reputation within his own ranks for being rather stingy.

Al Qaeda even alienated the Taliban, which hosted bin Laden and his training camps in Afghanistan for years. Since 9/11, many Taliban officials have complained that bin Laden repeatedly violated their agreement not to do anything that would harm Afghanistan or their own rule. The 9/11 attacks instead led to the Taliban's ouster.

In the official Taliban magazine, Taliban propagandist Abu Walid al Masri also openly mocked bin Laden for his flimsy do-it-yourself Islamic scholarship.[30] The Taliban propagandist charged that al Qaeda's whole strategy had grossly miscalculated.

"The majority of the population is against al Qaeda," Abu Walid wrote, in a series of Internet interviews with Australian counterterrorism specialist Leah Farrall. "Jihad has become synonymous with the explosive belt and the car bomb . . . and this is a real disaster because war is not indiscriminate killing."

Bin Laden, he added, had become an authoritarian leader who launched the "first private sector jihad in Muslim history." The Taliban's ruling council had decided to "disengage" from al Qaeda. Bin Laden and many of his allies, Abu Walid wrote, were no longer welcome in Afghanistan.[31]

* * *

THE COUNTER-JIHAD IS not just the work of individuals. Whole communities, both large and small, have also begun to resist extremism. The mobilization is often referred to as an "awakening." It plays
out differently, depending on the country and catalyst. But it is usually
a reaction to the failure of Islamist political ideologies to fulfill utopian
promises. Militants excelled at destruction but were unable to provide
constructive solutions to the basic challenges of everyday life, from education to health care and employment. And rather than help societies
move into the twenty-first century, they often rolled them into a dark
past.

The awakening was most vivid in Iraq, where al Qaeda's grip on
Anbar Province in 2006 led the US military to concede it had "lost"
Iraq's largest region.[32] A classified assessment warned, "The social and
political situation has deteriorated to a point that US and Iraqi troops are
no longer capable of militarily defeating the insurgency in al-Anbar,"
the *Washington Post* reported. "Nearly all government institutions
from the village to provincial levels have disintegrated or have been
thoroughly corrupted and infiltrated by Al Qaeda in Iraq, or a smatter-
ing of other resistance groups."

Future prospects also looked "dim," the report concluded, "and there
is almost nothing the US military can do there." As if to rub it in, the assessment coincided with al Qaeda's declaration of a new "Islamic state of
Iraq" in Anbar.[33]

The loss of Anbar in 2006 was the greatest single setback to the US
intervention. Politically, the desert province was the Sunni heartland.
And without the Sunnis, fragile multiethnic Iraq could never be whole.
Militarily, Anbar provided bases for al Qaeda and Iraqi insurgents to run
operations in other key provinces against both the US military and the
fragile Shiite-led Iraqi government. Strategically, Anbar bordered Saudi
Arabia, Jordan, and Syria. Through Anbar, al Qaeda of Mesopotamia also
could gain access to the three key Arab countries.

But al Qaeda's branch in Iraq went too far. It wrested control of Anbar
by intimidation, kidnappings, torture, and executions that eliminated respected tribal leaders. In many parts of the Middle East, tribes are still
the basic source of identity and protection, far more than the central
state. So eliminating the tribal structure upset the long-standing social
order. Al Qaeda also usurped the tribe's main businesses, smuggling
routes, and extortion rings—all major sources of income.

So just as the United States was giving up on Anbar, the province's tribal elders began turning against their Sunni brethren in al Qaeda. And the Awakening—or the *sahwa* in Arabic—was launched.

Sheikh Abdul Sattar Abu Risha,[34] a charismatic young tribal chief famed for his elegant white robes, pearl-handled revolver, and Gucci sunglasses, led the campaign. He was not inspired by any altruistic or ideological epiphany. He turned on al Qaeda for quite practical reasons. Al Qaeda's thugs murdered his father and two brothers. They then took over the tribe's powers and businesses—reportedly including oil smuggling and highway banditry, neither unusual in Iraq's wild west.[35]

The issue was simple survival.

Still in his thirties, Sheikh Sattar responded by mobilizing other tribal elders in the first Awakening Council to wrest back control of Anbar. Over the next year, the council recruited more than 90,000 men for a new militia and police force to expel al Qaeda.

The tribal elders reached out to the US military for arms and aid. "Our American friends had not understood us when they came," Sheikh Sattar said at the time. "They were proud, stubborn people, and so were we. They worked with the opportunists. Now they have turned to the tribes, and this is as it should be." [36]

The alliance was always a marriage of convenience, not a common political cause. "We did not support the U.S. forces or anyone else," Sheikh Sattar made clear. "We fought on behalf of our people and defeated al Qaeda." [37]

Iraq's Awakening, which began in late 2006, started to shift the balance of power in Anbar and then help turn around the vicious war in 2007. The American surge of troops in 2007 would not have succeeded without the Iraqi Awakening. The US military had cleaned out big cities like Ramadi and Fallujah before, at great human cost, only to lose them again. The Anbar elders' decision to turn against their militant Arab brethren was the key to al Qaeda's banishment the second time around.

Within Iraq, the charismatic young sheikh—not the American military—soon came to symbolize al Qaeda's defeat. Along the way, he also became a frequent al Qaeda target. Its thugs finally succeeded in the fall of 2007. Sheikh Sattar was assassinated when his car hit a roadside bomb outside his home just one day short of the first anniversary of the Awakening Council. He died just one week after meeting President

George W. Bush during a surprise visit to, by then, the comparatively peaceful province.

S MALLER-SCALE AWAKENINGS HAVE happened elsewhere, usually in reaction to violence and the imposition of extremist rule.

Pakistan's Swat valley is a lush 3,500-square-mile tourist paradise famed for its alpine vistas, fruit orchards, bubbling streams, and honeymoon resorts. It was popularly known as the "Switzerland of Pakistan." But between 2007 and 2009, the tranquil valley turned into a war zone as zealots from Pakistan's Taliban moved from lawless areas near the Afghan border deeper into the country's heartland. They got as far as Swat, just eighty miles from Islamabad, the capital. In a scramble to stop the advance, the government agreed to a political compromise allowing Islamic law to be imposed on Swat's 1.7 million people.

The decision was initially welcomed in Swat. The region had grown increasingly frustrated with the government's slow and flagrantly corrupt legal system. Justice often went only to those who could pay for it. But support for the deal and the local Taliban did not last long.

Led by a charismatic radio preacher named Maulana Fazlullah, Pakistan's Taliban banned girls' education and destroyed some two hundred schools for both genders. Women were ordered to cover not just their heads but also their faces. Barbers were banned from shaving men's beards. Shops selling music and entertainment videos were forced to close. Polio immunizations were halted. Cosmetics shops were trashed. The popular ski resort at Malam Jabba was burned down.

Justice became swift but also arbitrary and extreme. Armed men in bulky black turbans imposed gruesome punishments. They cut off the ears or noses of opposition figures. And they sold videos of police beheadings to intimidate the locals.[38] Corpses often hung for days in the public squares of Mingora, Swat's capital, as warnings. The body of a dancer was dumped at a crossroads after her execution for leading an unIslamic life; DVD recordings of her performances were strewn around her body.[39] Women were also punished simply for shopping or going out in public alone.

Within three months, the locals became disillusioned enough to act. The awakening in Swat was sparked partly by the public flogging of a teenage girl named Chaand. A widely circulated cell phone video showed three men pin the veiled teenager facedown to the ground as a fourth man whipped her hard across the back and bottom three dozen times.

"Please, *please* stop it," she wailed, writhing in pain with each new blow. "Either kill me or stop it."

Her crime was unspecified immoral behavior. One local version claimed she had stepped out of her home without a male member of her family. Another version claimed she was accused of violating Islamic law after she turned down the marriage request of a Taliban commander.

The Taliban circulated the video to scare the locals. It instead infuriated them.[40]

Pakistani columnist Shafqat Mahmood called Swat's new rulers "ignorant cavemen masquerading as fighters of Islam." The "barbarian horde" was after power, not Islam, he wrote.[41] When Pakistani troops moved back into the valley in May 2009, the Swatis led them to the militants' hiding places and tunnels where their weapons were stashed.

"These people, six months ago, weren't willing to share anything," said a Pakistani military official.[42]

The Taliban were soon ousted from Swat. More than 1,000 militants were killed in the process. National sentiment had grown decisively against them. In Islamabad, protesters waved placards and stuck cards in their caps with marching orders, "Go Taliban Go."

"Islam is our identity and our system of life, but variety and choice are part of it. People should dress modestly but women don't have to cover their faces and men don't have to grow long beards," Khurshid Ahmad, an Islamic scholar and national legislator, told the *Washington Post*.

"The Koran is very clear that there should be no coercion in religion. You cannot cram it down people's throats," he said. "This is where the Taliban destroyed their own case."[43]

Once again, however, the people of Swat did not turn on the Taliban because of any new political affinity or affection for the central government—especially its clumsy judicial system. Many in the scenic province, an autonomous princely state that only came under Pakistan's full control in 1969, still wanted to return to the inexpensive and quick customary law that is much like Sharia.[44] The Taliban remained a threat because the central government again failed to deal with inept local government, sweeping poverty, and a corrupt judiciary after the militants retreated.

Yet polls showed that support for al Qaeda and Pakistan's Taliban had plummeted nationwide. In 2009, more than 60 percent of Pakistanis viewed al Qaeda unfavorably—almost doubling the number from just one year earlier, according to the Pew Global Attitudes Project.[45]

Nine out of every ten Pakistanis surveyed said suicide bombs were "never justified." And almost 80 percent of Pakistanis expressed concern about extremism generally.[46]

The pivotal shift in the public mood was evident even in largely ungoverned tribal areas along the remote border with Afghanistan. Several villages mobilized local militias to regain control of their lands and lives. It was no tipping point, like Iraq's Awakening. They did not get sufficient backup in arms or aid, as in Iraq. They had both successes and retreats—and many deaths along the way.

"The tables are turned against the Taliban now," said political scientist Rasul Baksh Rais. "They are marginalized."[47]

The assessment may have been excessively optimistic, given the array of dedicated extremist groups that often shared resources, training facilities, and agendas in Pakistan. But the new confidence to challenge extremism did reflect the beginning of a starkly different trend, even in the world's most dangerous country.

The counter-jihad now has roots in every Muslim country, albeit in differing degrees.

"Today, al Qaeda is as significant to the Islamic world as the Ku Klux Klan is to the Americans—not much at all," reflected Ghada Shahbender, an Egyptian poet and activist who was out on the streets during Egypt's uprising. "They're violent, ugly, operate underground, and are unacceptable to the majority of Muslims. They exist, but they're freaks.

"Do I look at the Ku Klux Klan and draw conclusions about America from their behavior? Of course not," she told me. "The KKK hasn't been a story for many years for Americans. Al Qaeda is still a story, but it is headed in the same direction as the Klan."

3.

The Big Chill

**The perpetration of terrorist acts supposes a
rupture of such magnitude with Islamic teaching
that the individuals or groups who have
perpetrated them have stopped being Muslim.**

—Islamic Commission of Spain[1]

The symbolic turning point for the counter-jihad was in 2007.
It was reflected in an open letter written by Sheikh Salman al
Oudah* to Osama bin Laden on the sixth anniversary of the 9/11
attacks. The letter was long. It was quite personal. And it was bluntly
scathing.

"I say to my brother Osama, how much blood has been spilt?" the
Saudi cleric wrote. "How many innocent people, children, elderly, and
women have been killed, maimed, or banished in the name of al Qaeda?
Will you be happy to meet God almighty carrying the burden of these
hundreds of thousands, if not millions, of innocent people on your
back?"[2]

The letter was stunning because Sheikh Salman, as he was known to
his followers, had been one of bin Laden's earliest role models. The mis-
sive marked his total repudiation of the al Qaeda chief. To drive it home,
he released the letter to the media and on the Internet. He then went on
television to discuss it.

By 2007, bin Laden's most potent enemies were no longer Western
armies. They were increasingly Islam's own clerics.

---

* Oudah's name is also transliterated phonetically as Oodah, Ouda, Awdah, and Awda.

Sheikh Salman and bin Laden were actually contemporaries. Both were born in the mid-1950s. Both came of age as the Islamic revival swept the Middle East in the late 1970s. Physically, both had bushy, untrimmed beards. Devout Muslims believe shaving or trimming a beard is *haram,* or forbidden. Both also wore a shortened *thobe,* the white cotton garment for men that looks like a long shirt with deep side pockets. It is normally worn ankle-length, but the ultraorthodox and militants often wear it shorter to signify humility.

Their political views were also initially identical. As a young cleric in the early 1980s, Sheikh Salman had publicly endorsed an armed jihad against Soviet troops in Afghanistan. Bin Laden had been part of it. His adventures in Pakistan and Afghanistan launched him into a life of extremism.

Sheikh Salman's real influence on bin Laden's life, however, was a fatwa in 1990 against the Saudi government. American troops had just deployed in the kingdom for Operation Desert Storm, the seven-month campaign to end Iraq's occupation of neighboring Kuwait. The Saudi cleric condemned the monarchy for inviting foreign forces to deploy in Islam's birthplace. It was sacrilege, he declared, to rely on Americans and other infidels to protect sacred soil.

By several accounts, Sheikh Salman's fiery protests helped turn bin Laden against the House of Saud, which had made bin Laden's poor Yemeni emigrant father ludicrously rich off construction contracts in the 1970s and 1980s. Bin Laden, fresh off jihadist adventures in Pakistan and Afghanistan, denounced the royal family for blasphemy with the same zealous energy.

"The Saudi regime is but a branch or an agent of the United States," he later complained. "By being loyal to the U.S. regime, the Saudi regime has committed an act against Islam. And this, based on the ruling of Sharia, casts the regime outside the religious community . . .

"The regime," he railed, "has stopped ruling people according to what God revealed."[3]

A vast realm of oil-laden deserts and sun-bleached cities, Saudi Arabia can be a deceiving place. The largest of the twenty-two Arab countries has had a long relationship with the United States, which helped develop its oil industry between the 1930s and the 1980s and then armed and trained its military. Their leaders have walked hand in hand; they have visited each other's private retreats. The kingdom's shopping malls are filled with American goods. Jeddah, the cosmopolitan port city on the Red Sea, is dotted with Western chains like Starbucks, Fuddruckers, Hardee's, Applebee's, TGI Friday's, and Ruby Tuesday—sometimes several on the same street. There's even a McDonald's near the entry to Mecca, Islam's holiest city.

Yet it is no coincidence that Saudi Arabia has been the main breeding ground for al Qaeda. The kingdom's history has been defined by religion, militancy, and xenophobia.

The Prophet Mohammed's army spread the new faith by defeating, then uniting tribes across the Arabian Peninsula in the seventh century. The first Saudi state was created more than a millennium later in a merger between a tribal chief and the founder of Wahhabism, the most rigid branch of modern Islam. Together, tribal warriors and religious clerics conquered much of the peninsula in the eighteenth century.

The current version of Saudi Arabia—one of only two countries named after an individual—was created after another tribal takeover, by their descendants, in the twentieth century. Generations of Saudi youth have been brought up on tales of King Abdel Aziz ibn Saud's epic early battles. As the self-anointed "guardian of Islam's holy places," the kingdom has resolutely resisted outsiders, especially non-Muslims. Mecca and Medina are off-limits except to the faithful.

Saudi Arabia's ties to the United States have always been sensitive. Given its history of regional might, the kingdom's dependence on the American military to protect it has been particularly embarrassing. The arrival of US troops in 1990 sparked fury among pivotal players.

In his propaganda videos, bin Laden extolled Sheikh Salman for his daring criticism of the royal family. He called the dissident Saudi cleric "my ideal personality" and lauded him as "a savior who was the first person to demand the withdrawal of US troops from Saudi Arabia."[4] He later cited Sheikh Salman's fatwas and statements to justify his own campaigns.

The cleric returned the compliment. "It's an honor for me to be one of the soldiers of Abu Abdallah," Sheikh Salman reportedly told a bin Laden aide.[5] (*Abu* means father. Abdallah was bin Laden's first son, born in 1976. Historically, many Arab men have been named, formally or informally, after their firstborn son.)

For his fiery denunciations of the House of Saud, bin Laden was forced into exile in 1991. He was also stripped of his Saudi citizenship. He ended up in Sudan for a few years and later—after pressure from the United States, Saudi Arabia, and Egypt to expel him—back in Afghanistan.

For his incitement against the monarchy, Sheikh Salman was arrested in 1994.

The sheikh's imprisonment was another seminal moment in bin Laden's life. After the cleric's arrest, he "found myself forced" to assume the role of "enjoining what is right and forbidding what is wrong," he told CNN.[6] He issued an open letter from Sudan chastising Saudi Arabia's grand mufti for supporting the arrest of fellow clerics and endorsing the 1993 Oslo peace accord between Israel and the Palestine Liberation Organization. He treated the two acts as if they were comparable misdeeds.

Bin Laden lacked any religious or scholarly credentials, but he soon tried to step into the sheikh's shoes. He began issuing fatwas. He even started referring to himself as an "emir."

Bin Laden's first fatwa in 1996 condemned the monarchy for Sheikh Salman's imprisonment and for hosting US troops, even though the bulk of combat forces had long gone. The main American mission was by then training. But the presence of any Americans soldiers on sovereign Muslim territory, in bin Laden's eyes, was an occupation. The Saudi regime, he charged, had become accomplices to "crusaders."

The twenty-two-page diatribe was entitled *Declaration of War against the Americans Occupying the Land of the Two Holy Places.*

"The latest and greatest aggression incurred by Muslims since the death of the Prophet is the occupation of the land of the two Holy Places—the foundation of the house of Islam, the place of the revelation, the source of the message," bin Laden railed. Acting on American orders, he alleged, the Saudi government had arrested scholars, preachers, and young people. "Among them," he lamented, "the prominent Sheikh Salman Al-Oudah."

Then he declared a holy war against the United States.

Clearly, after Belief, there is no more important duty than pushing the American enemy out of the holy land . . . Due to the imbalance of power between our armed forces and the enemy forces, a suitable means of fighting must be adopted using fast-moving light forces that work under complete secrecy. In other words, initiate guerrilla warfare, where the sons of the nation, and not the military forces, take part. The best martyrs are those who do not turn their faces away from battle until they are killed . . . They have no intention except to enter paradise by killing you.

Bin Laden's 1996 fatwa, which became al Qaeda's manifesto, was largely ignored by the outside world. But it outlined everything that followed. From his bases in Afghanistan, bin Laden and his lieutenants plotted an ingenious series of attacks: In 1998, two truck bombs almost simultaneously destroyed the American embassies in Kenya and Tanzania. In 2000, a bomb-laden dinghy rammed into the USS *Cole* while it was refueling in Yemen. And in 2001, three airplanes flew into the Pentagon and the World Trade Center.

By then, however, Sheikh Salman's life had begun to take a different turn.

I WENT BACK TO Saudi Arabia, a country I've visited dozens of times, to explore what had happened in the decade since 9/11. Since my first visit in 1981, thousands of Saudis had joined extremist causes on three continents, from the rugged mountains of Afghanistan to the deserts of Iraq, from teeming Pakistan to the steamy Philippines, and from the failed state of Somalia in east Africa to Chechnya's war-ravaged enclave in Russia. Saudis were the largest group of foreign fighters in Iraq. Fifteen of the nineteen 9/11 hijackers were Saudi. Most had adopted the xenophobic Salafi creed that advocates returning to the ways of Islam's founders. *Salaf* means "forefather." Saudi Arabia's Wahhabi sect is the most pervasive form of Salafism today.

As long as jihadist sentiment remains strong in Saudi Arabia, the counter-jihad cannot succeed. So the clerics are key in a country where both the state and the national identity are based on religion.

Sheikh Salman was released from prison in 1999. After five years in jail, he emerged with somewhat tempered views. He began talking about peace and coexistence, purportedly after "gaining a deeper understanding of Islam." He gave lectures on human rights. He issued fatwas on dialogue "as a religious obligation." He launched a website in four languages, including English, to publish his evolving views.

After the 9/11 attacks, he even published a pamphlet critical of killing innocent civilians.[7]

It was not an instant or absolute transformation. In 2001, he told a

New York Times reporter that a suicide attack in Jerusalem was "within the realm of resisting occupation. Is there any international law that denies people the right to resist with any means they can?"[8] His controversial views led Jordan to deport him just hours before he was to deliver a lecture in 2002.[9]

In 2004, Sheikh Salman was also one of twenty-six Saudi scholars who signed a fatwa endorsing resistance against American troops in Iraq. It declared that fighting foreign forces was a "defense jihad" against "the big crime of America's occupation of Iraq" and therefore the duty of all who were able to fight. And in 2006, he supported Lebanon's Hezbollah during its month-long war with Israel.

"This is not the time to express our differences with the Shiites," the Sunni sheikh wrote, "because we are all confronted by our greater enemy, the criminal Jews and Zionists."[10]

He remained a Wahhabi elitist and a Salafi; he advocated returning to the ways of the first three generations of Muslims. Islam has witnessed at least three major waves of Salafi revivals—in the ninth, fourteenth, and eighteenth centuries. The most recent was led by Mohammed ibn Abd al Wahhab, the founder of Wahhabism.

Yet by 2007, Sheikh Salman's views had taken a notable turn. In April, he issued a fatwa renouncing violence against both Muslims and non-Muslims. He called on Islamic scholars, preachers, and people with influence to take a stand against aggression. He called it a crime that "disgraces" Islam.

"It does not matter if the victims are Muslim or not. The lives of all people are inviolable," he wrote on his popular website www.islam today.com.

"Do they think we are supposed to kill everybody who disagrees with us? Do they think we are supposed to point weapons at their throats?" he wrote. "Is that how problems are solved?"[11]

The final turning point, however, was Sheikh Salman's open letter to bin Laden five months later, on the sixth anniversary of the 9/11 attacks. It was a stunning rebuke.

"We, as scholars of Islam, reject what Osama does," the cleric wrote and later read on an Arabic television program. "The Muslim nation has not given anyone the right to declare war or be its spokesman."

The letter, both angry and anguished, condemned bin Laden's lust for power. It also held bin Laden at least partly accountable for the aftermath of 9/11, including the deaths of thousands, displacement of millions, and vast destruction during the US interventions in Afghanistan and Iraq. Sheikh Salman effectively repudiated his own position on Iraq three years earlier.

> What have we gained from the destruction of a whole country as in the case of Iraq and Afghanistan? These wars have brought on civil wars, misfortune and destruction about which Muslims are not happy . . . What do a hundred people in Algeria, or double that number in Lebanon, or likewise in Saudi Arabia hope to achieve by carrying out acts of violence—or, as they say, suicide attacks? These acts are futile. Let us say that these people manage to take power somewhere in the world. What then? What can people who have no life experience hope to achieve in the sphere of good governance? People who have no knowledge of Islamic law to support them and no understanding of domestic and foreign relations?

The Saudi cleric also condemned bin Laden for sponsoring al Qaeda offshoots across the Islamic world. He warned of the consequences to the al Qaeda leader—and Islam itself.

"Is Islam only about guns and ammunition? Have your means become the ends themselves?" he said. "Is reaching power the goal? Is this the solution? Are [you] determined to come to power, even if it is over the bodies of hundreds of thousands of police, soldiers, ordinary Muslims or innocent people? . . . How shall we appear when we meet our God, when so much blood has been shed under our patronage?"

Bin Laden, the sheikh concluded, had brought ruin to the entire Muslim world. The cleric's fatwa provoked headlines throughout the Middle East and even in the Western press. Its import was obvious.

SHEIKH SALMAN'S OPEN letter to bin Laden reflected a broader trend: By 2007, bin Laden's jihad inside Saudi Arabia—his homeland as well as the birthplace of Islam—had basically failed.

Al Qaeda had certainly tried. After the 2001 US invasion of Afghanistan, most of al Qaeda's members were forced to flee the network of extremist camps. Many Saudi militants ended up back at home. Dozens regrouped in two covert networks.[12] Saudi security uncovered one cell in 2002. But the other cell went undetected.[13]

Between 2003 and 2005, the normally sleepy kingdom was hit hard by terrorism. The first attack was in Riyadh, the Saudi capital, on May 12, 2003. Shortly before midnight, suicide car bombers struck three separate housing compounds used by foreign workers, including many Americans. Almost three dozen people were killed; some two hundred were wounded. A new wing of bin Laden's movement—which dubbed itself al Qaeda in the Arabian Peninsula—claimed credit.

The next day, I toured the site of the deadliest attack. The acrid stench of cordite still hung in the hot air. All of the compound's sand-colored buildings were damaged. Thick palm trees had been decapitated or snapped in half by the blast's impact. The attackers had deliberately detonated four hundred pounds of explosives in front of a four-story apartment block that housed seventy trainers, mainly Americans, for the Saudi National Guard. The sleeping inhabitants had been hurled in all directions.

With its front sheared off, the shattered building looked like a giant dollhouse. A twisted American flag dangled high on the side of the building. The explosives left a crater in the road at least ten feet deep and ten feet wide. The eerily quiet streets were littered with glass shards, bits of concrete and steel, odd pieces of furniture, and personal belongings that had been blown from the building. Just walking through the debris-strewn compound seemed like an invitation for a tetanus shot.

The attacks were sophisticated and tightly coordinated. All three bombs went off within a five-minute period in different parts of Riyadh. They involved breaking through security gates and past armed guards, a complex operation requiring stopwatch precision and coordination. The perpetrators had clearly been well-trained.

In November 2003, the new wing of al Qaeda struck again. But the second operation backfired. The sixteen victims, including several children, in another Riyadh housing compound were all Arabs and Muslims.[14]

The pace escalated in 2004. Over a two-month period, al Qaeda in the Arabian Peninsula launched a wave of operations against Westerners nationwide. Dozens were killed. Militants opened fire on foreigners at a business complex in Yanbu on the west coast. They assassinated five Westerners in the center of the country. And they shot up a foreign residential compound in Khobar on the east coast. In one of the most gruesome attacks, they kidnapped and later beheaded Paul Johnson, an

American engineer. Al Qaeda capped the year off in December by attacking the US consulate in Jeddah.[15]

In the end, however, al Qaeda in the Arabian Peninsula did not have sufficient popular support to survive in the kingdom, a report by West Point's Combating Terrorism Center said in 2010. "From his exile in Sudan and Afghanistan," it reported, "bin Laden overestimated popular resentment of the US military in Saudi Arabia and underestimated the Saudi public's aversion to domestic unrest."[16]

Saudi jihadis were prepared to go fight foreign forces in Iraq, but they were not willing to use violence to overthrow their own regime. Bin Laden, the study said, had basically lost touch with grassroots sentiment in his own homeland.

"Bin Laden's declaration was not the result of an organized domestic social movement," the report concluded, "but rather an ideological experiment by radicalized activists living in exile."[17] Bin Laden had issued his 1996 fatwa from Afghanistan. And from the early 1980s, with very brief interludes, he had spent most of his adult life outside the kingdom.

The surge of suicide bombings, the West Point study noted, happened during a "momentary discrepancy," when jihadis returning from Afghanistan were well organized and Saudi intelligence was not.[18]

After 9/11, Saudi Arabia had taken tentative steps to counter terrorism. But the monarchy did not really begin to employ its extraordinary coercive powers until it too became a target in 2003. It then outlawed funding for Islamic charities abroad, except when channeled through the government, and tried to track violators. It vetted extremist sympathizers within its security forces. It monitored mosques and Internet sites used for recruiting. And it launched a public relations "name and shame" campaign to publicly discredit any individual with extremist ideas.[19]

In a massive sweep, the kingdom also arrested some 9,000 suspected jihadists or their sympathizers between 2003 and 2007.[20] Almost sixty Saudi security forces in new counterterrorism SWAT teams died in shoot-outs with militant jihadis.

The core of al Qaeda, on the defensive, literally blew through its human resources. The turning point was a showdown between Saudi security forces and notorious chieftain Abdel Aziz al Muqrin. He was a high school dropout who had fought the Soviets in Afghanistan and the Serbs in Bosnia, fomented extremism in the Horn of Africa, and run guns from Spain to Algeria. He was the first leader of al Qaeda in the Arabian Peninsula. He was killed in a shoot-out in Riyadh on the same day that Paul Johnson, the American engineer, was beheaded.

By 2007, bin Laden was unable to regenerate momentum or critical mass for a new campaign at home. Saudi security kept one step ahead of his followers. More importantly, his sources of legitimacy were drying up. Even his early hero had publicly turned against him.

In his 2007 letter, Sheikh Salman reprimanded bin Laden for wasting the lives of Saudi youth—for nothing.

> My heart pains me when I think of the number of young people who had so much potential—who would have made great contributions to society, who had so much to offer that was constructive and positive—who have been turned into living bombs. Here is the vital question that you need to ask yourself and that others have the right to demand an answer for: What have all these long years of suffering, tragedy, tears, and sacrifice actually achieved?

By 2011, three decades after he first turned to extremism, bin Laden and his early hero held vastly different views.

"Oh God!" Sheikh Salman wrote in his 2007 letter, "I plead my innocence to you from what Osama is doing and from all those who are affiliated with him or work under his banner."

BY 2007, SUPPORT for al Qaeda and its suicide tactics was plummeting across the Islamic world.

Between 2003 and 2007, Muslims expressing confidence in bin Laden to do "the right thing" dropped by 36 percent in Jordan, 18 percent in Indonesia, and 15 percent in the Palestinian territories. For the West, any support was too much. But the tide had turned. Only 1 percent of Lebanese and 5 percent of Turks expressed confidence in the al Qaeda chief, according to a survey by the Pew Research Center.[21]

Muslims started to take action too—and persevered against the odds. In Iraq, the Anbar Awakening that took root in 2007 continued even after Sheikh Sattar's assassination by al Qaeda. His last surviving brother took over. The Awakening ended most of the violence in Anbar for the next four years. The combination of the Awakening and the US troop surge in 2007 allowed Washington to begin drawing down troops in 2009. In 2010, Washington announced the formal end of the seven-year combat mission.

Algeria witnessed a similar shift. In 2007, al Qaeda in the Magreb—created by the merger of al Qaeda and the Salafist Group for Preaching and Combat—carried out a series of suicide bombings that killed dozens of Algerians. Public sentiment also increasingly turned against al Qaeda.

The counter-jihad's most critical components, however, were the clerics who originally inspired and conferred legitimacy on al Qaeda. By 2007, religious leaders who had once been bin Laden's allies were increasingly denouncing him from their pulpits. Many issued fatwas against al Qaeda's campaign of terror. The common theme was condemnation of its tactics, targets, and most of all, twisted interpretations of Islam.

In 2007, even al Qaeda's chief ideologue—an Egyptian physician whose nom de guerre was Dr. Fadl—reversed course.

His real name was Sayyed Imam al Sharif and he was a founding member of al Qaeda. He wrote two how-to books on extremism. The first was *The Essential Guide to Preparation,* meaning for armed jihad. It was written in 1988, the year Fadl met and merged forces with bin Laden in Pakistan. The extremist struggle against nonbelievers, he wrote, was a religious duty for all Muslims. Martyrdom was life's greatest prize; it promised divine rewards.

His second book was *The Compendium of the Pursuit of Divine Knowledge.* It was written in 1994, while Fadl was in exile with bin Laden in Sudan. The tome, over 1,000 pages, condoned killing anyone, in any religion, who disagreed with al Qaeda. It also provided the intellectual framework for jihadism. It has often been called al Qaeda's *Das Kapital.*[22]

In 1994, however, Fadl had a falling-out with bin Laden and Ayman al Zawahiri, reportedly in part over the second book. In a huff, he moved to Yemen and returned to work as a physician. He laid low for seven years, until shortly after the 9/11 attacks, when his past caught up with him. Yemen detained him for three years. In 2004, he was deported to Egypt, where he began serving a life sentence for extremist activities.

In Cairo's notorious Tora prison, Fadl joined the so-called prison debates among the hundreds of jailed extremists about what constituted a justifiable jihad. Like Sheikh Salman, Fadl had an epiphany in 2007.

His response was a third book, released in serial form in Egyptian and Kuwaiti newspapers, called *Rationalizing Jihad in Egypt and the World.* Fadl reversed course completely. He fully renounced extremism.

"There is nothing that invokes the anger of God and His wrath like the unwarranted spilling of blood and wrecking of property," Fadl wrote. Muslims were "prohibited" from committing aggression against people of any faith.

There is nothing in the Sharia about killing Jews and the Nazarenes [Christians], referred to by some as the Crusaders. They are the neighbors of the Muslims . . . and being kind to one's neighbors is a religious duty . . . God permitted peace treaties and ceasefires with the infidels, either in exchange for money or without it—all of this in order to protect the Muslims, in contrast with those who push them into peril.[23]

Fadl specifically condemned al Qaeda's terrorism spectaculars—the four 9/11 attacks in 2001, the four bombings at Madrid train stations in 2004, and the triple bombings of London's subway system in 2005—as unlawful slaughter.

"Ramming America has become the shortest road to fame and leadership among the Arabs and Muslims," Fadl wrote. "But what good is it if you destroy one of your enemy's buildings, and he destroys one of your countries? What good is it if you kill one of his people, and he kills a thousand of yours?"

The fact that the serialized book had been faxed from an Egyptian prison clearly made it suspect. It could not have happened without government permission and even encouragement. But I subsequently interviewed two former jihadis in Cairo who knew Fadl and had been part of the prison debates. They were convinced his change of heart was genuine.

From prison, al Qaeda's former chief ideologue declared that the 9/11 attacks were a "catastrophe" for the Islamic world.[24]

KHALED AL HUBAYSHI was enemy combatant number 155 at Guantánamo Bay. He arrived at the American detention center, in blindfold and manacles, not long after fleeing the mountains of Tora Bora. Al Hubayshi had spent twenty-seven days with Osama bin Laden in the snow-capped caves region. The battle of Tora Bora was the al Qaeda chief's last stand in Afghanistan.

By mid-December 2001, the relentless American bombardment—700,000 pounds of bombs in one three-day period alone—forced the three hundred surviving jihadis to flee. Bin Laden finally sent around word that the fighters should head for Pakistan and report to their respective embassies. Al Hubayshi walked with more than two dozen others through the frigid mountains for six days.

When he got to the Pakistan border, however, he was arrested. He was then turned over to the United States. He arrived at Gitmo on January 17, 2002.

In 2009, I met al Hubayshi for coffee, many cups as it turned out, in Jeddah. Born in 1975, al Hubayshi still looked younger than his years, partly because of his light facial hair. In lieu of a beard, he had long sideburns that arched under his cheekbones until they petered out, a mustache of fine black hair, and a few wisps on his chin. He was only of medium height; he was neither beefy nor athletic. He was wearing a long shirtlike white *thobe* and a red-and-white-checked *ghutra* draped over his head, secured with a thick black circular cord on top. He had a pen and wire-rimmed sunglasses in his breast pocket. He was surprisingly candid. He occasionally even laughed as he recounted his story.

By any standard, however, al Hubayshi was hard-core. He had spent six years as a jihadi, eventually specializing in remote control bombs and instructing others how to make them.

"We'd build bombs during training, and then we'd try them out. We'd blow up walls and things," he told me. "But not people. Not during training."

He was teaching explosives to Chechen rebels in Kabul on 9/11, when he was warned to leave. The Afghans no longer wanted their Arab brethren around. Al Qaeda had become a liability.

Al Hubayshi spent three years and six months at Guantánamo Bay. He was repatriated to Saudi Arabia on July 19, 2005.

Ten years after 9/11, al Hubayshi represented the ultimate challenge for Saudi Arabia's sheikhs: The very men who had once urged young Muslims to go off and fight for an Islamic cause were suddenly tasked with weaning them off war and keeping them at home.

Al Qaeda's hold over its cadre, especially the large Saudi component, was put to the test in the kingdom's unconventional rehabilitation program. It was set up after the 2003–2004 bombings. Saudi clerics ran it. Their strategy was not just to change criminal behavior. The centerpiece was reeducation using the same tool employed by al Qaeda—Islam. The goal was essentially to reverse the kingdom's long mix of religion and militancy.

After talking with Hubayshi and other released Gitmo graduates, I visited the sheikh who started the program. "This is where we are now fighting one idea with another idea," explained Sheikh Ahmed Jilani, a portly man with a slightly scruffy beard and a genial manner.

The program had evolved almost accidentally out of Jilani's experience with a senior al Qaeda official who returned home in 2004. The wave of suicide bombings had scared Saudi Arabia into offering a thirty-day amnesty to militants willing to renounce violence.[25] He took it. The government asked Jilani to stay with the al Qaeda defector and provide counseling until it figured out how to prevent him from returning to radicalism. The two men lived together for months.

To Jilani's surprise, the al Qaeda official voluntarily started to talk about his experiences. He explained how he had been recruited. He disclosed what he had done as part of the militant network. He even outlined the group's operations inside the kingdom.

"It was an important lesson. We discovered that it didn't take force to get them to talk," Jilani told me. "We could do it with open conversation." The kingdom then adapted the idea to convince other captured or arrested extremists to cooperate.

The rehab program has two parts. The first and larger part was launched in 2004, after the wave of bombings led to the arrest of thousands of suspected extremists and sympathizers. Notorious for its strict penal code and tough jails, Saudi Arabia commissioned five new state-of-the-art prisons especially to hold the jihadists. (They were built, ironically, by the bin Laden family construction company.) The facilities mix maximum security with extensive counseling. Televisions in every cell play religious lectures by visiting clerics; they focus on dozens of topics all relating in some way to the "correct" meaning of jihad. Inmates have intercoms to engage in discussions. Personal counseling—with sheikhs, psychologists, and social workers—covers everything from anger management to trauma therapy and family life.

In a state where Islamic law is the only law, the use of religion with lawbreakers is not new. The kingdom has a long history of releasing

prisoners early if they memorize the Koran.[26] Clerics have also traditionally played a role in counseling prisoners, helping families after a
member has been arrested, even intervening on a prisoner's behalf with
the government. But the rehab program involves a far wider role for the
clergy.

Ironically, many jihadis actually had little in-depth knowledge of their
faith, even though they lived in the land of Islam's two holiest sites. In
2004 and 2007, the government conducted surveys of imprisoned extremists. Among the common denominators: Many came from large
families—with seven to fifteen children. Their parents had limited education. About one-quarter of the militants had criminal pasts, often related to drugs or alcohol. And virtually all the prisoners had little formal
religious training. Their exposure to Islam was often heavily influenced
by seeing jihadist videos or visiting extremist websites.

The former Guantánamo Bay detainees I met reminded me of the
British mercenaries I encountered during the Angolan civil war in the
1970s. The mercenaries had been misfits, fleeing personal or criminal
problems, poorly informed about international affairs, in debt, or had reacted emotionally to a crisis in the news. They had known little about
the Soviet-backed Angolan government or the two US-backed guerrilla
movements trying to unseat it. One mercenary even thought Angola
was the capital of the Congo.

Al Hubayshi was a similar story. He had first tried to join the jihad
in the mid-1990s after seeing a video of the Bosnian war, including
gruesome pictures of women and children killed by a Serb militia. One
woman had been decapitated. The Srebrenica massacre of some 8,000
Bosnian Muslims in July 1995, which was the largest genocide in Europe
since World War II, generated a huge reaction throughout the Muslim
world.

"The stores were selling the videos," al Hubayshi told me. "I felt I had
to do something." He called a number at the end of the video, to find out
how to join up, only to find the war had ended.

"The guy said to me, 'Don't you read the news? They've signed the
Dayton Peace Accords,' " he recalled. "I was pretty naïve. The only gun
I had ever used was in the desert for hunting. And I didn't know much
about Bosnia—or the world."

Al Hubayshi's story was often an amateur's odyssey. And he was an
on-again, off-again jihadi. The details were impossible to verify, but the

short version of his long tale is that he started looking for other causes after Bosnia fell through. He considered Chechnya and opted instead to join the Muslim insurgency in the Philippines in 1996, during an "extended-vacation jihad" from his job at a Saudi government utilities company.

Al Hubayshi spent a few weeks on the island of Mindanao with the Moro Islamic Liberation Front but grew frustrated and went home. "The training was very poor, and I wanted to be professional," he told me. "The most experienced fighters said going to Afghanistan was like going to college."

In 1997, al Hubayshi tried again. He quit his job, flew to Pakistan, hooked up with other young Arabs, drove across the Khyber Pass to Afghanistan, and joined a training camp in Khost run by Abu Zubaydah, a big-name Saudi militant.

"I learned jungle war, city war, but then I specialized in explosives—how to blow up buildings, where to put explosives, the mathematics of how many kilos it takes to destroy certain size buildings or train rails," he told me, as if we were discussing cooking measurements.

He spent about a year in Afghanistan, he said, then developed surprisingly mundane problems with his passport, was jailed briefly in Pakistan when he crossed the border to renew it, and ended up working for Abu Zubaydah's operation in Pakistan for several months.

In 1999, al Hubayshi again decided to go home. He resented some of the menial work, including grocery shopping. By that time, the main action in Afghanistan also pitted Afghans against each other in a civil war.

"If I was going to die," he told me, "I wanted to die fighting for something meaningful." He flew to Yemen on a fake passport, stayed for a few weeks with men he had met in Afghanistan, then slipped across the desert border to Saudi Arabia.

"Thousands walk across that border," he explained. "It's a little like Mexico, long and very porous."

Al Hubayshi intended to start a new life in Jeddah. "I was a little disillusioned," he told me. But two years later, he claimed, he was wooed back when two Saudi jihadists contacted him with a warning that Saudi authorities wanted to question him. (He later decided this may not have been true.) So on his younger brother's passport, he returned to Afghanistan.

By May 2001, he told me, bin Laden had consolidated his control over the various camps of foreign fighters in Afghanistan. During his previous stint, the camps had been a loose network. He had considered himself affiliated with Abu Zubaydah rather than bin Laden. But when he returned, "al Qaeda was like a corporation," he said.

Al Hubayshi recounted being courted by bin Laden personally after he arrived in Kandahar. They sat on carpets in the al Qaeda chief's office and nibbled off a platter of fruit.

"He told me he was a little busy," al Hubayshi recalled. "In 1997, you could sit with him for days, but in the summer of 2001, just before 9/11, he was busy." Rumors were rampant about an impending attack, although specifics were scarce. But bin Laden clearly thought al Qaeda was secure in Afghanistan long-term. "Osama told me, 'We will find land for you and help you build a house. You can stay and get married here,' " al Hubayshi recalled. "He said, 'We're not going to let you down.' "

For four months, al Hubayshi learned more about explosives and electronics, including how to use cell phones or light switches as remote controls to detonate a bomb. He trained other foreign fighters too. When the al Qaeda hijackers flew into the World Trade Center and the Pentagon, however, the political environment changed abruptly. Al Qaeda and its foreign fighters were no longer welcome. Al Hubayshi soon ended up in Tora Bora.

"Sometimes, Osama was a little crazy," al Hubayshi recalled. "He thought the Americans would come and we would fight them man-to-man in the mountains. He came and told us it was going to be really hard and we had to be tough, but that it was going to cost America a lot—a hundred to two hundred million dollars a day. He kept telling us, 'The Americans will lose this war.' "

He paused in thought. "But we had nothing to stop B-52s dropping bombs," he said. "It was all bullshit. It was just to encourage us."

Al Hubayshi was particularly angry that bin Laden could not be bothered, at the end, to personally talk to the fighters with him at Tora Bora. He was instead the first to escape. The others had to fend for themselves.

Among the other Saudi men I interviewed, the decision to join al Qaeda sometimes seemed almost whimsical. They struck me as adventure seekers in search of a mission, a job, an identity, a sense of purpose, or escape from personal problems or the law. Anger and emotional issues often influenced decisions far more than any militant ideology.

Al Hubayshi's twin brother had traveled with him to the Philippines in the mid-1990s. He also went to Afghanistan in 1997. But Yasser al Hubayshi soon decided he did not like Afghanistan and went home. He then went to the United States. He spent time in Oregon and Arizona and ended up marrying an American. Their three children, al Hubayshi told me, had American passports.

"My twin brother is fat," al Hubayshi said, laughing lightly. "He didn't spend five years in Guantánamo Bay." Al Hubayshi's older brother had also lived for a few years in the United States. After what he called his "lost decade" as a jihadi, al Hubayshi had grown cynical about jihadis who signed up for al Qaeda's cause.

"In the beginning, you think all the people are like you and they came to help Muslims," he told me. "Then you find, no, they're human. Many are looking for position, for power, for money. They weren't heroes. They were greedy."

SAUDI ARABIA'S REHABILITATION program has tried to exploit al Qaeda's weaknesses. After he was flown home from Guantánamo Bay, al Hubayshi was sentenced to a year in prison, mostly for passport infractions. At the end, he went through the original rehabilitation program.

To reeducate extremists, the Saudi government has blended religion with reality therapy. Reality therapy and choice therapy were developed by American psychiatrist William Glasser in the 1960s. Both focus on personal choice, personal responsibility, and personal transformation. They acknowledge past experiences and focus on what can be learned from them, but they move as quickly as possible to dealing with current needs and building a future. Bonding with a counselor is key, especially for nonvoluntary or resistant patients.

For Jilani, who started the program, the bonding began at Guantánamo Bay. He flew to the island to pick up most of the twelve batches of Saudi detainees released between 2003 and 2009. The Saudi government recruited 150 other sheikhs and religious scholars to counsel its militant inmates. Several were deliberately selected because they were known as independents or critics of the monarchy. They were instructed not to lecture but to engage in dialogue, to draw out prisoners, and "to speak to them like brothers," Jilani explained. The first step was listening to the jihadis' personal journeys.

"We use reality therapy to help them treat themselves or correct their thoughts themselves, to see their problems and agree if they made a mistake," Jilani told me. "It's crucial to let them speak out. The new ideas must come from them. We go with them until they believe in these ideas."

Sheikh Salman al Oudah—who had earlier fostered extremism, criticized the monarchy, and endorsed the war for Iraq as a legitimate jihad—was among the clerics selected to counsel the Gitmo grads.[27] He publicly endorsed the program. In his 2007 open letter to bin Laden, he praised the men with "brave hearts" and "courageous minds" who had defected from al Qaeda.

"Many of your brethren in Egypt, Algeria and elsewhere have come to see the end road for al Qaeda's ideology," he wrote bin Laden. "They now realize how destructive and dangerous it is."

Backed by psychologists and social workers, Saudi Arabia's clerics basically tried to convince jihadis that they had been suckered by al Qaeda, exploited for others' gains, and taught an errant version of Islam. They too were effectively victims. The sheikhs gradually led prisoners to different views of three controversial issues—jihad, *takfir*, and relations between Muslims and non-Muslims.

As the basis of discussions on jihad, rehab sessions included videos and newspaper pictures of gruesome bombings.

"I asked them, 'What is our opinion of what you have seen?' " Jilani said. "Is this the right way? Does Islam support this kind of act? Does Islam approve of destroying or killing things?"

Jihad, he explained, is only for governments, not individuals, to declare—and then only rarely for a rational cause to defend the faith. And certainly, he added, no one in al Qaeda was qualified to declare jihad.

The second issue was use of *takfir*, or accusing others of apostasy. Al Qaeda often cited *takfir* as justification of violence. Bin Laden's rambling 1996 fatwa accused Middle East governments, Muslim leaders worldwide, and anyone opposed to al Qaeda's ideology of being apostates, thereby justifying their deaths. Invoking *takfir* condoned tactics ranging from suicide bombings to beheadings. But bin Laden's fatwa, Jilani explained, did not reflect the faith. Only clerics can declare *takfir*—and again only in unusual cases. Basically, Jilani said, bin Laden's fatwa was null and void.

The third and most sensitive issue is how Muslims deal with non-Muslims. It is also at the heart of jihadism.

"We teach them that the Prophet dealt with Christians and Jews, who lived with him in Medina, through dialogue," Jilani told me. "One of the important verses in the Koran is that you can't force anyone to be Muslim. We tell them that Islam has a message of peace with Muslims *and* non-Muslims.

"Al Qaeda," he said, "has destroyed this by creating a culture of death and hate."

In 2007, the symbolic turning point for the counter-jihad, the Saudis introduced a second rehabilitation program. It is smaller but more intense. The men who have gone through it fall into three categories: Some were al Qaeda operatives, including intercepted suicide bombers captured in the kingdom. A second group fought in Iraq with al Qaeda of Mesopotamia. The third set, picked up in Afghanistan or Pakistan, were detainees returned from Guantánamo Bay. The men entered the program as the last part of their prison terms.

The final tug-of-war for jihadi loyalties between the Saudi government and al Qaeda takes place at a former resort outside Riyadh. Its gardens are an oasis in the desert. I met Jilani and his staff at the facility; we talked in a large tentlike structure complete with four chandeliers and a lush green carpet. Among its amenities, the Care Rehabilitation Center has a swimming pool, wide-screen televisions, PlayStations, Ping-Pong tables, art therapy classes, and a foosball table.

"You know," Jilani said, when he couldn't think of the name for this last activity, "that game they play on *Friends*." The rehab facility has often been referred to as the Betty Ford Center for terrorists.

Extremists abandon their causes for disparate reasons. A major factor is disillusionment with ideology, killing civilians, the hard life, or the internal politics and power games, according to former prisoners and Saudi officials. Some begin to see their lives or the world through a different prism. Others leave because they are aging; the daring adventures of youth no longer seem so tantalizing. Sometimes the whim that led them to join also led them to depart.

I asked Hubayshi what specifically triggered his own transformation.

"The media today says it's wrong, but they didn't then. The sheikhs too," he told me. "Now they say don't go to Iraq—not because we don't feel sorry for what is happening, but because we will be used. The stores don't sell those videos anymore either.

"Now, people who had that experience are also more cynical. We went to Afghanistan to help our Afghan brothers, but in the end the Afghans wanted us to leave. They asked us to go," he said. "That made us *very* angry."

THE SAUDI GOVERNMENT has also used its oil wealth to buy out extremists, just as it once channeled petrodollars to support jihadist causes. Punishment and reeducation have been balanced with benevolence in the form of financial incentives and security. During a prisoner's incarceration, the state provides welfare for his family, usually including an income, health care, children's schooling, or emergency aid—a common practice with ordinary criminals too. Saudi officials claim they have no choice.

"Those radicals don't leave these guys alone," Abdulrahman al Hadlaq told me during my visit to the Care Rehabilitation Center. He was director general of the Ministry of Interior's ideological security division.

"They keep trying to rerecruit them!" he said. "They use many tactics. Just to give you an example—a guy is released, and soon after he goes home, they will put an envelope under his door with money that says, 'This is from your brothers.' "

The government's goal has been to preempt hardship and the temptations of radicalism. The program includes vocational training, usually in modest skills such as carpentry and computers, to help foster alternative professions. After a prisoner's release, the government's "aftercare" has included a job, a car, a dowry for marriage, down payments on a home, and a monthly stipend. Sometimes it has thrown in a scholarship for a younger brother, dental work for a mother, and other family assistance.

When I was in the kingdom, a popular joke was making the rounds. "What's the best way," it went, "to get a good job, a beautiful wife, a fine car, and $20,000 for wedding expenses?" The answer: "Become a repentant terrorist."

The government tried to build in financial safeguards. It gave the dowry money, for example, directly to the bride's father. "No, no," said al Hadlaq, with a chuckle. "We don't want them to have that much cash!"

After his rehabilitation, al Hubayshi was given a new Toyota Corolla and a monthly stipend of eight hundred dollars. His family found a wife for an arranged marriage, still a common practice in Saudi Arabia. And the government gave him 100,000 riyals—about $28,000—for a dowry and furniture. When his wife was unable to get pregnant, al Hubayshi also asked for help to pay for fertility treatments.

Without the financial aid, al Hubayshi told me, he might not have made the transition. "When you get back, your only experience has been learning to kill. No one wants to have anything to do with you," he said. "Where do you think you will be welcome? Only Iraq or Afghanistan. The government helped me start again."

"Otherwise," he added, "I might be in Iraq right now." Saudis were among the largest number of foreign fighters in Iraq.

A decade after 9/11, the rehabilitation program had scored several successes as well as notable setbacks and failures. The "soft" counter-terrorism strategy had a rough beginning. Suspicions ran deep. Some die-hard al Qaeda members were unreachable. They preferred prison to renouncing their ideology.[28]

"A minority, a small minority," a security official told me, although he refused to give a precise number.

Some graduates also returned to terrorism. By mid-2010, almost 10 percent of the three hundred jihadis who went through the second program at the Care Rehabilitation Center had rejoined radical jihadist causes.[29]

The figure was higher among former Guantánamo Bay detainees, the government conceded. Twenty-five of 120 former Gitmo detainees had returned to extremism.[30] (Overall, the United States reported in 2010 that about 20 percent of the 550 Guantánamo Bay detainees released to all countries had returned to terrorism.)[31]

At least ten Saudis had escaped to Yemen, where they joined a rein-carnation of al Qaeda in the Arabian Peninsula. It claimed responsibility for the plot to blow up Northwest Airlines Flight 253 from Amsterdam to Detroit on Christmas Day 2009. Umar Farouk Abdulmutallab, a Ni-gerian, had hidden the explosives in his underwear. In October 2010, the group was also linked to two sophisticated bombs planted in printer car-tridges that were shipped by FedEx and UPS to Jewish synagogues in Chicago.

Two of al Qaeda in the Arabian Peninsula's top leaders—Othman Ahmad al Ghamdi and Said Ali al Shihri—both graduated from the Care Rehabilitation Center. The group's bomb maker was also a Saudi.

The father of Said Ali al Shihri said his son initially appeared to be adjusting after six years in Guantánamo Bay, followed by a short imprisonment and rehabilitation in Saudi Arabia. But then he suddenly disappeared after several visits from four men, including two other former Guantánamo Bay detainees. Al Shihri's father publicly denounced his son.

"I say it loud and clear that my son is a deviant member of society who must be removed. He was not upright like the rest of the Gitmo returnees who benefited from the lessons of the past and showed their gratefulness for the assistance they were provided," he said.

He also appealed to his son to repent—again. "Resort to reason, stop this deviation of yours, keep your pledges, and don't follow the whims of Satan and his helpers," he said.[32] Despite the kingdom's investment in Shihri and Ghamdi, both ended up on its Most Wanted list.

Saudi Arabia's rehabilitation efforts also failed to address fundamental flaws. The program did not deal with the core teachings in the kingdom's own schools—in a country where the majority are now young. In 2010, some two-thirds of Saudi Arabia's 29 million people were under thirty years old. Despite modest recent revisions, schoolbooks were still openly hostile to the West and derogatory about non-Muslims, both ideas central to extremism.

Wahhabi xenophobia and arrogance are also still strong. A list of government-approved fatwas includes one that commands Muslims not to initiate greetings with non-Muslims. It only allows them to respond to overtures initiated by Christians and Jews with "the same to you." It also permits Saudis to provide charity if the non-Muslims are needy.[33]

Finally, Saudi Arabia's young are still growing up on heroic—and often wildly exaggerated—tales of Saudi jihadis fighting the decade-long Soviet occupation of Afghanistan. Most actually had minor combat roles, and many never fought the Soviets at all. But the inflated lore has fueled romantically noble ideas about armed jihad.

Yet by 2010, more than 3,000 men and a handful of women had passed through the rehabilitation programs. Almost one-half had renounced militancy, served their time, and been released.[34] The overall relapse rate was under 10 percent. In the United States and Europe, recidivist rates for former prisoners are between 60 and 70 percent within three years of their release. And more than one-half end up in prison again.[35]

By 2010, Saudi Arabia had also eradicated all but a few amateur extremist cells. The hard-core professional wing of al Qaeda in Saudi Arabia, which began to peter out in 2006, had largely disappeared a decade after 9/11. Saudi intelligence nabbed new cells before they could carry out attacks. It was also key to uncovering the plot to send two printer cartridge bombs by FedEx and UPS from Yemen to Jewish synagogues in Chicago. In an unusual public statement on intelligence issues, the White House publicly commended the kingdom for its role in thwarting the attacks.

Saudis acknowledged the ongoing challenges. "We are not fully successful, but we are trying," Jilani told me. "At least now we are sure we are going in the right direction."

At the end of a long conversation with al Hubayshi, I asked him about his core political views.

"I thought of myself as a jihadi. I'll be honest with you," he said. "You start with good intentions. But over time, the environment around you makes you extreme. Think about it—you wake up every day in Afghanistan. You see poor people. The food is not good. You see sick people who can't get medication. So who do you blame? The world. The United States. Saudi Arabia. You feel the world has to do something. So I stayed. I thought, 'I will live the same shit life they do.'

"There is a thin line between jihad and terrorism," he reflected. "And sometimes you move to the other side and you don't notice. Then you find yourself." It sounded like something Jilani and his fellow sheikhs might say in their counseling sessions.

I also asked al Hubayshi what, looking back on his own experience, he thought of bin Laden.

He laughed. "Maybe you thought Osama was smart, but he wasn't," al Hubayshi said, shaking his head. "He made rash decisions, like to do 9/11. He should have known that these attacks would bring trouble for the Afghans. He never thought the Taliban or Pakistan would give him away. His bodyguard told me that Osama was really shocked when the Pakistan government sided with the United States."

Al Hubayshi did not raise his voice, but he was clearly angry.

"Osama had only one idea—how he could kill Americans and how he would become famous," he told me. "He liked the media a lot. I know. Before [the US embassies were bombed in 1998 in] Kenya and Tanzania, he talked a lot about the media. He would say, 'So-and-so interviewed me. Japanese television asked to interview me.'

"He used young people for his benefit," he added. "His children and wives, they had a good life in Afghanistan, a privileged life. He made it safe for them. The rest of us had a hard life. And the food was terrible."

I asked al Hubayshi, who admitted he was bored with his utilities job, if he talked with other former combatants or toyed with the idea of joining up again. A few of the Gitmo detainees kept in touch, he said.

I asked what they talked about. He laughed. "Mostly the guards," he replied. "'Remember this guy? Remember that guy?'

"No, when I go to bed, I compare myself—with my wife next to me, in a nice room and a comfortable bed—with Gitmo and Afghanistan and the caves. And I think sometimes I was crazy then. I try to forget that it ever happened."

4.

A Midsummer's Eve

**Now our people have felt in their skin, flesh
and bones that the only way to save the country
is peaceful coexistence of different tastes, walks of life,
ethnicities, religions and schools of thought.**

—IRANIAN PRESIDENTIAL CANDIDATE
MIR HOSSEIN MOUSAVI[1]

On June 12, 2009, Neda Agha Soltan went out to vote in Tehran. The twenty-six-year-old beauty, who had mischievous eyes, full lips, and long brown bangs, had no inkling that her decision would lead to her death eight days later. She had never been interested in politics before, so she would surely have been surprised that she might someday symbolize the failure of the Islamic world's most controversial ideology.

Neda—as she is now commonly known—reflected a common dynamic in the region's political rebellions. Newcomers are spurred from apathy to activism by unexpected catalysts. Most are young. They are not among the elites, the educated, the talented, the privileged, the wealthy, or the well connected. Most are self-recruited; no charismatic leader or novel ideology has galvanized them, as in previous eras. And most are political nobodies.

Like the majority of Iran's population, Neda was born after the 1979 revolution. Her life was unremarkable. She married her first love, divorced three years later, and moved back in with her mother and father, who worked for the government. She talked about becoming a travel agent. She loved music, including the violin and piano. She briefly studied Islamic philosophy but dropped out in her second year.[2]

"She used to say that the God they are teaching us at these universities is different from the God I worship," her older sister Hoda later recalled. "Her professor taught them about a vengeful God, but Neda said, 'This is not my God. The God I worship is a compassionate and loving God.' "[3]

Neda instead became part of Generation U—the Muslim young under age thirty who were unfulfilled, unincluded, underemployed or underutilized, and underestimated. They have been thoroughly unhappy with the status quo. And they are totally into YouTube.

Generation U was important because Iran has one of the region's youngest populations. After Iran's 1979 revolution, the new theocracy called on its women to breed an Islamic generation. It offered incentives, including stipends per child. It also lowered the marriage age from sixteen to nine, the official age of puberty. Women complied. By 1986, the average Iranian woman was bearing seven children. Iran's population—some 34 million in 1979—soared by more than 20 million during the revolution's first decade.

The logic was explained by a ranking cleric. "We'd just had a revolution that faced threats from both internal and external enemies," said Ayatollah Nasser Makaram-Shirazi. "We wanted to increase the number of people who believed in the revolution in order to preserve it."[4]

The numbers instead almost overwhelmed Iran, because the Islamic Republic could not afford to feed, clothe, house, educate, and employ those numbers. It eventually reversed policy, but too late to avoid a huge baby boom generation—that was coming of age but still under age thirty by 2009.

On election eve, Iran could only generate about 300,000 of the roughly 1 million new jobs needed yearly to absorb young people entering the job market. Youth between the ages of fifteen and twenty-nine accounted for about 70 percent of the unemployed. Among young men, almost one in four was unable to find work. Even with a university degree, the average waiting period for a job could be three years.

Iran also had one of the youngest voting blocs. The revolution originally lowered the voting age to fifteen. As the baby boomers gained disproportionate say, the regime raised the voting age to eighteen in 2007. But the young could still be the decisive factor in an election.

The emergence of Generation U was also significant because Iran has been a trendsetter in the Islamic world for a century. In 1906, its Constitutional Revolution produced the first republican constitution and parliament in all of Asia.* It was one of the Islamic world's early modernizers, dating back to the 1920s and 1930s. Its 1979 revolution introduced political Islam as a modern ideology, the climactic act in the revival's first phase.

Each turning point in Iran influenced other parts of the region. Each dealt with core issues—of identity and agendas, power and justice—common in predominantly Muslim nations. And each reflected the broader struggle to navigate a workable balance between an old faith and new republicanism, between tradition and modernity—the central tension in politics in the twenty-first century even more than in twentieth.

More than any other country, the Islamic Republic of Iran tried to accommodate both the old faith and the new republicanism in two parallel ruling systems. It had a republican wing with separate executive, legislative, and judicial branches of power outlined in a constitution and secured by a conventional army, navy, and air force. But it also had an Islamic wing with parallel institutions based on Islamic law that were empowered to override presidential, parliamentary, and civil court decisions; this wing was secured by its own more potent military. The system was topped by a supreme leader who had powers, comparable to an infallible pope, over both systems.

By 2009, three decades after the revolution, the balance clearly did not work. The system was riven: An Islamist faction—well organized and tight-knit—wanted society to uniformly adhere to a powerful and absolute single truth, intolerant of all other opinions, whatever the cost. A republican faction—amorphous and disorganized—wanted society open to a diversity of beliefs, even if it weakened the single truth that founded the state, in order to win wider support. The rival visions ran against each other in Iran's 2009 presidential election. And Generation U was critical to the outcome.

President Mahmoud Ahmadinejad represented the principlist move-

---

* The Ottoman Empire experimented briefly with a constitutional monarchy in the late nineteenth century but did not have a republican constitution until the early 1920s.

ment, so-called for its adherence to a single and narrow set of principles. Ahmadinejad was a small man with shrewd instincts. He did his doctorate in traffic management, a nightmarish problem in chaotic Tehran, which reports hundreds of car accidents daily. He served in the Revolutionary Guards during Iran's war with Iraq in the 1980s. As a provincial politician, he was noted for being less corrupt than many ruling clerics; he flaunted his fashion preference for what he called a janitor's jacket. He was briefly mayor of Tehran, a position elected by members of the city council.

But Ahmadinejad became a divisive figure after winning the presidency in 2005. He rejected the tentative reforms of his predecessor and instead created a ruthless hard-line government. The Islamic Republic was gradually militarized as he named members of the elite Revolutionary Guards to political and economic jobs; he appointed its veterans to be provincial governors. Revolutionary Guards businesses won no-bid government contracts—in the petroleum, automobile, telecommunications, electronics, and manufacturing industries—worth tens of billions of dollars, despite their often questionable qualifications for the assignments.

All in the name of revolutionary Islamic principles, Ahmadinejad's government generally muzzled society. Censorship was tightened, media outlets closed. A women's rights campaign was quashed; so were labor organizations. Leaders of both were arrested. Universities were scrutinized; some faculty members were squeezed out. Arrests, prosecutions, and executions all soared. Many Iranians were picked up on vague charges of un-Islamic activity rather than for specific criminal acts.

During his first term, Ahmadinejad also grossly mismanaged the economy. Iran earned as much in oil revenues during his first five years in office as it did during the first quarter century of the revolution.[5] The price of oil soared to $146 per barrel in 2008—up from lows of just over $3 per barrel in the 1980s—but he managed to run through most of the oil reserve fund. He doled out money almost recklessly to pet projects without parliamentary approval; he approved loans to supporters that had interest below inflation, making the loans instant money losers. He then dismissed Central Bank chiefs and cabinet members who dared to disagree with him.

In foreign policy, Ahmadinejad defied the world. In 2006, Tehran also reneged on an agreement with the international community to suspend uranium enrichment, a key step for both peaceful nuclear energy and production of a bomb. The regime then refused to fully cooperate with the United Nations or allow weapons inspectors full access to Iranian sites and scientists. It also refused to budge, despite new sanctions imposed by the United Nations, the United States, the European Union, and more than one hundred international financial institutions.

Iran increasingly meddled in Iraq, Afghanistan, and Lebanon. Ahmadinejad personally challenged Israel's right to exist. He denied the Holocaust and hosted an international conference in 2006 to question it. Among the speakers was David Duke, former Imperial Wizard of the Ku Klux Klan.

By 2009, Iran was also more doctrinaire than at any time since the revolution's early reign of terror. It was more isolated internationally than at any juncture since the 444-day crisis over the US Embassy seizure between 1979 and 1981. And it was more troubled economically than at any time since its costly eight-year war with Iraq in the 1980s.

NEDA VISITED NEIGHBORING Turkey as the campaign began. She started to date again. She took music lessons. Her mind was elsewhere, her family later recalled. Many young Iranians were disillusioned with politics after Iran's flirtation with reform failed abysmally under Ahmadinejad's predecessor. For a country with almost 40 million voters, Iran's election seasons are also famously short, usually a few weeks, allowing limited time for interaction between candidates and constituents.

But the regime was so self-confident that it made three serious miscalculations.

The first involved candidates. Hundreds of Iranians, including forty-two women, registered to run for president. At every election, the Guardian Council—a part of the regime's Islamic wing and made up of twelve scholars and jurists—vets candidates for their Islamic credentials. In 2009, only three men were allowed to run against Ahmadinejad. All were from the revolutionary elite and had impeccable Islamic credentials: Mir Hossein Mousavi had been prime minister throughout the 1980s. Mehdi Karroubi had twice been speaker of parliament. And Mohsen Rezaie had been commander of the Revolutionary Guards for sixteen years.

The regime wanted to limit choice. But it misjudged basic republican instincts in the twenty-first century—and the resistance to rigid Islamic rule. All three candidates challenged some aspect of the principlists' absolutist policies. Mousavi and Karroubi campaigned for tolerance of political diversity, more press freedoms, women's rights, and transparent economic management.

"Everything is at stake," a political scientist told me when I visited Iran as the campaign began.

The second miscalculation was to broadcast presidential debates for the first time. In the past, candidates each hosted their own rallies; they had little interaction. But in 2009, six debates were held on state-controlled television during the campaign's final ten days. Each session pitted two of the four candidates against each other. Each ninety-minute debate was live, uncensored, and unedited. The ability to compare candidates in televised challenges ignited a new political energy. Voters suddenly sensed options.

Neda got quite caught up in the campaign's spirited final days, her family recalled. After the evening debates, Iranians started turning out on the streets to debate again what had been said. It was a spontaneous reaction, as friends and neighbors talked excitedly about politics. Neda was among them.

"Neda called Mom and told her, 'You're missing these scenes. Everybody is out,' " her sister recalled. The crowds grew larger after every debate.

The debate between Ahmadinejad and Mousavi was especially riveting. The president, who showed up with two thick files, menacingly threatened to disclose classified secrets about Mousavi's wife, a national figure in her own right. Zahra Rahnavard was the first female university chancellor after the revolution. In another first, she actively campaigned for her husband; in three decades, no other political wife had hit the campaign trail. But she often appeared at rallies, usually in bright floral scarves. The couple even held hands in public. The Iranian press dubbed her "the Michelle Obama of Iran."

"I have a dossier on a lady. You know the lady," Ahmadinejad said. "In your campaign, she sits next to you, which is against all the regulations." (He was wrong. Men and women related by blood or marriage are allowed to touch each other and sit together in public.)

Ahmadinejad alleged that Rahnavard's academic degrees were ill-gotten. He portrayed her—and therefore her husband—as beneficiaries of nepotism and corruption.

"She got a PhD without attending the university entrance exam," Ahmadinejad alleged. "And now she is an assistant professor without having qualifications. She is now heading a faculty. This is *lawlessness*! This is what I am opposed to—grants and concessions going to some people and depriving others."[6]

In a scene unprecedented in Iranian politics, Mousavi unleashed a stinging rebuke. He charged on national television that Iranians did not want a government that kept secret dossiers on its citizens. He countered that Ahmadinejad's policies were based on "delusion and superstition."[7] He belittled a sitting president for libeling his wife and others, including two earlier presidents never charged with any crime. And he claimed he emerged after twenty years away from politics because Ahmadinejad's policies were so dangerous.

"She is one of the country's intellectuals!" he said of his wife. "She worked for ten years for her PhD in political science, and we have all the documents to prove it. You have created the wrong impression of her."

Mousavi's pride in his wife's accomplishments resonated among Iranian women. Zahra Rahnavard was actually the most dynamic player in the whole campaign. After the debate, she held her own furious press conference and charged Ahmadinejad with lying, disparaging all women, and undermining the Islamic revolution. Mousavi, a soft-spoken architect and a somewhat boring speaker, got a huge boost from her dynamism. (She was later selected as one of one hundred global thinkers in 2009 by *Foreign Policy,* an American publication. She was third on the list—after Federal Reserve chief Ben Bernanke for preventing another great depression and Barack Obama for "reimagining America's role in the world.")[8]

The debates generated a querulous final campaign; the barrages got fiery. At a rally in Isfahan, Mousavi charged that Ahmadinejad had so sullied the country's image that Iran was as discredited as Somalia, a failed state famed most for its piracy and rampant poverty.

"Our people have not given you the right to disgrace them," Mousavi said.[9]

Even former Revolutionary Guards commander Mohsen Rezaie blasted Ahmadinejad for his provocative foreign policy. "When we say we are revolutionary, it does not mean that we are seeking adventures," he said. "It means we have wisdom and discretion."[10]

Momentum also grew behind Mousavi because he was the one politician who had a record of standing up to Iran's supreme leader—the symbol of the Islamic Republic.

In the 1980s, Mousavi had been prime minister and Ayatollah Ali Khamenei had been president, then the weaker position. Mousavi led Iran through its tough eight-year war with Iraq, when Tehran was isolated internationally and oil prices sank below four dollars per barrel. Khamenei was always in the background. In 1989, not long after the war ended, the constitution was amended and an executive president replaced the prime minister. Mousavi went back to architecture and painting; Khamenei was selected as supreme leader.

Two decades later, Mousavi began a comeback, even though he lacked charisma or support from the regime he once led. He drew large crowds excited about less rigid theocratic rule.

On election eve, Ahmadinejad's presidency appeared in real jeopardy.

By election day, Neda decided she wanted to vote.

On June 12, 2009, a Friday, she set out to cast a ballot. At the first polling station, she discovered that there were no observers from opposition candidates, her family said. She then went to a second polling site, but it also had no monitors. She found the same thing at a third polling station.

In what would prove the ultimate irony, Neda opted not to cast a ballot.

Iran's elections use paper ballots. The results of almost 40 million votes are hand-counted, not computerized. At minimum, many Iranian analysts expected a runoff between Ahmadinejad and Mousavi. A winner must get over 50 percent of the vote, tough in a four-way race. Iran often had runoffs between the two highest vote-getters. Four years earlier, Ahmadinejad had faced a runoff against Akbar Hashemi Rafsanjani, a two-term former president in the 1990s, parliamentary speaker in the 1980s, and Iran's wiliest politician.

Yet less than two hours after the polls closed, state-run television began announcing that Ahmadinejad was winning a decisive landslide. After less than twelve hours, the government confirmed that he won 64 percent—an unprecedented victory, also with the highest turnout ever—against the three other candidates.

Iran's supreme leader heralded the outcome as "divine intervention." It was the regime's third miscalculation.

Mousavi called the results "a dangerous charade." His internal polling indicated he had won the first round outright; the official results gave him only one-third of the vote. He alleged an array of irregularities: His representatives had been expelled from polling stations. Two key provinces had ballot shortages. Polling stations had closed unusually early. Security forces had intimidated voters. And millions of ballots had no registration numbers.

The election was unusual in other ways. The early results showed Ahmadinejad ahead by a margin of two to one virtually everywhere. But initial tallies always came from urban areas where Mousavi was considered strongest; rural areas, Ahmadinejad's base, were last. The final vote also showed identical—and historically unprecedented—voting patterns across 98 percent of the country, despite deep ethnic and economic differences in the world's eighteenth-largest country. They were an aberration from every previous Iranian election.[11]

"Today, the people's will has been faced with an amazing incidence of lies, hypocrisy, and fraud," Mousavi said. He demanded a recount.

So did Karroubi, the former parliamentary speaker and most charismatic candidate. The official results reported that he came in last with only 300,000 votes—fewer than the number of spoiled ballots. When he had run for president in 2005, he had garnered 5 million votes.[12] In 2009, he even lost his hometown. The outcome "was so ridiculous and so unbelievable that one cannot write or talk about it," he said. "It is amazing that the people's vote has turned into an instrument for the government to stabilize itself."[13]

Millions of Iranians did not believe the official results either. Iran's celebrated grapevine buzzed with inside stories of regime pressure, creative vote-rigging, and concocted results. An employee of the Interior Ministry, which conducted the election, told the *New York Times* that the government had plotted the outcome for weeks, purging personnel who did not aid and abet the effort.

"They didn't rig the vote," he said. "They didn't even look at the vote. They just wrote the name and put the number in front of it."[14]

WITHIN HOURS OF the final results on June 13, tens of thousands of people spontaneously poured onto Tehran's streets. The rage was visible in several parts of the capital. In one protest downtown, several thousand people chanted, "Death to the coup d'état." Many Iranians wore green, the color from Mousavi's campaign. He had taken to wearing a green scarf given to him by a supporter. His wife had picked up on it, often wearing green items of clothing and waving a green ribbon at rallies. Green is also the color of Islam.

The regime tried to stem the unrest. Universities, often hotbeds of dissent, were closed. Opposition websites were hacked; the Internet was censored. Cell phones and text services were cut off. Opposition figures were arrested. On the streets, paramilitary zealots on motorbikes and antiriot police with shields tried to beat back protesters. Within twenty-four hours, the first death was reported.

Yet with a stubborn determination, the momentum only grew. By day three, cities across Iran were swarming with public processions. Protesters carried green placards, green posters, and green banners that said, simply, "Where's my vote?" In Tehran alone, the mayor—a former Revolutionary Guards officer—estimated that up to 3 million people were on the streets.[15] After dark, thousands turned out on rooftops in Tehran and other cities to proclaim their fury. Chants of "Death to the dictator" echoed through the eerie night.

The new opposition dubbed itself the Green Movement.

The young were at the forefront of the largest public outpouring since the 1979 revolution. They helped mobilize many other sectors of Iranian society: shopkeepers as well as construction workers, doctors in white coats as well as taxi drivers in shirtsleeves. Even government employees dared to turn out. Among the most striking sights were the females— young girls with pushed-back scarves exposing their coifs who brought along an older generation clutching their enveloping black chadors. The women often walked boldly out front.

Neda was among the demonstrators. "She joined the others in protest because she felt the Iranian people had been insulted," her sister Hoda later recalled. "Even if she hadn't voted herself, her mother, her sister, and her friends had voted."[16]

"Neda went to every single demo, all of them," her sister said. "It was during one of those protests that a woman in a black chador came up to her and said, 'My girl, why don't you dress a little bit more conservatively for these demos because I know these animals. They have real psychological issues and usually go after the beautiful ones, and you are a really pretty girl.' "[17]

On day four, a massive protest in Tehran ran more than a mile long.

The regime became so nervous that it revoked press credentials for visiting foreign correspondents; they were told to leave Iran altogether. Local reporters were instructed to remain inside their offices. The government tried to cut off all images of unrest from reaching either other parts of Iran or the outside world.

But Iranians are tech savvy. By 2009, more than 30 million Iranians used the Internet—up from 250,000 in 2000.[18] Iran also boasted the largest number of bloggers in the Middle East. So, in a pattern that established a precedent for the subsequent Arab revolts, Iranians increasingly conveyed their own images and news from cell phone cameras and videos through email, via YouTube, Twitter, and Facebook accounts, and on a flood of new opposition websites.

Ahmadinejad dismissed the demonstrators as akin to soccer fans who had lost a big game. His backers organized counterdemonstrations. At one Tehran rally, a crowd estimated at 10,000 shouted, "Rioters should be executed."[19] To show his own indifference, Ahmadinejad then departed for a regional security conference in Russia. Ignoring the situation at home, he instead gave a speech about the global balance of power.

"The current political and economic order," he blithely declared, "is approaching the end of its mastery of the world."[20]

Neither ploy had much impact. As protests mushroomed, Iran appeared on the brink.

So one week after the vote, on June 19, Supreme Leader Ayatollah Ali Khamenei intervened to stem a political showdown that increasingly looked like a threat to the whole system, not just to Ahmadinejad. He addressed the nation in a televised sermon at Friday Prayers.

The supreme leader's role was originally to arbitrate disputes. But Khamenei came down firmly on Ahmadinejad's side.

"The Islamic state would not cheat and would not betray the votes of the people," Khamenei told worshippers. He conceded possible election glitches but resisted allegations of rigging. "Perhaps one hundred thousand votes, or five hundred thousand, but how can anyone tamper with eleven million votes?" he said, evoking laughter from the crowd.

Iran's supreme leader then issued an ultimatum: stop the turmoil—or else. He angrily put the opposition on notice about the dangers—and consequences—of refusing to accept the election results.

"I'm asking everyone to end it ... This is not the correct way," he said.[21] "If the political elite ignore the law—whether they want it or not—they will be responsible for the bloodshed and chaos."[22]

THE NEXT DAY was midsummer's eve, June 20. It was hot in Tehran. The eighth day after the election was also tense. Immediately after Khamenei's speech, calls had gone out for people to defy the supreme leader and return to the streets.

"Neda didn't sleep at all the night before," her sister Hoda later recalled. "My mom pleaded with her not to go out. Mom was really worried. But Neda said, 'If I don't go and others like me don't go, then who's going to go?' "[23]

Neda's father said his daughter knew the risks. Dressed in jeans, a knee-length black shirt, and a black scarf, she left home in midafternoon, promising to keep in touch. Then she met up with her music teacher, Hamid Panahi, a white-haired man with a big white mustache. When she did not call, her mother tried her cell phone. Neda answered from the noisy chaos on the streets.

"She said, 'There are so many government forces out here. I've never seen so many in my life before,' " her mother recalled.

"I asked what are they doing, and she said, 'What do you think they're doing? They're chasing us and beating us.' I pleaded with her to come back home. She said, 'Mom, I will. Don't worry.' "

Her mother called again in a half hour, and Neda reported that security forces had started using tear gas. Their eyes were burning so badly that Neda had taken refuge at a clinic. Again, she promised to return home soon.

Neda, Panahi, and two others piled into her old Peugeot. But the protests had overwhelmed Tehran traffic, and they soon got stuck. The car's air-conditioning also did not work, so Neda parked on a side street near another demonstration. The four got out and started walking.

It was just after 7 p.m. and still light on the eve of the year's longest day. The next fifteen minutes unfolded quickly.

Arash Hejazi, a writer and former medical student, was standing close to Neda and Panahi. "We knew that something was going to happen," he later told makers of a PBS documentary. "After Khamenei's remarks, we knew that he had allowed his guards to open fire on the crowd."[24]

Hejazi was immediately struck by Neda's angry energy, even as her music teacher tried to hold her back. "I was really looking at her with admiration because she was a woman, a young woman, so courageous," he said. "I was dying of fear out there, and she was just moving around and shouting." [25]

Antiriot police with batons were chasing protesters, who fled in their direction. "We ran, and Neda was running beside me," Hejazi said. "Her music teacher couldn't run as fast as the others, so Neda turned back all the time to see if he was okay."

Then a single gunshot ripped through the air. Eyewitnesses claimed it came from the rooftop of a private home across the street.

Hejazi turned and watched Neda look up briefly in astonishment. "I'm burning. I'm burning," she mumbled. It was the last thing she said.

Hejazi and Panahi grabbed Neda as she slumped to the ground. "Without her throwing a rock or anything, they shot her," her music teacher said in disbelief later that day. "It was just one bullet." [26]

The end of Neda's life was caught on a grainy cell phone camera as she looked up and then dropped in the middle of a side street. Her arms fell raised up, as if she were being arrested. Her black scarf slipped onto the ground, exposing dark brown hair.

Bending over her, Panahi pleaded, "Neda, don't be afraid. Don't be afraid. Neda, stay with me. Stay with me, Neda."

Hejazi said the shot almost surely hit her heart. He used his medical training to try to stop the bleeding. "I put pressure on the wound," he said. "From what I saw, the bullet had hit her aorta and lungs. When the aorta is hit, the blood drains from the body in less than a minute. There's nothing you can do." [27]

The cell phone video captured the blood streaming from Neda's mouth, then her nose. It ran across her face in a strikingly distinct pattern. Neda's eyes were the most haunting part of the video. One eye was covered by the fast-flowing blood, the other remained wide open.

The entire video lasted forty seconds. She was dead by the end of it.

But the impact of her life had only begun. By the end of midsummer's eve, the heart-wrenching video was being relayed around the world. Hundreds of television stations broadcast it, some many times. Thousands of websites posted it. It was forwarded through tens of thousands of Twitter and Facebook accounts. Millions saw it on YouTube.

No death has ever been seen by so many people, in so many places, especially so quickly. It was gruesomely captivating.

Many other Iranians had already died—numbers were widely disputed—in the tumultuous eight days after the presidential election. But because of the gripping video, Neda instantly became the face of the opposition.

The implications of her murder were reinforced when the crowd who watched her die then nabbed a man they thought was her killer.

"I realized that a crowd was pulling someone towards us and that person was shouting, 'I didn't kill her,' " recalled Hejazi. "People were starting to beat him, and they took off his clothes and his shirt. They started discussing what to do with him," he said. "They searched his body. They took out his wallet. They took out his ID cards and starting shouting, 'He is a Basij member. He's one of them.' "[28] The Basij was a paramilitary unit operating under the Revolutionary Guards and specializing in internal security.

A second video posted on YouTube showed demonstrators holding him and a militia card identifying him as Abbas Kargar Javid.[29]

"We are all Neda" became the Green Movement's rallying cry. It was shouted from rooftops at night. Pictures of Neda—many from her death video—were adapted to posters, T-shirts, artwork, even masks on sticks for protesters to put in front of their own faces. Facebook pages and websites in English and Farsi were dedicated to her. Songs and poetry were written about her heroism. In statements and interviews the opposition candidates deferred to her bravery.

In posters and pictures, the distinct pattern of blood that oozed across her face was adapted to the Islamic Republic's flag. In one particularly damning picture, the same blood pattern was imposed over the supreme leader's face, implicitly blaming him for her death.

Iranian officials scrambled to come up with their own version of what happened, but the stories did not match up. State television initially called the video a fake—and claimed that Neda was an actress who had splashed fake blood on her face, only to be murdered later by friends. One official claimed that she was alive and living in Greece. The Iranian ambassador in Mexico suggested on CNN that she had been assassinated by the CIA.[30] Another version even blamed Hejazi, the former doctor who had stepped in to try and save her.[31]

The regime later aired its own documentary about her death. In yet another version, it reported that an unidentified woman had approached Neda and, using a gun hidden in her purse, shot her. But no one was arrested or prosecuted for her death.

NEDA WAS BURIED quietly on midsummer's day in Behest-e Zahra, or Zahra's Paradise, the sprawling cemetery on Tehran's bleak desert outskirts. Her family had been called to retrieve her body. She was then given a ritual washing and laid to rest the same day under an unmarked mound. The government refused to allow the family to hold a funeral service.

"We weren't allowed to put up a notice on a local board to announce her death. None of the mosques would take us," Hoda later recounted. "None of the halls or restaurants would give us a place to hold a ceremony in Neda's memory." [32]

The regime, however, could not contain the damage. Neda became the new face of martyrdom, a concept central to both Shiite Iran's revolutionary zeal and the Sunni extremism of al Qaeda.

Neda, coincidentally, means "voice" in Farsi.

In Shiite Islam, martyrdom has been a central tenet since Islam's so-called second sect split off in the seventh century, soon after the Prophet Mohammed died. The schism was triggered by a dispute over political leadership. The Prophet's family believed that Ali, the first convert to Islam as well as the Prophet's cousin and son-in-law, was his rightful successor. Shiite literally means "follower of Ali."

But the Prophet's inner circle of advisers countered that Mohammed had left no instructions; they insisted that a new leader should be chosen from among them. They prevailed; the first three caliphs came from outside the family. The Prophet's cousin Ali did eventually become the fourth caliph, but he was murdered five years later. Leadership then moved beyond the Prophet's family to the new Umayyad dynasty, from which mainstream Sunni Islam emerged.

The Prophet's family made one final stand. They believed it was better to die fighting for justice than to live with injustice—a principle that has defined martyrdom and shaped both politics and personal practices among Shiites ever since. Ali's son Hussein challenged the Umayyads with a small band of fewer than one hundred followers. They knew they were likely to be massacred by a more powerful army, as they were in the battle of Karbala, an ancient Mesopotamian city in what is now southern Iraq.

Hussein's sacrifice made protest and revolt against tyranny a Shiite tradition—a duty to God. Shiites still reenact Hussein's martyrdom in an Islamic passion play every year, just as Christians on Good Friday re-enact Jesus' procession to Calvary before his crucifixion. The Shiite holi-day is called Ashura.

Iran's 1979 revolution was actually sparked and then spurred on by the Shiite rituals of martyrdom. The first clash between the shah's troops and his opposition produced the revolution's first *shahid* or "mar-tyr" in January 1978. Shiite deaths are commemorated in a cycle on the third, seventh, and fortieth days. The first shahid's death was commemo-rated forty days later, which generated another clash, another death, an-other commemoration—and an ongoing cycle of martyrdom that fueled fury against the monarchy for months. One year later, on January 16, 1979, the shah was forced to abandon the Peacock Throne.

Over the next three decades, the regime made martyrdom an inte-gral part of both domestic and foreign policy, most spectacularly during Iran's eight-year war with Iraq. It was the Middle East's bloodiest mod-ern conflict.

After Saddam Hussein's army invaded Iran in 1980, more than 123,000 Iranians became shahids to hold off Iraq. Many more were in-jured trying to become martyrs. Even preteens and old men volunteered to be human minesweepers, cannon fodder, or tank traps. Tales about particularly heroic acts of martyrdom were glorified in Iranian society. Streets, schools, and clinics were named after martyrs, complete with the "shahid" before each name as an honorific. Iran created special martyrs' sections in cemeteries with display stands above each grave to include pictures and personal memorabilia.

The war ended in 1988, but two decades later the faces of famed mar-tyrs were still emblazoned across big billboards. In Isfahan, one of the world's most beautiful cities, the biggest billboard on the airport road showed a sea of military helmets laid out on the ground above the slo-gan "Martyrs get to see first what God created." Several cities started their own martyrs' museums; display cases contained bits of a shahid's uniform, a last letter to or from a loved one, a personal Koran, a last will and testament—and always the story of the martyr's final deed. Tehran's martyrs' museum is two blocks down the street from the old United States Embassy.

The Islamic Republic also used martyrdom as a tool to export its ideology. It fostered, funded, and armed extremist cells throughout the Middle East. Its offshoots and allies were initially Shiite, but its reach eventually expanded to include some Sunni groups as well. Hundreds of Iranian-backed shahids—both males and females decked out in bomb-laden vests, belts, backpacks, and even fake baby bumps—transformed the region long before Osama bin Laden.

But Neda's dramatic death began to redefine martyrdom. It suddenly became the symbol of opposition to the regime's ruthless, narrow "principlist" rule—not the instrument of its extremist ideology.

"I was there. I saw that innocent girl dying just in front of my eyes, and I know that Iran will never be the same after Neda's death and after that video," said Hejazi, who had tried to help her. "People of the world will never look at Iran the same way they looked at it before Neda's death." [33]

"Neda symbolizes a generation that this election was all about and this Green Movement was all about," he said. "She didn't want to take power. She wasn't looking for politics. She wasn't looking for anything other than some individual freedom and some freedom of speech. Basic rights. That's why she crystallizes all those hopes and dreams that were shattered after the election." [34]

The regime felt sufficiently threatened by the new type of Iranian martyrs that it stationed security forces near Neda's grave. It also banned the traditional Shiite commemorations at her gravesite, especially the fortieth-day memorial. On July 30, thousands of Iranians, including two of the opposition presidential candidates, struggled to reach grave 41 in row 32 of area 257 in Zahra's Paradise for a final farewell. [35] Security forces tried to turn them all away, then used tear gas to disperse the crowd—to keep them away from the grave of a young woman.

The regime reportedly tried to tempt Neda's parents with the same pension allocated to a martyr's family in exchange for publicly blaming her death on the regime's opponents—and proclaiming that she had been a martyr instead for the Islamic Republic. They refused. [36]

* * *

Aᴄᴛᴇʀ Nᴇᴅᴀ's ᴅᴇᴀᴛʜ, the bitter confrontation between protesters and the regime flared for six months. Dozens more died, even by the government's reluctant admission. Thousands were detained, including a former vice president, the former head of parliament's foreign affairs committee, and a member of parliament whose brother had been president. Some who were later released—both men and women—told horrific stories of torture and rape in prison. Detainees also began to die in custody. One of them was the son of a noted former Revolutionary Guard officer; his father said his son's face had been smashed. The judiciary also carried out Stalinesque show trials.

Public demonstrations grew increasingly difficult in the summer, so the Green Movement turned to civil disobedience in the autumn. It launched a boycott of all goods—from eggs to cell phones—that advertised on state-controlled television. Under the dark of night, it put up posters of detainees, demanding their freedom. The regime tried to intimidate protesters by posting their pictures on the Internet; the opposition responded by posting their own pictures of security forces who beat protesters.

In an imaginative move, Green Movement members orchestrated a word-of-mouth campaign to deface the national currency with antiregime slogans and images. Stamps were made for mass production: One was a caricature of Ahmadinejad with "People's enemy" inscribed underneath. Another was a simple *V*—in green. A third declared, "Long live freedom." Many carried handwritten messages, such as "Cheater Khamenei and power-hungry Ahmadinejad."

The most moving stamp reproduced a picture of Neda from her death video, complete with the distinctive blood patterns. The regime tried to take the defaced currency out of circulation. It threatened not to honor defaced notes. But it eventually backed down due to sheer volume.

Throughout the fall, the Green Movement used long-scheduled commemorations—when the regime normally urged the public to turn out for rallies—as cover for their own marches. The opposition candidates were unable or unwilling to take the lead, so the young did most of the organizing. More youths were arrested, more tried, more brutalized.

As demonstrations became more difficult, public anger also deepened. The focus shifted from Ahmadinejad's reelection to the supreme leader. Graffiti all over Tehran—on buildings, campuses, buses, fences, and underpass walls—proclaimed "Down with Khamenei."

The young daringly tried individual initiatives. Mahmoud Vahidnia, who had won a gold medal in the National Math Olympiad, was invited to a special meeting of Iran's student elite with the supreme leader. The academic forum was broadcast live on national television. In a message clearly aimed at Iran's youth, Khamenei set the tone in opening remarks by warning that any challenge to the election results was the "biggest crime" in Iran.

Vahidnia was a tall, thin youth with big glasses. When it came time for his turn, he spoke softly into the microphone, but with a bite that stunned the television audience. He warned that the supreme leader lived in a bubble and was not aware of what was happening inside Iran.

"I want to ask you something: Why does nobody in this country dare to criticize you?" he admonished the septuagenarian cleric, who had been the most powerful figure in Iran for two decades.

"Do you think that you never make mistakes? Isn't this ignorance?" he said. "You have been changed into a kind of inaccessible idol that nobody can criticize. I don't understand why everybody is forbidden to criticize your choices." [37]

Vahidnia spoke for twenty minutes. He did not mention Neda, but he evoked her death by chastising the regime for its ruthless crackdown on peaceful dissent. "Wouldn't our system have a better chance of preserving itself if we were using more satisfactory methods and limited the use of violence only to essential circumstances?" he asked. [38]

The mild-mannered math student then implied that the supreme leader was personally responsible for human rights abuses, including torture and rape of detainees. "You, who have the role of a father, when you deal with your opponents in such a manner, your subordinates will likely behave similarly, as we have seen in the prisons," Vahidnia said in the October meeting.[39]

Iranian television abruptly cut off the nationwide broadcast, but not before most of Vahidnia's exchange had been recorded by viewers. It too almost instantly appeared on YouTube.

The young even used the anniversary of the United States Embassy seizure to mobilize protests. Iran commemorates the takeover every November 4. It usually lets schools out for the day and buses pupils to the old diplomatic compound for anti-American rallies. The gatherings always resonated with shouts of "Death to America."

But in 2009, the opposition converted the anti-American event into an antiregime rally. "Death to No One" was the new student slogan. "Iranians scream peace with all peoples of the world," they chanted.

The pace of protests picked up in December. So did public rage at the regime. December 7 is National Students Day in Iran; it commemorates the "martyrdom" of three students from 1953 protests against the monarchy. Before the 2009 anniversary, several activists were expelled or warned that they faced expulsion if they participated. They did anyway. Student protests erupted in at least fourteen Iranian cities.[40]

Each new round of protests produced new posters and angrier slogans. This time, the cry across the campuses echoed, "Our curse, our shame, our incompetent supreme leader."

Iran's young dissidents used social media as their members were picked up.

Majid Tavakoli spoke to one of the Tehran rallies. When police pursued him, he tried to escape by cloaking himself as a woman. He was eventually caught. The regime published a mug shot of him in female disguise, then charged him with "insulting the supreme leader" as well as "collusion against the regime." He was sentenced to eight years in prison, plus a five-year ban on political activity and another five-year ban on leaving the country.

Iran's young launched a "We are all Majid Tavakoli" campaign. Men took pictures and videos of themselves dressed in women's hejab and posted them on YouTube, Facebook, Twitter, and opposition sites. They also Photoshopped the blue and black hejab worn by Tavakoli and superimposed it on pictures of Ahmadinejad and the supreme leader. Both circulated widely. Both reflected public scorn for Iran's leadership.

The intrepid uprising against rigid theocratic rule rallied more than just Iran's fledgling republicans. It also won support from key clerics. The most important was Grand Ayatollah Ali Montazeri, a man who was almost supreme leader. For years, he had been the designated heir of revolutionary leader Ayatollah Ruhollah Khomeini (not to be confused with Ali Khamenei). But his criticism of the regime's practices and executions led to his dismissal just a few months before Khomeini died in 1989. Khamenei, then president, was selected instead.

Since his dismissal, Montazeri had been ostracized by the regime; he faced house arrest for long stints in the holy city of Qom. But he still had a huge following as the leading clerical dissident. He used the Internet to transmit his thoughts, fatwas, and criticism of the regime.

Shortly after Iran's disputed election, Montazeri had issued a fatwa dismissing the results. He urged Iranians to continue "reclaiming their dues" in calm protests. He also warned security forces not to follow orders that would eventually condemn them "before God."

As the regime's crackdown widened, Montazeri wrote a scathing letter to fellow clerics. "The [revolution's] goal was not simply to change the names and slogans but then keep the same oppression and abuses practiced by the previous regime," he told them.

"I feel ashamed of the tyranny," he wrote. "What we now see is the government of a military guardianship, not the guardian of Islamic scholars."

Among the clergy, debate had raged since the revolution about what an ideal Islamic state should look like. The clergy even argued over whether an Islamic state was good, long-term, for Islam. Many of Islam's ministers feared that the human shortcomings of an Islamic government would in turn taint Islam.

Two weeks after the big student demonstrations, on December 19, Montazeri suddenly died. His passing triggered an outpouring that the government could not stem. Hundreds of thousands of Iranians converged on Qom, the holy city and center of Islamic learning, for his funeral. Qom had earlier been off-limits to the opposition. But the procession carrying Montazeri's coffin quickly turned into a mass protest. The moment symbolized the merger of the largest sector of Iranian society with the intellectual heft of clerics who had once been central to the revolution.

"Dictator, dictator, this is your last message!" the demonstrators shouted. "The people of Iran are rising."

The demonstrations culminated eight days later on Ashura—the holiday honoring the first Shiite martyr fourteen centuries earlier in a fight against injustice. The commemoration is especially serious in a country with the world's largest Shiite population. In cities across the country, hundreds of thousands turned out for separate religious ceremonies that turned into raging protests.

But in 2009, Neda's death resonated as much as Hussein's martyrdom.

"She couldn't stand the injustice of it," mused Hamid Panahi, the music teacher who had been with her when she died. "All she wanted was the proper vote of the people to be counted."

The youth-led rebellion briefly appeared to be gaining an edge. Then, as on midsummer's eve, Iran's security forces opened fire. This time, they were no longer hiding on rooftops. This time, they shot en masse. Ashura was the bloodiest day since the election. The faith was coming full cycle.

The theocracy reexerted control in early 2010. But the cost was unprecedented. The world's only modern theocracy, which had aspired to be the model for God's rule on earth, basically had to militarize to hold on to power. It was discredited among millions of its own people—and even more in the Islamic world. And the opposition, even from the political sideline or prison cells, still provided the vision of an alternative Iran.

In 2011, the young sporadically tried to mobilize again after the Tunisian and Egyptian upheavals. They launched short hit-and-run demonstrations in Tehran. They gathered briefly, marched short distances, chanted against the regime, and took videos to post on YouTube, Facebook, Twitter, or opposition websites.

"Whether Cairo or Tehran, death to tyrants!" they shouted.

Then they broke up, slipped into cars already positioned on streets, and made their way to another spot for another short protest.

"Mubarak and Ben Ali," they chanted about the ousted Arab leaders. "It's your turn next, Khamenei!"

The Green Movement's rebellion against radical Islamic ideology represented a particular irony: a regime that seized power through revolution, exported extremist ideology, taught suicide tactics, and was suspected of a covert nuclear weapons program suddenly faced its biggest challenge to date from peaceful civil disobedience. For the Islamic world, Iran was again a trendsetter.

PART TWO

A Different Tune

5.

Hip-Hop Islam

**There is a cool Islam out there, Yusef.
You just have to find it. You have to sift through
all the other stuff, but it's there.**

—MICHAEL MUHAMMAD KNIGHT,
GODFATHER OF MUSLIM PUNK[1]

Throughout the Islamic world, rap is now providing the rhythm of resistance. Its songs are the twenty-first-century anthems against both autocrats and extremists.

In November 2010, a young Tunisian rapper who called himself El General posted a song on his Facebook page and YouTube. He had no alternative. The government of President Zine al Abidine Ben Ali had virtually banned hip-hop. Its musicians were not on government-approved playlists for state-controlled television or radio. They were rarely able to get permits to perform in public. And most were barred from recording CDs.

El General—whose real name is Hamada Ben Amor—also had no resources of his own. At twenty-one, he faced the problems of many young Tunisians. He was without reliable work and still living at home with his parents. For Tunisia's rappers, the only regular gigs were on the Internet. So he recorded the song underground.

"I had two friends," he later explained. "One filmed my songs on a small video camera, and the other edited the videos and put them up on YouTube."[2]

The song was entitled "Rais Lebled," a play on the term *rais el-bled,* meaning the president of the republic. It raged against the problems of poverty, unemployment, hunger, and injustice—and boldly blamed them all on Ben Ali.

> *Mr. President, today I speak to you,*
> *In the name of all who are suffering.*
> *People dying of hunger,*
> *They want to work to survive.*
> *Go down to the street and look around you,*
> *People are treated like animals.*
> *Look at the cops,*
> *Their batons beat everyone with impunity,*
> *Because there's no one to say no,*
> *Not even the law or the constitution.*

The four-minute video was haunting and raw. It showed the young rapper sauntering through a darkened, sewage-strewn alley to a secret site to record. The makeshift studio had graffiti spray-painted on the wall. He beat out the song in front of an old-fashioned mike, with no one else in sight. Afterwards, he ambled back down the alley into the night. His face was never in the light, his identity remained unclear. Going public was too dangerous.

> *We're suffering like dogs,*
> *Half the people living in shame.*
> *Misery everywhere,*
> *People are eating from garbage cans.*
> *Today I'm speaking for the people,*
> *Crushed by the weight of injustice.*
> *I've chosen to speak,*
> *Even though many have warned me against it.*

El General's song was an instant sensation. Its outrage resonated especially among the young. It broke through the climate of fear in a country where no politician had dared to criticize a president in power for almost a quarter century. His incendiary rap quickly rippled across the Internet. The amateur video was even picked up by Al Jazeera, the twenty-four-hour Arabic news channel.

The song had a transformative influence. It set the stage for the Jasmine Revolution that broke out a month later. It did what many Tunisians dared not do—speak out.[3]

They steal in plain sight.
No need to name them,
You know very well who they are.
A lot of money should have gone to development,
To schools, to hospitals, to housing.
But the sons of dogs,
Are instead filling their stomachs.
Mr. President, your people are dead.[4]

A few weeks later, a government inspector demanded a bribe from Mohamed Bouazizi, the street vendor in Sidi Bouzid. She confiscated his produce and his scales. When he could find no recourse, he set himself on fire over the same problems that echoed through the plaintive rap lyrics. As protests over Bouazizi's plight spread across the country, El General's rap became the rallying cry. Verses were sung by tens of thousands of Tunisians in street demonstrations demanding the president's ouster.

For El General, the words proved personally prophetic. As the Jasmine Revolution gained momentum, he wrote another song entitled "Tunisia Our Country." Its blunt condemnation bordered on treason. At 5 a.m. on a cold winter day, government security forces showed up at his door in Sfax, a former commercial center on the Mediterranean coast.

"Some thirty plainclothes policemen came to our house and took him away without ever telling us where to," his brother told news agencies. "When we asked why they were arresting him, they said, 'He knows why.' "[5]

The young rapper was taken to a prison in Tunis. He was put in solitary confinement. And he was repeatedly interrogated about possible political connections. But in the breathtaking speed of the first Arab revolt, the revolutionary anthem had also already made him famous. Demonstrators began demanding his release as well as the president's resignation.

"They asked me, 'Please stop singing about the president and his family, and then we'll release you,' " he later recounted.[6]

The government, as one of the growing concessions to appease demonstrators, let him go after three days. El General, little known before his protest song, had become almost as famous as Bouazizi. "That's when I realized that my act was really huge, and really dangerous, because the police got so many calls about my incarceration," he said. "Once I stopped being scared, I had this huge pride."[7]

Two weeks after the Tunisian president abruptly fled, El General performed in public for the first time. Wearing the Tunisian flag draped around his shoulders, he belted out his anthem for a crowd of thousands. His appearance brought the Jasmine Revolution full cycle. Mannoubia Bouazizi, the mother of the young street vendor whose self-immolation launched the uprising, had traveled to Tunis to share the stage. The two young men had transformed political activism in Tunisia—and in turn the entire Arab world.

El General's song became the anthem of revolutions across the region. It was sung in street demonstrations from mighty Egypt to tiny Bahrain. Through Facebook, he had many requests to join the protesters at Cairo's Liberation Square. He had no passport, so he opted to work instead on a rap ode to Arab revolution.

"Egypt, Algeria, Libya, Morocco," the chorus went, "all must be liberated too."

I N THE DECADE after 9/11, hip-hop also became an increasingly potent voice of the counter-jihad.

On May 16, 2003, Muhammad Bahri was performing at a small piano bar in Casablanca. It was some two hundred yards down the road from the Golden Tulip Farah, a luxury hotel on one of the bustling city's wide boulevards. It was shortly after 9 p.m.

At just that moment, a taxi carrying Youssra Oukaf, a modelesque Moroccan singer who performs under the single name Soultana, stopped at a traffic light near the Golden Tulip. When the light turned green, the cabbie put his foot on the accelerator.

As Bahri performed and Soultana's taxi started down the street, a bomb exploded in the Golden Tulip. The blast ripped through the lobby and into the night. The force reverberated so far down the road that Bahri initially thought it was seismic activity.

"The room was shaking badly," he later told me. "We thought it was an earthquake."

The explosion was one of five coordinated suicide bombings that echoed across Casablanca within a mere thirty minutes. Years later, Soultana still remembered the fear that gripped Morocco's commercial center.

"My father called me on my cell," she said. "He told me to get home. He said there were bombs all over the city."

The worst carnage was at the Casa de España social club, where people were dining and playing bingo. Bodies or their parts were blown across the room. The explosion set off a fire that incinerated part of the building. A bomb also went off at a Jewish community center, which happened to be empty but would have been packed the next day. Suicide bombers then blew up prematurely near a Jewish cemetery and near the Belgian Consulate, an attack that may have been intended for a Jewish-owned restaurant.[8]

The bombings, in diverse parts of the sprawling port city, were Morocco's first international terrorist attacks. They happened just four days after the triple bombings in Saudi Arabia by al Qaeda in the Arabian Peninsula.

In Casablanca, the government blamed another al Qaeda offshoot, the Moroccan Islamic Combatant Group. It too was spawned in Afghanistan. The five attacks followed a fatwa from Osama bin Laden charging that Morocco—a former French colony and a gateway between the West and the Arab world—was "straying from the righteous path of Islam."

The death and destruction sparked an unexpected reaction. Instead of being cowed by al Qaeda, the wave of extremism instead spurred a cultural counterattack in Morocco. Bahri and Soultana started rapping against bin Laden and his cohorts.

A decade after the 9/11 attacks, the young throughout the Islamic world are, literally, singing a different tune.

"The idea came to me after the bombings," explained Bahri, who was part of Morocco's first rap group, CasaMuslim, and now performs solo under the name Barry. "I went to the hotel and saw all the damage. It was a disaster. I had so many questions: Were these people really Muslim? Really Moroccan?"

He later recorded a song entitled "Who Are You?" The translation from Darija, the local Arabic dialect, loses the rhythmic beat but not the message.

Who are you? Who are you today?
Your politics are dark . . .
You're wearing long pants [Afghan garb],
You're hiding behind your beard
Behind your [Muslim] cap.
You speak of resistance,
But you're doing all these ugly things.
You forgot about the Prophet's guidance.
You are monsters.
If you understood the Koran,
There wouldn't be bombs.

In the early twenty-first century, hip-hop has given new voice to young Muslims, who now dominate the faith from Morocco to Malaysia, Iran to Indonesia, and Somalia to the Palestinian territories. Rappers are now among the most potent new messengers of political change. Hip-hop has emboldened the young to lash back at both extremists and autocrats. Its songs have become the anthems of protests across the Arab world. It has also been a bridge to other cultures, fostering a sense of commonality rather than a clash.

"I hate bin Laden," Soultana told me when we met in Casablanca, not far from the Golden Tulip. She is an unusually tall Moroccan with exotically high cheekbones and hair that falls in dozens of tiny braids to her waist. She was wearing tennis shoes with pink laces.

"He's changed everything for Muslims—even the meaning of Islam. He's created more problems for us than he has for you!" she said, with a long angry sigh. "He wants conflict between the West and Muslims, but the young today don't. We hate extremists. We look away from militants with their beards and robes. They don't attract the young anymore."

In one of her early songs after 9/11, Soultana raged at bin Laden,

You bring hell to our world, you bring misunderstandin' . . .
Now you represent no Muslim, because al Qaeda is hell . . .
Shame on you, shame on your people.
Peace for all, a love will cure this sickness you bring.
God willing, soon we will be able to change the world,
To bring a new safe generation to take the lead.

In the Islamic world, hip-hop serves the same function that rap did when it emerged in the 1970s among young American blacks in the South Bronx. The original hip-hop street parties were a reaction to years of gang violence. They provided nonviolent outlets for pent-up anger and energy.

Two years after the Casablanca bombings, rap groups joined forces for a three-city concert series called "I Love Hip-Hop in Morocco." The North African country's first hip-hop tour became a popular documentary of the same name. The film chronicled the newcomers' struggles, their shoestring funding, the drama of rapping in a Muslim country—and the extraordinary turnouts. More than thirty-six thousand Moroccans turned out to hear the new groups perform.

At the concert in picturesque Marrakesh, the rap group Fnaire introduced a song that became a hip-hop sensation in the Arab world.

Hands off my country, land of my ancestors,
People dear to my heart, land of mine and my grandchildren.
I refuse terrorism in my country, and I cry it out loud,
Hands off my country, land of my ancestors.

Hip-hop has now created an alternative subculture among the young across the Islamic world. Rap is its voice in a 4/4 beat. Muslim rap is replete with beeps, bops, and beatboxes, although without the materialism, misogyny, vulgarity, and "gangsta" violence that later emerged in Western hip-hop. Muslim rappers' messages, however, are just as bold and blunt.

For the Muslim world, hip-hop is not only a radical departure in music and message. It is a radical challenge to religious taboos too.

Beyond basic percussion for religious chants, many hard-line clerics forbid music altogether. Saudi Arabia's strict Wahhabism basically bans any form of modern dancing, singing, and music in public. The kingdom allows only the traditional and painfully slow sword dances—by men.

So for the Muslim world, rap group names are especially defiant. Dam and Rapperz were early Palestinian groups. Kla$h is a Saudi. Afrock and Da Sole are Tunisia rappers. Desert Heat came from the United Arab Emirates. Disso R Die and ThuGz Team are Kuwaitis. Rappers DJ Outlaw and Chillin came from little Bahrain. Hich Kas—which means "nobody" in Farsi—was among the first of many Iranian rappers. Boyz

Got No Brain are Indonesian rappers. MC Kash is an Indian rapper in Kashmir.

Islamic rap has emerged even in the West. Mecca2Medina was Britain's first Muslim hip-hop group. Miss Undastood, an American Muslim who wears hejab, has been called the first lady of Islamic rap.

Hip-hop is a microcosm of the Islamic revival's fourth phase—and its many complex facets.

The rejection of extremism by young Muslim rappers, first and foremost, does not mean they have embraced secularism. Many of the rappers are strikingly religious and observant. Throughout the Muslim world, hip-hop and Islam are now thoroughly entwined. Soultana even raps about her faith.

"I sang that there are a lot of practices we need to remember," she told me. "In one song, I say,

> You can pray five times a day, it's simple.
> You can give during Ramadan, it's simple.
> You can't drink or do drugs, you're Muslim.
> It's not hard to be a real Muslim.
> You will be satisfied.

Soultana does not wear hejab, but she has many friends who do. During a performance in Rabat, three men told her that female singers were *haram*, or "forbidden," to perform in front of men. She simply countered, "I read the Koran." Then she went on singing.

At a summer concert in 2009, Soultana told me, she and the rap group Fusion stopped to observe the final daily call to prayer. Many of the young in the audience followed suit. Islamic hip-hop has become a genre, somewhat like Christian gospel hip-hop and rock.

In 2007, MTV launched a new MTV Arabia channel. Its flagship show was *Hip-Hop Na*—or "Our Hip-Hop." It auditioned the top local rap groups in seven Middle Eastern cities. One of the finalists was Dark2Men, a group so underground in Saudi Arabia that not even the boys' parents knew about their pastime.[9] Dark2Men's most popular song was an ode to Islam:

> We're the ones who care about women and family.
> We're the ones who care about neighbors and community.

And after all that, how dare you people call us terrorist.
I'm proud to be Muslim.
Islam is the deepest peace.
And no matter what they say or do,
I am, I am, I'm Muslim.

By 2009, even conservative Saudi entrepreneurs were tapping into the trend with the launch of 4Shabab—"For Youth"—the first full-time Islamic music video channel. The founder won financial backing by showing Saudi investors the provocative programs watched by young Arabs on other channels; then he showed them the numbers of viewers.[10]

In its first year, 4Shabab's most popular program was a music competition called *Soutak Wasel,* or "Your Voice Is Heard." It was quickly nicknamed *Islamic Idol.* The rap and rock singers—all male, performing to an audience segregated by gender—crooned about the challenges of leading a virtuous life and completing daily prayers.[11]

Islamic hip-hop reflects the counter-jihad because it does not embrace American or Western culture, even as it embraces its musical forms. For most of the decade after 9/11, anger at the West increased especially among the young. It was linked largely to the US wars in Iraq and Afghanistan, the Palestinian-Israeli dispute, American drone strikes in Pakistan, and aid and arms sales to autocratic regimes. The "war on terror"—which often appeared to Muslims to be targeting them all—triggered a big backlash that, in turn, only deepened religious identity. Soultana rapped:

They said we are terrorists because we are Muslims,
Because one criminal did it wrong in the name of Islam.
Our Islam is peace, love, respect.
We are the generation calling for peace.

The godfather of Muslim punk, Michael Muhammad Knight, put it more succinctly. "In this so-called war of civilizations," he said, "we're giving the finger to both sides."[12]

Hip-hop was the first voice of political opposition, even before the street protests that erupted in 2011. With its defiant political rhythm, hip-hop became the idiom to protest hardships, injustice, and oppression. Rap spawned a new bad-ass sass in countries where the state controlled the media, banned the opposition, orchestrated elections, and arrested the outspoken—conditions that have in turn fostered alienation and extremism. The angry lyrics, the in-your-face moves, and the irreverent words have redefined the way young Muslims express themselves on domestic politics.

"Hip-hop is now the battleground for Muslims," Soultana explained. "And rappers have become the revolutionaries in Morocco and the Arab world.

"Arabic music is usually about love or cheating boyfriends or girlfriends," she said. "But when you listen to rap, you find ninety percent of it is about our real problems, even the taboo topics—things no one else is willing to bring up in public. You can let it out in rap."

And there is a lot to rap about. Problems abound for millions of young people in some of the world's most troubled countries. Their numbers alone are a challenge. The young make up the majority in all Muslim countries, in some places close to 70 percent.

Pakistan is one of the five most-populous Muslim countries, along with Indonesia, India, Turkey, and Bangladesh. In 2010, 63 percent of Pakistanis were under twenty-five.[13] But only one out of every one hundred children entering kindergarten was likely to complete high school. One out of every four teachers in the South Asian nation did not even show up for school—*every day*. In Karachi, Pakistan's financial center and largest city, more than 1 million school-age children—out of 4 million total—were not in school at all. The United Nations ranked Pakistan 163rd out of 177 countries on education.[14]

In Iran, the government generates only about 300,000 of the roughly 1 million jobs needed annually to absorb young people entering the labor market. Even among college graduates, it takes an average of three years to find a job. Between 1990 and 2010, unemployment among Iranian youth almost doubled.[15]

In the neighboring Arab world, more than 10 million children between the ages of six and fifteen were not enrolled in any schooling in 2009, according to the United Nations. The already volatile Middle East accounts for one of the world's youngest populations. More than 50 percent of the region's 300 million people are under twenty-five years old.[16] They also represent the world's fastest-growing labor force and highest youth unemployment (proportionately). In 2010, one-half of the region's jobless were also under the age of twenty-five—roughly double the world average.

In Egypt, the most populous of the twenty-two Arab countries, one-quarter of the population was between eighteen and thirty years old in 2010. And 90 percent of Egypt's unemployed were in that age group, the United Nations reported.[17]

"These increasingly restive youths are particularly vulnerable to those who would preach radicalism and hostility toward the West, especially the United States," Dubai's Emir Mohammed bin Rashid al Maktoum warned in a 2009 op-ed in the *Wall Street Journal*.[18]

In Jordan, Queen Rania said that unemployment among Arab youth was "a ticking time bomb." At a gathering of business leaders, she warned that the number of unemployed people under thirty years old in the Middle East could increase from 15 million in 2008 to 100 million in 2020—or just twelve years.[19]

The employment vacuum has in turn opened the way for militants and anti-Western militias to step in—often as a means of survival more than for the ideological draw. Many Afghan fighters claimed they joined the Taliban largely for a livelihood.

As American troops started to withdraw from Iraq in 2009, more than one-quarter of Iraqi men under age thirty were out of work, the United Nations reported.[20] In 2010, the problem became political. The United States had funded the 90,000 Sunni Muslims who banded together in the Sons of Iraq militia to push out extremists. The Anbar Awakening in Iraq's most volatile province was the pivotal turning point that allowed Washington to begin a pullout three years later. But Iraq's Shiite-dominated government then ordered the militia disbanded and failed to provide promised jobs for the young Sunnis. Many former fighters threatened to rejoin the insurgency.

Even oil wealth has not protected the rich kingdoms from demographic realities. Saudi Arabia is one of the youngest countries in the region. In 2010, 70 percent of the population was estimated to be under thirty years old.[21] The kingdom's population almost tripled between 1970 and 1989, fueled partly by soaring oil prices and family incomes. The vast majority of Saudi jihadis have come from this generation.

Saudi Arabia is also a microcosm of a broader problem. In many Muslim countries, conservative religious authorities have long had veto power over education. Their control—over both what was taught and who taught it—has been an unspoken deal with governments in exchange for not meddling in state affairs. In the kingdom, the royal family has controlled politics. The Wahhabis, clerics from Islam's most rigid sect, have controlled mosques and schools—and minds.

The heavy emphasis in Saudi schools has been on rote learning and religion—an extension of education once centered on memorizing the Koran—rather than critical thinking and science, technology, engineering, medicine, or business. As a result, many young Saudis have not developed employable skills needed in a globalizing world.[22] Other Muslim countries have similar problems.

Since oil prices quadrupled in the 1970s, petro-wealth has allowed Saudi Arabia to buy foreign professional talent as well as manual labor. But it also produced a serious unemployment problem—over 10 percent in 2009—mostly among the young.

In Morocco, almost 40 percent of young people between the ages of fifteen and twenty-nine were unemployed in 2010. The national rate was 9 percent.[23] And at least one out of every three Moroccans was still illiterate. But even the well-educated had problems finding jobs.

Morocco's youth increasingly took out its anxiety and anger in hip-hop. Soultana has rapped as furiously at her own government as at al Qaeda. In Darija, the local dialect, she railed,

> They said they'd bring a new system for our country,
> But reforms are no more than hallucinations.
> They said "Vote" because we have transparency and credibility,
> But when they won, they closed their doors and nothing
>   happened.

The song's refrain resonated with personal fury.

> Every day I see youth dying.
> I see guys and girls with diplomas unemployed.
> I see children in the streets searching for food.
> I see women prostitute themselves to feed their babies.
> Thirty-eight percent illiteracy—as if we don't have schools.
> Twenty-five percent unemployment—as if we don't have
>   capabilities.

Seventy-six percent violence against women
And one hundred percent of poverty and silence.
So how can you build a good new generation?

Not surprisingly, protests also erupted in Morocco in 2011. Thousands of Moroccans took to the streets in Casablanca, Rabat, Marrakesh, Tangier, and beyond to demand a new constitution, an end to corruption, and a limit on the king's power. Their slogans picked up the rappers' beat. "We too want change," they cried.

TAMER NAFAR IS the lead singer of DAM, the first Palestinian rap group. A lanky Palestinian with a close-cropped haircut and fashionable facial stubble, he wears the rapper's baggy jeans, oversized T-shirt, and sometimes a baseball cap backwards, although no jewelry bling. He started rapping as a teenager and formed DAM with his younger brother Suheil Nafar and friend Mahmoud Jreri in 1999, initially as a sideline. Rap was hardly profitable in a poor Palestinian community. The three grew up in the slums of Lod, a mixed Arab and Israeli town just south of Tel Aviv. They are among the so-called '48 Arabs, Palestinians who have lived in Israel since its creation in 1948.

Hip-hop has become an outlet even in the Middle East's most volatile corner. Just as rap initially provided an alternative to gang violence for young blacks in the Bronx, hip-hop has offered an alternative to suicide bombs and Molotov cocktails among Palestinians.

"Every village now has hip-hop," explained Nafar. "Hip-hop is our CNN."

DAM has triple meanings. It is the acronym for Da Arabic MCs. (Rap is called MCing or emceeing.) It also translates as "eternity" in Arabic. In Hebrew, it means "blood."

"So it's 'eternal blood,' " Nafar told me, "meaning we will stay here forever."

DAM's lyrics ooze with rage—uncensored and unapologetic—at Israel. The words are often raw. In a track entitled "I Don't Have Freedom," the trio rapped,

We've been like this more than fifty years,
Living as prisoners,

Behind the bars of paragraphs,
Of agreements that change nothing.

Onstage, Nafar combines the cocky swagger of a rapper and the fury of a Palestinian protester. He palms the microphone, leaning into it as he beats out the words, then raises it over his head and claps it in his hands between verses. With some songs, he struts to the beat across the stage. With others, he dances a blend of hip-hop and rhythmic Arabic dancing.

DAM gained fame with a highly controversial 2001 song called "Who's the Terrorist?" The trio sang it after a devastating suicide bombing of a Tel Aviv nightclub; twenty-one young Israelis died and dozens more were injured. DAM's song raged at the world for not understanding the desperation Palestinians felt because far more of their own people had been killed by Israeli forces over the previous year.

"The world stood still, didn't do nothing," Nafar later explained. "Then a Palestinian guy got into Tel Aviv, and he committed a suicide bombing, which led to twenty-one victims, young kids, to get killed. Twenty-one versus thousands of Palestinians and suddenly the world stands still and says, 'Let's stop the war, and let's stop the murder. Let's stop the terror.'

"We saw that as an unfair thing, like to shut down one eye and to open the other one—to legitimize the killing of Palestinians, but to fight their reaction."[24]

"Who's the Terrorist?" was downloaded more than half a million times from YouTube. Its popularity reflected the conflicting sides of the Islamic revival's fourth phase. The lyrics, sometimes vile, lashed out in language that could not be more offensive to Israel. The song compared Israel's occupation of the Palestinian territories to Germany's occupation of Europe in World War II.

Democracy? I swear you're Nazis,
With all the times you raped the Arab spirit.
It got pregnant and birthed a boy called the suicide bomber.
And here you are calling us terrorists.
Who's the terrorist? I'm the terrorist?
How am I the terrorist, when this is my homeland . . .

But the song also then ached for coexistence.

I don't want to be misunderstood.
We reach for peace. I'm for coexistence fifty/fifty,
Not ninety-nine percent for you and we split the rest as well . . .
I'm not against peace, peace is against me.

For all their fury, DAM's songs also do not urge, threaten, or organize violence.

"I have a lot of rage, but I express it with a microphone, not a weapon," Nafar explained to a Jewish publication in 2007—in Hebrew.[25] The DAM trio has repeatedly condemned extremism and violence—by both sides—even as their songs try to explain the context of suicide bombs.

Music as an outlet is a stark contrast to the two uprisings, or intifadas, that created the most radical generation of young Palestinians.[26]

The first intifada erupted in 1987 and lasted five years. It was dominated by haphazardly organized young Palestinians who threw rocks, burned tires, and lobbed crude, homemade Molotov cocktails at Israeli forces. Israel's response was increasingly tough. Casualty estimates vary, sometimes widely. Between 100 and 200 Israelis died.[27] More than 1,000 Palestinians were killed.[28] And over 120,000 Palestinians were reportedly arrested.[29]

The second intifada erupted in 2000 and also lasted five years. It was far more violent. Well-armed militias led the uprising. Dozens of suicide bombers from militant groups blew themselves up in public venues— shopping malls, buses, a pizza parlor, a school, hotels and restaurants, even a disco. Palestinian militias also fired dozens of rockets into Israel. Israeli forces responded with aerial bombardments and so-called targeted assassinations.

By the time a cease-fire was declared in 2005, more than 2,820 Palestinians had died. More than 1,000 Israelis had been killed.[30]

In the opening single on the 2007 album *Dedication*, DAM rapped, "Our album is the new intifada, the lyrics are the stones." But its songs preached boycotts rather than bombs.[31] The trio actually devoted more song time to issues of crime, drug use, and kindergartens for Israeli Arabs surrounded by sewage. Its debut album was entitled *Stop Selling Drugs*.

Hip-hop has filled a social and communications void for what is arguably the most important sector of Palestinian society—and the largest. In 2010, more than one-half of Palestinians were under twenty-five years old.[32] But neither the government nor the private sector could absorb them, and jobs in Israel were no longer an option. Unemployment was a staggering 35 percent among West Bank youth and over 50 percent among the young in Gaza, the United Nations reported.[33] And there were few outlets—and fewer funds—for entertainment.

For this generation, life experience and worldviews have also been largely defined by conflict—the two intifadas and the three-week war between Israel and Gaza in 2008 and 2009. After the Gaza war, the *Washington Post* reported on the show-and-tell in a seventh-grade Palestinian class. The twelve-year-old kids got up in class and told how their families in Gaza had been killed, their friends injured, their neighbors' homes damaged, and their own homes destroyed.

"The F-16 bombed my uncle's house," Mohammed Abu Hassan told the class. "His stomach got ripped out, and he died." Another explained how the top two floors of his building had been burned by the shelling, so twenty people were living in the cramped ruins of the ground floor.[34]

Among their peers in twenty-two Arab countries, Palestinian youth may best reflect the rival trends of the counter-jihad. Young Palestinians have witnessed the greatest violence in their lifetimes. Anger has never been greater. Alienation has never been deeper. And in 2009, four out of every five Palestinian young people said they were depressed, a United Nations survey reported.[35]

"If the situation continues like this, most of the kids will become drug dealers," Nafar told me. "There's no life here, no art." The slum where the three rappers lived was already notorious for drug problems.

Yet a decade after 9/11, the majority of young Palestinians also rejected violence. Nearly 70 percent of young adults over the age of seventeen said that they did not believe the use of violence would resolve the Palestinian-Israeli conflict, the United Nations survey reported. Only 8 percent called violence "an important tool."[36]

Rap has captured the popular mood. In 2006, DAM recorded "Change Tomorrow," which urged their Palestinians peers,

> *Don't grab a gun, but grab a pen and write*
> *I'M AN ARAB like Mahmud Darwish* did.*

---

* Mahmud Darwish, who died in 2008, was widely considered the Palestinian national poet.

I'll never kill the others just to live.
My heart is screaming, we are human beings,
My head is held high, in the name of Palestine.

Jewish groups have criticized DAM's songs for promoting an anti-Zionist message. And some clearly do. In "Stranger in My Country," DAM rapped,

A democratic Zionist regime is ruling us
Democratic to those who are Zionist,
And Zionist to those who are Arab . . .
What is forbidden for him is forbidden for me,
What's allowed for him is forbidden for me.
And what's allowed for me is undesirable for me,
Because it denies my existence.

Yet Nafar broke into hip-hop in the late 1990s collaborating with Israeli rapper Subliminal. The two fell out during the second intifada almost a decade later. As with many on both sides of the divide, passions polarized.

Nafar also rapped in Hebrew to reach an Israeli audience. In "Born Here," he sang in Hebrew that he felt like "a dove trying to survive under the hawk's regime."

After the second intifada ended, the Palestinian trio also collaborated with the Israeli band Shotei Hanuveh on the track "Generations Demand Peace" and performed at peace rallies.[37]

By 2007, DAM had developed a following among young Israelis and performed at Jewish clubs. At Café Barzilay, fans lined the street to get into a show beginning at midnight—on a weeknight. At the nightclub Levontin 7 in Tel Aviv, DAM performed in a hip-hop *sulha* (Arabic for "reconciliation") with Israeli rappers.[38] The trio also appeared on an Israeli television program, speaking in Hebrew.

An Israeli music critic for *Time Out Tel Aviv* devoted three pages to the rising Palestinian group.

"Their CD sounds exactly the way a high-quality hip-hop album is supposed to sound—exploding with aggressive energy . . . on the one hand, with complex musical compositions and sophisticated production on the other hand. Samples from traditional Arabic songs . . . integrate

perfectly with the heavy bass and insistent beat of contemporary Western hip-hop," reviewer Shai Fogelman wrote.

"Anyone who thinks that DAM is simply a curiosity," he added, "is
destined to be surprised when they explode in our faces." [39]

A documentary about DAM's young rappers, still in their twenties,
premiered at the Sundance Film Festival in 2008. I saw a special showing
of *Slingshot Hip Hop* at a Washington, DC, cinema four blocks from the
White House. I talked to the three Palestinians afterwards, then watched
them perform at the local Hard Rock Café. A packed crowd—Christians,
Jews, and Muslims, including some young women wearing hejab—
rocked in rhythm to DAM's beat. They sang,

> *This is for the small kids in this big world,*
> *Lost, don't know what is happening.*
> *Barely opened your eyes, you saw tears*
> *Barely opened your heart, you felt pain,*
> *Barely joined us, you saw that we are separated.*
> *Jews, Christians, and Muslims,*
> *None of these sides wants to understand the other.*
> *Every side thinks they're better than the other,*
> *Claiming that he's the only one going to heaven,*
> *Meanwhile, making our lives hell.*
> *But you're different from us, your heart is still pure.*
> *So don't let our dirt touch it.*
> *Keep asking for a life full of equality.*
> *And if someone asks you to hate, say no.*
> *I am the child of today, the transformation of tomorrow.*

A MONG YOUNG MUSLIMS, hip-hop is the counter-jihad in nimble ca-
dence. But it is more than an alternative voice to extremism's creed.
It can also be a way out.

Kanaan Abdi Warsame—known professionally as K'naan—is a wispy
Somali who fired his first gun at the age of eight. It was a Kalashnikov
assault rifle. With a bayonet attached, the AK-47 rifle was taller than the
Somali youth.

"My uncle taught us," he told me years later. "We were handed AKs,
and we shot them. When you fire an AK, and you're that age, the butt

of it jerks back and hits your shoulder. My brother was better at it than I was."

K'naan had a lot of exposure to weapons growing up in strife-torn Somalia. At the age of ten, he discovered a live grenade as he washed lessons off the slates at his school, a small makeshift building with a tin roof. In the dirty water, it looked at first like a rotten potato. "We threw it around—and it began to look less like a potato," he recalled. "Then the pin slipped out. I threw it as fast and far as I could. It blew away most of the school."

A year later, K'naan barely escaped a group of gunmen in Mogadishu. Three of his friends could not run fast enough. They were shot, their inert bodies left in the streets.

In a land dominated by Islamic militants, political gangs, clan warlords, and criminal gunmen, kids also became lawless. When he was thirteen, K'naan's older brother was arrested in connection with the bombing of a court building.[40] An aunt, a well-known Somali singer, reportedly helped him escape a firing squad.

K'naan had close calls too. "When I was a teenager and the country was in turmoil, I was a really hot-tempered kid," he told me. "In my neighborhood, kids would steer clear of offending me, as I was really extreme in my response to things. So if someone said something about me or about something I'd done, my reaction would be violence more suitable to someone who killed. I had no meter.

"When I was a teenager," he said, "kids called me 'psycho' or 'wild man psycho.'"

Hip-hop turned around his mean-streets life—and his attitude. When K'naan was thirteen, his father worked as a New York cabbie. He sent money home to the family; once he also sent his sons a cassette of hip-hop. Somalia has a long and strong poetic tradition. For K'naan, the music had deep appeal. He soon tried his own rap, rhyming words that he picked up from the cassette; he often had no idea what they meant.

K'naan fled Somalia as it disintegrated into civil war a year later. Mogadishu was in the early stages of chaos, with the government collapsing and foreign embassies packing up shop. With his mother and brother, he made it out of a poor neighborhood nicknamed "the river of blood" on the last flight before fighting closed the airport. They ended up in Harlem.

In a foreign country with a foreign tongue, hip-hop was his most accessible resource. "It helped me learn words, but it also helped me learn the culture," he later recalled. "When Nas rhymes, 'I want all my daughters, to be like Maxine Waters,' I was able to find out who she was, and that led me to Toni Morrison." [41]

Hip-hop eventually gave him a career. K'naan began performing as a teenager to help support the family after they moved to Canada. His mellow, funky rap had broad appeal. He was invited to perform with bigger names like Mos Def and Adam Levine of Maroon 5. Reviewers started comparing him to Bob Marley, the Jamaican musician who championed Africa. K'naan later recorded with Marley's son. He has now performed on four continents.

I caught up with him at a hip-hop festival in Virginia. K'naan looks a bit Bohemian rap retro. Born in 1977, he is still small and lean. His most distinguishing feature is a modest afro, usually topped by a hat positioned at a cocky angle. He has a small mustache and light fuzz on his chin.

Rap provided K'naan a political voice as well as a personal lifeline. Except for the United Nations, he has become the most vocal and visible spokesman for Somalia, rapping about "the most forgotten people in the world" living on "the meanest streets in the universe." His songs are anthems against aggression by extremists, warlords, clans, tribes, and even pirates. His most famous song is "Wavin' Flag."

> So many wars, settling scores,
> Bringing us promises, leaving us poor.
> I heard them say "love is the way,"
> "Love is the answer," that's what they say.
> But look how they treat us, make us believers,
> We fight their battles, then they deceive us.

The battle for the hearts and minds of Somalia's youth is now playing out in hip-hop—on all sides.

Omar Hammami, better known as Omie as he was growing up, represented the extremist side. He was born in Alabama, grew up celebrating Christmas, went to Bible camp, reportedly loved *Tom Sawyer*, and was elected president of his sophomore class in high school. His mother was a Southern Baptist, his father a Syrian-American. In his late teens, however, he was seduced by extremism. He married a Somali, moved to Mogadishu, and in 2006 joined al Shabab. He was only twenty-two.[42]

Al Shabab is the most dangerous of Somalia's many armed factions. *Shabab* means "youth" in Arabic. The movement launched its insurgency campaign in 2006. It declared an alliance with al Qaeda in 2007. Its battles against Ethiopian troops supporting the central government forced 400,000 people to flee Mogadishu. The youth militia adopted classic al Qaeda tactics—suicide bombs, assassinations, and beheadings—to target government officials, terrorize aid workers, and intimidate African Union peacekeepers. Its goal was to create an Islamic state in Somalia—and then an Islamic caliphate from East to West.

In 2009, al Shabab gained control of a large part of southern Somalia, where it set up its own leaders and courts. In one particularly gruesome judgment, it took a thirteen-year-old rape victim into a soccer stadium and, with spectators watching, stoned her to death. By 2010, al Shabab was a major player in the global jihad.

Hammami was al Shabab's most famous foreign recruit. He took the nom de guerre Abu Mansoor al Amriki, a play on the Arabic word for America. He soon became the face of al Shabab in propaganda videos.[43]

In one slightly wacky recruiting video, in 2009, the young Alabaman appealed to his brethren abroad. "The only reason we're staying here, away from our families, away from the cities, away from—you know—ice, candy bars, all these others things, is because we are waiting to meet the enemy . . . If you can encourage more of your children and more of your neighbors and anyone around you to send people . . . to this jihad . . . it would be a great asset for us."

Amriki also incorporated plenty of hip-hop in his propaganda, reflecting rap's appeal to all sectors of Muslim youth. In an eighteen-minute video in 2009, he rapped,

Mortar by mortar,
Shell by shell
Only going to stop,
When I send them to hell.[44]

The rap rivalry was pivotal because an estimated 69 percent of Somalia's population was estimated to be under thirty in 2011.[45] Two decades

after the east African country began to disintegrate, only one in five Somali children attended school; most were unlikely to finish it, the United
Nations reported.[46] Between 1991 and 2011, many schools were simply
deserted or turned into military bases. And one out of every six Somali
children was acutely malnourished.

Child soldiers were also a chronic problem. Thousands of children,
some as young as ten, joined clan armies, local militias, extremist movements, and even the government army. Boys and girls, the latter for
cooking and cleaning, were recruited from schools, on soccer fields, by
force in poor neighborhoods, and on the radio.[47]

K'naan captured the problem in a song called "Dreamer."

"I'm barely thirteen, and I pack dirty," he rapped. "Old Russian fire-
arm, that shoots thirty."

By 2010, almost eight out of every ten soldiers in Somalia's many
rebel forces were children, according to Somali human rights groups. So
were about 20 percent of government troops.[48] In his songs, K'naan has
often rapped about childhood in Mogadishu as the only place worse than
Kandahar, the former Afghan headquarters of the Taliban and Osama
bin Laden. In "If Rap Gets Jealous," he sang,

> Sure I've waited about pop, pop, pop, pop,
> That's four cousins shot . . .
> I got circumstances, but let me stop dancing 'round the issue.
> And tell you straight forward, I'm poor,
> A refugee, been in prison and survived the war.
> I come from the most dangerous city in this universe,
> Where you're likely to get shot at birth.

K'naan's debut album was *Dusty Foot Philosopher*, named after one
of his young friends gunned down on a Mogadishu street. In the theme
song, he rapped about "kids who play cops and robbers—but not with
water guns." The album, which won Canada's equivalent of a Grammy
for best rap recording, fused hip-hop and a touch of reggae with African
percussion. It dealt with both the wealth and poverty of the human soul.

The young rapper retained his credibility among Somalis partly because he remained deeply observant of his faith, despite living in the
West and touring with other hip-hop groups. He too reflected the para-
doxical part of the Islamic revival's fourth phase.

"I'm practicing," he told me. "I pray during the day despite the music world I'm in, the lights and glamour and fast life, and the people I'm around. I don't smoke anything, don't do drugs, never had alcohol in my life. My struggle is to find time for my person and my God.

"God protected me in so many different circumstances," he added. "The biggest protection was not that I didn't get shot but that I didn't kill anyone. That's huge. If you kill someone, you carry their burden. I'm fortunate. I have friends who've had to kill people. Family too."

K'naan took his message to the wider world in 2010. After Haiti's devastating earthquake, several of the world's top young singers—Justin Bieber, Avril Lavigne, Nelly Furtado, and others—assembled in Vancouver after the Winter Olympics to record an all-star version with K'naan of his "Wavin' Flag." The song, collectively recorded by "Young Artists for Haiti," debuted as number one on the Canadian singles chart. All the profits went for earthquake relief.[49]

Well beyond Somalia's borders, K'naan had also become something of a rapper-philosopher in the Islamic world. In "Take a Minute," he sang,

> *How did Mandela get the will to surpass every day?*
> *When injustice had him caged and trapped in every way?*
> *How did Gandhi ever withstand the hunger strikes and all?*
> *Didn't do it to gain power or money, if I recall . . .*
> *And that's the reason why I could never play for me,*
> *Tell 'em the truth is what my dead homies told me.*
> *I take inspiration from the most heinous of situations,*
> *Creating medication out my own tribulations.*
> *Dear Africa, you helped me write this,*
> *By showing that to give is priceless.*

6.

The New Chic

It has to begin somewhere.
For each of us it may be a different issue.

—Egyptian activist Dalia Ziada

The convulsions across the Islamic world have involved tens of millions of people. But each has an individual story about why they got involved. Among the most telling are the women's tales. They reflect the depth of change—and how long it has been coming.

Dalia Ziada was twenty-nine when she joined the revolt against President Hosni Mubarak in Egypt. She had a particularly long journey to Liberation Square. It started when she was eight.

"I am a survivor of female genital mutilation," Dalia Ziada told me, as she stirred a steamy espresso in a Cairo café. "In 1990, when I was eight years old, my mother told me to put on my best party dress. It was supposed to be some kind of surprise, a celebration. I found myself instead in a doctor's office. I shouted and refused, but the doctor gave me a shot. I woke up in terrible physical pain."

Ziada's first protest was within her family. As a teenager, she tried to prevent the genital mutilation of her sister and her cousins. No female in her family had ever fought back. "And mostly," she conceded, looking up from her coffee, "I failed."

In Egypt, female genital mutilation spanned millennia, dating back to the pharaohs. In 2005, a United Nations report found that 97 percent of Egyptian females between the ages of fifteen and forty-nine still underwent one of four types of genital mutilation—clitoridectomy, excision, infibulations, or the miscellaneous pricking, piercing, incising, scraping, or cauterizing of the genital area.[1] The practice is cultural rather than religious, more African than Middle Eastern. Many Christian girls in Egypt have also been genitally mutilated.

But in 2006, at the age of twenty-four, Ziada had a long debate with an uncle about her seven-year-old cousin Shaimaa, the family's last female child.

"We talked most of the night. He was shocked at the blunt discussion," she recalled. "I told him that he had no right to circumcise her. I said I'd cut off Shaimaa's finger if he went through with it. He looked at me with surprise and said that would ruin her life, and I said, 'Now you get it.' I thought I'd lost. But he called me the next day and said I'd convinced him.

"That's when I realized I could do things. Because I had been able to save someone," she said, "I decided to see what else I could do."

Ziada, who comes from a traditional family, does not look the part of sex educator. She is doe-eyed and without makeup, so her pale chubby cheeks and colorless lips make her appear younger than she is. In public, she wears hejab coverings in bright florals, rich patterns, or fake designer prints; she changes her scarf daily. She is an observant Muslim, so not a wisp of hair shows. Judging from her eyebrows, her hair must be dark brown.

"Hejab is part of my life," she told me. "I would feel naked without it." She often jokes, with a robust laugh at herself, that her scarves are the most interesting part of her wardrobe. Yet her religious commitment defines her life.

"My ultimate interest," she wrote in 2006, in the first entry on her new blog, "is to please Allah with all I am doing in my own life."

Ziada soon became a leading activist among the so-called pink hejab generation, young women committed to their faith, firm about their femininity, and resolute about their rights. With three college classmates, she launched a campaign to educate women about genital mutilation and domestic violence. Then she moved into broader human rights.

"When I graduated," she explained on her blog, "my personal interest in having equal rights as a woman expanded to my country."

Her first big project was translating a comic book called *The Montgomery Story*, about Reverend Martin Luther King Jr.'s civil disobedience campaign in 1955. King mobilized a bus boycott after Rosa Parks was arrested for refusing to give up her seat to a white man. The comic book chronicled the Walk to Freedom, when many blacks went long distances by foot to work, school, and stores. Dozens of its leaders were arrested; a bomb was thrown into King's home, narrowly missing his wife and child. Yet the movement remained nonviolent. The Supreme Court ultimately ruled that bus segregation was illegal.

"When I read this story, I learned that someone must take the risk for others to follow," Ziada told me. "I wanted to be the Martin Luther King of Egypt!"

The Montgomery Story, originally an educational tool to advance civil rights among the young or less literate, ends with tips on nonviolent activism. One of several groups Ziada worked with distributed two thousand copies of her Arabic version across the Middle East, from Morocco on the Atlantic to Yemen on the Arabian Sea.

"Finding a way to explain civil disobedience was very exciting. It was something new for ordinary people," she said. "Then I started looking for other ways to use nonviolence and civil disobedience for my own campaigns."

Ziada is also a movie buff. She knows all the big stars in both the Islamic world and the West. She knows action films as well as chick flicks and comedies. So her next major project was organizing the first human rights film festival in the Arab world.

"People talk about wanting human rights," she said. "But frankly, most don't actually know what they really are."

Under President Mubarak, the regime tried to block the festival. "The government reacted as if we were planning a terrorist attack," she said, finishing her coffee.

Egyptian authorities originally assessed a stiff fee to show each film—even though they did not hold any rights to the movies—which Ziada and her backers could not afford. So she cut back from dozens of films to only seven. Then Egypt's censors denied approval of the films, even though she had avoided movies about Egypt. Undeterred, Ziada went to the censorship board's offices, waited by the elevator for its director, then rode up with him to plead her case.

"I think he was shocked that I would dare stop and question him," she told me, with a chuckle. "We talked all the way up the elevator. In the end, he was laughing and he gave me approval. Security didn't believe it. The government doesn't have the guts to tell you not to do something, so they try to stop you through the back door."

The harassment was not over, however. Authorities then shut down the theater that had agreed to show the festival's films. "The theater had been working for years without problems. Suddenly, industrial security officials went to the owner and said his theater was not equipped with the right machines—and closed it down through the end of the year," she said, rolling her eyes. "And it happened just two days before the festival was supposed to start!"

Ziada hastily arranged for various nongovernment organizations to host a different film and panel discussion every night for a week. The problem was how to organize a proper launch for the groundbreaking festival—and not get caught. With less than forty-eight hours before the launch, she scrambled to hire a tourist riverboat. On a cool November evening in 2008, a crowd of young politicos, human rights activists, academics, bloggers, and movie lovers showed up at a Nile River pier and boarded the Imperial cruiser.

"We looked like we were all young people celebrating something," Ziada recalled, the corners of her round eyes crinkling in a grin. "Once the ship moved, we put up posters and showed the first film. It was a fantastic night."

She was only twenty-six.

"We stopped letting them always tell us no. We started making decisions for ourselves," Ziada said, with a striking self-confidence. "And we were willing to challenge them when they stood in the way."

In 2009, facing the same obstacles, Ziada managed to sneak in twenty movies for the second Cairo Human Rights Film Festival. To get around security force restrictions, she provided the wrong schedule, imaginary venues, and different times. And again, she held opening night on a Nile riverboat. In a country with one of the region's most autocratic regimes, Ziada showed *Orange Revolution,* about the 2004 Ukraine uprising; *Flowers of Rwanda,* about the fate fourteen years later of victims from the 1994 genocide; *Burma VJ,* a documentary secretly filmed during the 2007 uprisings against Myanmar's military regime; and *Persepolis,* the 2007 French animated film about a young girl coming of age against the backdrop of the 1979 Iranian revolution.

For the second festival, Ziada dared to include Egyptian films too. She showed *N70.* The movie told the story of Emad el Kabeer, a twenty-one-year-old minibus driver who intervened with police when his cousin refused to pay them a bribe. El Kabeer ended up in prison. N70 was the Nokia cell phone model used to video el Kabeer's torture. He was stripped, beaten with sticks, and his legs held up in the air. Two Egyptian policemen then pushed a broomstick into his rectum and repeatedly sodomized him. The cell phone also captured the sounds of his haunting screams.

Egyptian police, who shot the original video, passed it around to warn other minibus drivers who resisted paying bribes. But an Egyptian human rights activist also got a copy and posted the video on his blog. It ended up on YouTube. Mubarak's regime was forced to prosecute the two policemen.

"I felt so humiliated," el Kabeer later told the Associated Press. "They were so brutal, as if they were slaughtering an animal and peeling off his skin." [2]

N70, a fictionalized version of the incident, focuses on what happened to el Kabeer after the ordeal. When he was released, Egypt's macho Arab culture exacted its own price. He lost his job. Colleagues and friends abandoned him. His fiancée left him. And his family struggled to deal with the shame, complicated by his mother's death while he was imprisoned. In the film, an actor playing el Kabeer is interviewed about the traumatic aftermath. In the fictionalized version, the young bus driver ends up committing suicide.

Ahmed Nader made the movie after meeting Ziada at her first film festival. "He asked if I'd promise to show the film if he made it. When I said yes, he said that's all he needed," Ziada told me. "Ahmed came to me six months later with the finished film. It's short, only twenty minutes. But it's very powerful. It even has the torture scene—the blood, not the whole broom.

"We're not just about politics," she added. "Young activists are all trying to change society's mind-set and to right wrongs for the people."

The festival featured three other Egyptian films. One portrayed ordinary Egyptians suffering economic injustice—now a chronic problem in the North African nation—and mobilizing to fight it. Another was a Romeo-and-Juliet tale about a young Christian boy who falls in love with a Muslim girl he can never marry. The most potent movie, however, was also the shortest. Please Spare Our Flowers was a one-minute film about female genital mutilation that shows ragged pinking shears slowly snipping off the tops of dozens of beautiful flowers, one by one by one, just as they're blooming—each producing a piercing scream from an unseen girl child or baby.

I asked Ziada why she had turned to films. "Oh, that was easy," she said. "*Everyone* loves movies! They carry the message in a nonviolent way to the widest audience."

As THE PINK hejab generation gradually chisels away at centuries of restrictions, young women are also redefining what it means to wear hejab—as a declaration of activist intent rather than a symbol of being sequestered. The change is visible in virtually every Muslim country. The young are increasingly shedding black and gray garb for clothing more colorful and even shapely, albeit still modest. Pink is the most popular color. Young women in their teens, twenties, and thirties also flavor their faith with shades of pastel blues, bright yellow, rustic orange, occasionally trimmed with sparkles, tassels, or even feathers. Hejab stores from Gaza to Jakarta now carry everything from long denim dresses with rhinestone designs to frilly frocks with matching scarves. *Hejab Fashion*, an Egyptian monthly magazine, was launched in 2004 for the pink hejab generation. It has nothing to do with religiosity. But it is also not just about fashion or vanity.

The Veiled—or al Motahajiba—is one of Cairo's new fashion centers combining Islamic feminism and cool. When I visited the shop in 2009, hejab wear was as elegantly displayed on glass shelves as designer scarves at Nieman Marcus. Shaimaa Hassan, a twenty-year-old salesgirl, told me that her favorite color was turquoise. She handed me a booklet of fashionable new hejab styles. The latest fad was the Spanish wrap, so-called because the scarf is tied with a large knot at the back, a version of hairstyles worn by flamenco dancers. As she demonstrated how to wrap it, Hassan explained that she had just finished vocational school in commerce and intended to open her own business someday.

Sabaya, which means "Young Girls" in Arabic, is a salon, boutique, and café in Cairo's trendy Heliopolis district. It was launched in 2008 by Hanan Turk, a famous Egyptian ballerina who was recruited for the cinema in 1991. The glamorous young actress appeared in more than twenty major films, both comedies and dramas, in which she often wore racy dresses or exposed ample décolletage. In 2006, she starred in the controversial film *Dunia,* or "World," about a young ballet dancer who explores her sexual identity and resists pressures to hide her femininity. The themes bordered on the taboo. The director struggled to get it past Egypt's censorship board.

Shortly after finishing the film, however, Turk opted to don hejab. The reaction in Egypt's arts world was electric. "She must have gone crazy," said Yusef Chahine, the director who gave Turk her early break into cinema.[3]

She was unfazed. "I had intended to take this step a long time ago," she announced in response, "but I never had the guts before."[4] A year later, she announced plans to launch a religious magazine with a noted singer. They called it *Hajj,* after the Muslim pilgrimage to Mecca. Two years later, she opened Sabaya for fashionable hejabis. A sign in neon lights outside called it a place of "veiled beauty."

Turk remained a fashion plate, devising ways to dramatically drape her curves in stunning colors—and replicate them for other women. In many pictures, she looked even more exotic than she did before hejab. The wares in her store reflected her style.

"There's a tendency among people who don't know Islam to think of the veil as a sign of conservatism, ignorance, or backwardness," Nagwa Abbas, the manager, told me over lattes at Sabaya's café. "It's just iden-tification. Underneath, we wear what everyone else wears. We're all for women having every opportunity. Our aspirations don't change just be-cause our clothing is different."

For many young women, hejab is now about liberation, not confine-ment. It's about new possibilities, not the past. It provides a kind of social armor for Muslim women to chart their own course, personally or pro-fessionally. For Ziada, hejab provides protective cover and legitimacy for campaigns she considers to be the essence of her faith—human rights and justice.

"Families feel much more comfortable allowing their girls to be ac-tive, to get higher education, or jobs, or even to go out alone at night when they are wearing hejab," she told me. "It's a deal between a Mus-lim girl and society. I agree that I will wear hejab in order to have more space and freedom in return."

In its many forms, hejab is no longer assumed to signal acquiescence. It has instead become an equalizer. It is an instrument that makes a fe-male untouchable as she makes her own decisions in the macho Arab world. It stamps authenticity even amid her demands for change. And it is a weapon to help a woman resist extremism's pull into the past. Militants cannot criticize or target her for being corrupted by Western influence.

"The veil is the mask of Egyptian women in a power struggle against the dictatorship of men," explained Nabil Abdel Fattah, author of *The Politics of Religion,* when I stopped to see him at Cairo's Al-Ahram Center for Political and Strategic Studies. "The veil gives women more power in a man's world."

And Muslim women are increasingly assuming those powers as basic rights.

I spent a couple of evenings on Lovers' Bridge, the site of the pivotal first battle in the bold protest to oust Hosni Mubarak. It spans the Nile's dark waters and is the hot spot for socializing in Cairo. Young couples canoodle on the bridge, occasionally interrupted by strolling flower salesmen laden with baskets of roses or red carnations. On a cool January evening, I met Shaimaa Ahmed and Hisham el Hefnawy on the bridge. Shaimaa was dressed in a pink paisley scarf and a floor-length denim skirt. A hospital social worker in Cairo, she wore no lipstick, but her dark eyes were elegantly outlined in black. Hisham was an agriculture student from outside the capital. It was their first formal date.

The young couple met, he explained, on an Internet site that roughly translates as "Tagged" and is a cross between Facebook and eHarmony .com. The Internet offers many other ways for Muslims to connect socially. The home page of Muslima.com, which features an attractive young woman in bright red hejab, offers a "matrimonial site bringing together thousands of Muslim women and men from around the world." It advertises widely on other Muslim websites. Internet cafés from Algiers to Amman, Beirut to Baku, Damascus to Dubai, Jeddah to Jakarta, and Tripoli to Tashkent are filled with young Muslims trolling these sites.

Hisham saw Shaimaa's profile and left her a message that he would like to talk. She checked out his home page. For a month, they texted on their cell phones and communicated by other remote Internet connections. He then came to Cairo for a family wedding and invited her to meet in person. She agreed. Their first date was on Lovers' Bridge. When I had walked up to them, each had one end of an iPod headpiece in their ears, listening to his collection of music.

I asked what they envisioned their life might look like if they ended up together. She immediately took the lead. "I don't want a traditional life," she said, with certainty. "I want to break routines. I want a career. I want to go out at night. I want to travel."

Hisham said he would prefer that his wife did not work.

Before he could go any further, she interjected, with a smile, "That's not for me. We'll have to talk about that." Hisham had no comeback.

Education has been a key to the transformation. A 2008 Gallup poll found that most Muslim women today are not only literate, they are a growing proportion of university students. Women have postsecondary education even in countries with strong religious sentiment—Iran (52 percent), Egypt (34 percent), Saudi Arabia (32 percent), and Lebanon (37 percent). Surprisingly, Gallup also reported that more women had postsecondary education in Pakistan (13 percent) and Morocco (8 percent) than in the Czech Republic (11 percent) and Brazil (4 percent).[5]

"Now, it's hardly something worth noting that in Egypt, universities are filled with women, in some cases more than men, and they are excelling," the Gallup poll reported. "The valedictorians of Cairo's elite medical school are famously known to almost always be female."[6]

Attitudes about female education have shifted markedly across the Muslim world, according to a 2009 Pew Global Attitudes survey. There are obvious exceptions, such as Afghanistan. But Muslims polled on two continents—Jordan (65 percent), Egypt (71 percent), Nigeria (78 percent), the Palestinian territories (85 percent), Pakistan (87 percent), Turkey (89 percent), Lebanon (96 percent), and in Indonesia (93 percent)—said it is as important to educate girls (and equally) as it is to educate boys.

Key countries witnessed large leaps in just two years—Pakistan up by 13 percent and the Palestinian territories by 11 percent. Most striking was the rise in public opinion in Gaza, the teeming little territory squeezed between Israel and Egypt that was taken over politically by Hamas in 2006 elections. In 2009, the number of Gazans who believed equal education was important for girls and boys was up 28 percent—to 83 percent.[7]

As a result, young women of all classes entering universities across the Islamic world are no longer dominated by English-speaking or Westernized elites. Young women in their pastel hejabs are highly visible on every Egyptian campus, including the American University of Cairo. Tunisia's autocratic government outlawed hejab in government offices, schools, and public facilities to stem the Islamic tide. Yet a decade after 9/11, some 80 percent of the girls and faculty at Tunisian universities defiantly wore hejab to class.[8]

Muslim women also like to point out that they have reached top political positions—a feat not yet claimed by many of their Western counterparts. In the late twentieth and early twenty-first centuries, five Muslim women became heads of state in Turkey, Indonesia, and Pakistan, and two in Bangladesh. All five were popularly elected. And three of the five wore hejab.

Yet in their push for equality in the twenty-first century, young Muslim women also increasingly cite females in Islam's early days as their role models.* The first convert to Islam was a woman—the Prophet's wife Khadijah. She was also his boss. She hired him, when she was a widow, to run caravans for her business. And *she* proposed marriage to *him*. Aisha, a later wife, also issued fatwas and left behind many of the hadith traditions.

Fatima, the Prophet's daughter, is the revered mother of Shiite Islam. And his granddaughter Zainab is often compared by Muslims to Antigone, the ancient Greek character who paid with her life for bravely defying authority over issues of justice and leadership—the two issues also at the heart of Islam's greatest schism. Zainab is buried in an elaborate tomb outside Damascus still visited by tens of thousands of Shiite pilgrims fourteen centuries later.

The mix—the pink hejabis and the globalized Internet world—is what makes this generation one of the most dynamic forces in the current social and political upheavals. After pledging her commitment to Allah, Ziada described herself on her blog as "a mix of Shakespeare's Brutus with his internal conflict of choosing between satisfying the selfishness

---

* Ironically, the only woman mentioned by name in the Koran is the Virgin Mary. Muslims embrace Judaism and Christianity as part of a single religious tradition and their prophets as important figures in Islamic history too. The Virgin Mary—or Maryam in Arabic—is a widely revered figure in Islam. Young women often write school papers about her as a role model. All other women in the Koran are referred to by position as the wife, mother, daughter, or aunt of a man. In contrast, the hadith mention women by name.

of the people he loves or protecting his beloved country against them, Dickens' Pip with his great expectations and unlimited ambition, and Austen's Elizabeth with her proven self-confidence and pride."

Like many of the pink hejabis, Ziada has little taste for Islamist politics. She rejects the Muslim Brotherhood, the Islamic movement founded in Egypt in 1928 that now has more than eighty offshoots around the world. She considers them hypocrites for promising to improve life for all Egyptians but then issuing a draft manifesto that would prevent women and Christians from becoming president.

"So the only person who can run is a Muslim man," she told me angrily. "What the hell is this? They talk about democracy all the time, but look at the party's own structure. They don't have elections for leaders. There are no women, except in a women-only branch. And when people make petitions to challenge them on something, they don't get answers.

"You know, ordinary people are not stupid," she said. "We discovered that they're working for their own goals, not our interests. They don't understand the duality of young people who want to be faithful to their religion *and* live a modern life."

Like the pink hejabis, Ziada also rejects all extremist groups. "People turned to extremism to escape from authoritarian regimes," she explained. "Sooner or later, we will get rid of extremism because people have realized that extremists can't deliver either. They just create a whole different set of problems."

In 2010, Ziada started organizing workshops for young Egyptians to encourage civil disobedience rather than confrontation. "Debate, don't hate," the promotion poster advertised. Working with a Muslim civil society group, she trained activists from other Arab countries about how to move from online activism to on-the-street action. Among the trainees were two Tunisian bloggers who, only months later, played critical roles in flashing the story of Mohamed Bouazizi's self-immolation across the Internet.

"You can see," she called me later, with great excitement. "It's paying off!"

Ziada continued her campaign at Liberation Square in 2011. After protesters set up a permanent camp in the Cairo center, she walked around the vast plaza distributing copies of *The Montgomery Story*.

"It was a good time," she told me, "to remind people of the techniques—

and to remind them that there were people who did it before us, and we can do it too."

THE UPHEAVALS ACROSS the Islamic world are not just political. They are also about the faith itself. A gender counter-jihad—both to end male domination of Islam and to reinterpret the religion's rigid tenets—has also been coming for a generation.

Amina Wadud is the movement's birth mother. She planted the first seeds during a trip to South Africa in 1994. It was an exhilarating time. The apartheid era had ended a year earlier with the election of President Nelson Mandela and the first multiracial government. South Africa's new constitution was the world's most progressive. It ensured equality not only for all races and religions but also for both genders. It outlawed discrimination against gays and lesbians as well as pregnant women. In a country long governed by an odious ideology, barriers were coming down everywhere. Wadud's visit also coincided with the three-hundredth anniversary of Islam in South Africa.

During a stop in Cape Town, Wadud broke another barrier. She was invited to become the first woman to publicly lead both men and women in Friday Prayers.

It was one of those accidents of history—a confluence of changing times, changing environment, changed thinking, and the right cast of characters. The idea came up informally after a conference. Wadud, who has a commanding charisma, was standing amid empty banquet tables discussing gender barriers with other Muslims, including progressive local imam Rashied Omar. The radical notion of a woman taking the pulpit in a mosque, always a man's realm, was thrown out in conversation.

Wadud embraced the idea. She was already challenging the patriarchy within Islam that has deferred for fourteen centuries to the male experience and way of thinking.

"I just don't believe that's all there is to God," she told me. "I've grappled for thirty years with how much of this is God and how much of this is human—and I'm continuously convinced that so much of it is the human *perception* of what God is. And therefore fears, culture, insecurities, and human questions all come into play, because our notion of God comes from us.

"God," she pronounced, with a comfortable certainty, "is more than we think God is."

A day after the Cape Town conference, the local imam summoned Wadud to the Claremont Main Road Mosque, a pale pink stucco mosque famed for its antiapartheid activities. He gave her only forty-five minutes' notice. She scrambled to come up with an appropriate sermon.

Allahu akbar. "God is great." She began the traditional prayer, standing in a room full of men. The women were segregated in a balcony upstairs. "All praise and thanks be to Allah, the Lord of mankind and all that exists," she intoned, the refrain that opens all Muslim prayers.

Wadud's appearance at the Cape Town mosque sparked a firestorm of feverish protests and threats from far beyond South Africa. Conservative Muslims tried to get Wadud fired from her university job and the progressive imam sacked from his mosque. Imam Omar described the "venomous" reaction "demonizing" him as one of the lowest points in his life.[9]

Wadud was actually annoyed about the experience too, since women had little to do with a major turning point in their own history. Muslim men had again made a key decision for them; she had not been consulted on the timing, venue, or content. She was also insulted, she later told me, because the men did not seem to care about (or listen to) her sermon on women's rights in Islam. She felt used. The event was more about form than substance.[10]

If she had been consulted, the event might never have taken place, because Wadud had her period. In Islam, observant women are not supposed to attend mosque during their menstrual cycles. "The most progressive Muslim male," she wrote years later, "cannot accommodate the relationship between biology, the politics of ritual, and the legal stipulations given historically."[11]

Wadud is a feisty woman with deep-set eyes, warm brown skin, and a handsome mole on her right cheek. She favors big, bold rings on many of her fingers, and occasionally a thumb, and long earrings that dangle below her hejab. She is reverent about her faith but irreverent about many of its customs. For four years, she covered her face under a black veil, the ultimate display of Islamic modesty. She now takes a decidedly different view.

"If you think that the difference between heaven and hell is forty-

five inches of material, boy will you be surprised," she reflected in
2006.

"I do not consider it a religious obligation, nor do I ascribe to it any
religious significance or moral value per se," she wrote in her groundbreaking book *Inside the Gender Jihad.* "It is certainly not the penul-
timate denotation of modesty as mandated by the Koran. It offers no
guarantee of respect or protection. Those who reduce women to their
sexuality will continue to do so." [12]

After Cape Town, Wadud began voicing a new feminist vision of
Islam. She started from scratch with God's revelations to the Prophet
Mohammed. The religion was always meant to be progressive, not re-
gressive, she argued. It originally offered new freedoms for its followers;
it only restricted unjust practices.

Most important, she noted, Islam was supposed to be universal in
time, place, and applicability. God's revelations were not petty—or at
least not as narrow-minded, restrictive, judgmental, or mean as many
interpretations added over the next fourteen hundred years. The revelations were never intended to be wedded through eternity to practices in
a desert culture at a fixed moment in time. They were not to ignore all
human progress thereafter. The faith instead has to be flexible to accommodate all people—throughout time—who want to believe.

In a series of sermons, lectures, and books, Wadud reinterpreted Islam's intentions by stripping away centuries of embellishments added
long after the faith was founded. She explored disparate definitions of
the Koran's Arabic words. She showed how the same grammar could be
read in different ways. She went back to pre-Islamic customs to frame
the radical improvements introduced by Islam as proof of the revelations' intent.

"For fourteen centuries, the Koran has been interpreted almost exclusively by men," Wadud told me in 2009. "It's only in the past couple of
decades that women have begun to say that *we* should look at the text
and come up with *our own* conclusions."

God's relationship to the individual is based on piety, not gender, she
wrote with a dismissive certainty in *Qur'an and Woman,* a book now
revered among Muslim women in the way *The Feminine Mystique* and
The Second Sex were read by Western women in the 1960s and 1970s.

Wadud invokes the Koran to support her positions. Rereading the sacred text from a woman's perspective, she wrote,

The mere fact that the Qur'an was revealed in seventh-century Arabia when the Arabs held certain perceptions and misconceptions about women and were involved in certain specific lewd practices against them resulted in some injunctions specific to that culture . . . Some prevailing practices were so bad they had to be prohibited implicitly and explicitly: infanticide, sexual abuse of slave girls, denial of inheritance to women, zihar,* to name but a few. Other practices had to be modified: polygamy, unconstrained divorce, conjugal violence and concubinage.[13]

The Islamic holy book, for example, honors female leadership. It celebrates Bilqis, the queen of Sheba, for both her political and her religious practices. "The Koran uses no terms that imply that the position of ruler is inappropriate for a woman," Wadud wrote. "No distinction, restriction, addition, limitation or specification of her as a woman who leads is ever mentioned."[14]

The Koran also does not require veiling. Long before Islam, women in wealthy Arabian tribes were veiled and secluded as signs of status and for protection. Islam embraced modesty, but its message was not about hiding women, Wadud claimed. It was instead about equality among believers.

"Modesty is not a privilege of the economically advantaged only: all believing women deserve the utmost respect and protection of their modesty—however it is observed in various societies," she wrote.[15] Veils were merely cultural reflections of esteem in one particular culture—a long time ago.

Wadud's interpretations on four issues are particularly controversial. They turn long-standing practices upside down.

On divorce, she argues, the Koran does not deny a woman's right to reject her husband. In seventh-century Arabia, a woman needed only turn the entrance of her tent in another direction to repudiate conjugal relations with a man. The Koran does not challenge the practice and instead imposes new measures to prevent men from abandoning or misusing women.[16]

On polygamy, Islam instituted the first rules—and limits—on what was already a widespread practice in seventh-century Arabia, Wadud

---

*Zihar is the pre-Islamic custom whereby a husband could divorce his wife by simply declaring, "Thou art to me as my mother's back."

contends. Islam's goal was to ensure that wives were equally treated and that widows and orphans were cared for at a time when states had no formal welfare nets. The Koran stipulates to men, "If you fear that you will not deal justly with the orphans, marry women of your choice, two, three or four. But if you fear that you will not be able to do justly, then only one . . . to prevent you from doing injustice." [17] The verse was intended, Wadud contends, to provide economic rights and security for children and women, not rights to multiple sexual partners for men.

On obedience and punishment, Wadud argues that the Koran never states that a woman's submission to her husband makes her a better Muslim. [18] Islam, which introduced laws to govern society as well as new spiritual beliefs, instead introduced social reforms to counter seventh-century practices often brutal to girls and women. "Most of the reforms were for the benefit of females," Wadud wrote. "No equivalent reforms benefiting the males were instituted!" [19]

Finally, on a woman's value, the Koran stipulates that when a debt is contracted, two male witnesses are required—and if not two men, then one man and two women. But the two women have different roles, Wadud contends. Only one is a witness; the other is a collaborator or backup in case the first becomes unavailable because of other duties. It has nothing to do with the value of a woman. More importantly, the law was for a certain type of transaction that is now obsolete. "It was not meant," Wadud wrote, "to be applied as a general rule." [20]

Wadud is an unlikely role model for the new Islamic feminists. She is a convert. She was born Mary Teasley in Bethesda, Maryland, a suburb of Washington, DC, in 1952. Her parents were Christian, her father a preacher. She credits her interest in religion, justice, and gender to the "light of belief that I inherited from my father, a man of faith and a Methodist minister who was born and died poor, black and oppressed." [21]

Her conversion to Islam was gradual. At the University of Pennsylvannia, she explored her own spirituality, probing Buddhism and Hinduism. Her first taste of Islam was a casual visit, more out of curiosity, to a Washington mosque near her mother's home. The turning point came after a neighbor passed along a Koran given her by a group looking for female converts. Its words, Wadud later recounted, "moved me to tears and awe." [22] She pronounced her *shahada*—the declaration of faith, and the first of Islam's five pillars—on Thanksgiving in 1972. She had just turned twenty.

Mary Teasley then took the name Amina Wadud. Amina means "honest woman" in Arabic. Wadud means "the loving one" or "the loving God of Justice." In Islam, it is one of the ninety-nine names of God—the forty-seventh, to be precise. After earning a doctorate in Islamic studies at the University of Michigan, she restlessly wandered the Islamic world. She taught in Malaysia, Libya, and Indonesia and lectured in dozens of other countries.

"I have experienced firsthand the despair and anguish, joy and exhilarations of being a Muslim woman," she likes to say.[23]

As in other faiths, debate rages about a female's role in Islam. Early Muslim tradition has only one well-documented case of a female preacher. In the seventh century, the Prophet Mohammed appointed Umm Waraqah bint Abdallah* to lead prayers in her community. She was an early convert to Islam. She memorized the Koran; she was reportedly among the few to hand down the sacred text orally before it was recorded in writing.[24] And she continued to serve as the local imam—or *imamah*, for females—long after the Prophet's death.

For fourteen centuries, the traditional interpretation was that Umm Waraqah was empowered to lead prayers in her home or among her community—of only females. Thousands of fatwas—by men—reinforced that position.

Today, Wadud and the new Muslim feminists argue that this interpretation is simply wrong. Various traditions, known as hadith, record the Prophet's appointment. But most credible hadith do not stipulate what "community" means—or that the Prophet was explicitly referring to a community of females. The Arabic word is *dar*, which is genderless. It can also refer to "home," "neighborhood," "village," the more general "area," or even "haven." Umm Waraqah's *dar* was so large, according to the same Islamic traditions, that the Prophet appointed a separate muezzin for it. And "home" does not mean strictly females anyway. Plus, Umm Waraqah was never explicitly forbidden to lead a mixed congregation.

Wadud is now among a growing number of scholars, jurists, *sheikhas*, *imamahs*, and ordinary Muslim women pressing for the powers of reli-

---

*The name means "mother of Waraqah and daughter of Abdallah," a common practice in identifying women into the twentieth century.

gious authority. From Morocco to Turkey, Syria to India, they are por-
ing over the Koran and hadith traditions. They are daring to inject a
feminine perspective into Islam's teaching and practices. The idea that
Islam can liberate women—rather than restrict them—has gained wide
traction.

E VERY MUSLIM COUNTRY now faces some form of feminine revolutionary. Many of the activists reject the "feminist" label as a
Western construct, but their aspirations—equal rights to education, employment, social advancement, and political participation—are the same
as their Western or secular counterparts. The new Muslim feminists instead want to win equality through Islam, not despite it.

The feminist counter-jihad takes at least four different forms, from
devout women focused on changing family laws to grassroots coalitions
with political goals. Morocco's Million Signatures campaign pressured
the monarchy to reform (if not totally overhaul) laws on women's rights
in 2004. In 2006, Iranian women launched a similar movement with the
same name to challenge discriminatory laws in the penal code, the economy, and family laws. In 2011, Egypt's women tried to mobilize a million women's march in Liberation Square after the ouster of President
Mubarak, but the initiative faltered under male pressure.

Feminist wings have even emerged within Islamist political parties,
including Egypt's Muslim Brotherood, Lebanon's Hezbollah, and the
Palestinians' Hamas. As Islamist parties started running for political office, they recognized the need to cultivate female voters. Women lever-
aged their importance, moved up the ranks, and soon developed their
own agendas. Hezbollah's female branch—al Haayat al Nisaayia—now
instructs women on their legal rights under Lebanon's constitution as
well as under Islamic law. [25]

The goals of Islamist feminists, however, are often viewed through
a slightly different prism. "We don't have the eternal complex of having to be equal with men," said Umm Mahdi, who heads the women's
branch of Hezbollah's financial wing. "We seek justice, not equality." [26]

The new feminists tackle the full range of subjects. In the United
Arab Emirates, Wedad Lootah wrote a daring book in 2009 calling for
equality—in sexual pleasure and orgasms. A family counselor in Dubai's

main courthouse, Lootah wears a conservative black *niqab* that covers all but her brown eyes. Her book *Top Secret: Sexual Guidance for Married Couples* is also filled with religious references and Islamic jurisprudence.[27]

Islam's feminists have even gone global. In 2009, the Musawah movement was launched in Kuala Lumpur by feminists from forty-seven Muslim countries. *Musawah* is the Arabic word for "equality." "Feminism that does not justify itself within Islam is bound to be rejected by the rest of society and is therefore self-defeating," explained Azza Karam, the Egyptian author of *Women, Islamism, and the State*.[28]

After centuries of sequestering women, some Muslim states have begun to respond to feminist demands—or at least tolerate them.

Turkey appointed its first class of *vaizes*, or female preachers, in 2004. Within four years, it had more than 450 *vaizes*. Fifteen provinces had women as deputy muftis. Women even led Turks on the annual pilgrimage in Mecca. By 2010, females made up the majority of students in several seminaries.[29]

"Turkey is a country that has accepted the idea of sexual equality," said Ali Bardakoglu, head of Turkey's religious affairs ministry. "And that must be reflected in religious practice."[30]

Egypt's Al Azhar University, the world's oldest center of Islamic learning, approved publication of the first Koranic interpretation by a woman. Souad Saleh, one of the world's leading female scholars on Islam, launched *Women's Fatwa* on an Arabic satellite television station to issue religious rulings from a female perspective.

Eman el-Marsafy is one of hundreds of Egyptian professional women memorizing the Koran and teaching it to other women at Cairo's al Sadiq Mosque. "We're taking Islam to the new world," she told me when I visited the mosque's community room, which was packed with women discussing the Koran. "We can do everything everyone else does. There's no conflict between living an Islamic life and living in this world. We want to move forward too."

Egypt's grand mufti, Ali Gomaa, issued fatwas that allowed women to initiate divorce, outlawed female genital mutilation, and declared that Muslim women have the right to become judges and lead nations.

"Islam extends equal political and social rights to both men and women," he ruled. Gomaa, one of the Muslim world's most influential scholars, also issued a stunning fatwa to protect women who have had sex before marriage.

In the Middle East, it is an open secret that many women, both Muslim and Christian, secretly undergo reconstructive hymen surgery before marriage to make their new husbands believe they are still virgins. In 2007, Gomaa ruled that the surgery is halal, or permissible. He also advised women not to tell their future spouses about their sexual pasts.

"If God wants us to know everything about each other," the sheikh ruled, "he would have given us the ability to read each others' minds, so why did he not do so?"

Gomaa, who has three daughters, also decreed that a married woman who engages in adultery but regrets her actions and asks God for forgiveness should not tell her husband. "According to Sharia, if a husband knew that his wife had sexual intercourse with anyone else, he should divorce her, so by not telling him she would be protecting their home and her life," he said. [31]

In 2010, Malaysia appointed two female judges to its Islamic court system, one of the last frontiers for Muslim women. Women have long served on Malaysia's secular courts, but it took a fatwa from the country's top religious authority in 2005 to approve the idea—and then another five years before the first appointments.

Morocco recruited the first women to serve as *murshidas*, or female religious guides, in 2008. They have the same training and perform the same functions as men. They teach the Koran; counsel the faithful; issue official religious opinions; visit schools, hospitals, and prisons; and appear on television and radio programs to address questions from the public. [32]

King Mohammed VI even invited a female scholar to give the Ramadan lecture at the royal palace. A woman had reportedly never been in the palace chamber for the event, much less spoken at the most sacred time of the year. Her lecture was attended by top government officials, the diplomatic corps, and even military officers. [33]

Yet a full decade after Wadud's groundbreaking Cape Town sermon in 1994, Morocco's new *murshidas* and Turkey's *vaizes* were still *not* allowed to lead Friday Prayers or give the weekly sermon in mixed company.

Wadud, however, persevered.

"In South Africa, there was an astounding awakening to the possibilities. I realized I'd never thought outside the box on leadership," she told me. "Yes, there were protests afterwards. And there was a lot of media coverage. But it seemed so natural to me. For the next ten years, I did more research and a lot of soul-searching. I was asked often to lead prayers, but I always said no." She paused for a moment.

"I was afraid of fooling myself. I had to make sure it wasn't just about ego," she added, looking at me over her reading glasses. "I wanted to make sure this was about a larger connection to Islam and its message. I had to challenge myself again, and again. It took a full ten years."

In 2005, Wadud finally agreed to lead Friday Prayers again—this time on her own terms in an event sponsored by the Progressive Muslim Union in New York City. Three mosques refused to provide a venue for her to preach. And the Sundaram Tagore Gallery in Manhattan—which hosts exhibitions and events for spiritual, social, and aesthetic dialogue—backed out after a bomb threat. So on March 18, her daughter's birthday, Wadud led a congregation of some sixty Muslim women and forty men in the community hall of St. John the Divine, the Episcopal cathedral in New York City. The call to prayer was given by another woman. In her sermon or *khutbah,* Wadud talked about the absence of gender in God.

"I don't want to change Muslim mosques," she said. "I want to encourage the hearts of Muslims, in their public, private, and ritual affairs, to believe they are one and equal."

Outside, protesters carried threatening banners. One rejected her as a Muslim. "May Allah's Curse Be Upon Amina Wadud," it read. Another warned, "Mixed-gender prayers today, Hellfire tomorrow."

Wadud's second appearance at an Islamic pulpit unleashed an even greater firestorm than had the first a decade earlier. She was called blasphemous and "a devil in hejab." In Saudi Arabia, the Institute for Islamic Jurisprudence demanded that she repent. It warned that the prayers of Muslims who attended her service were null and void—and should be repeated. The kingdom's top cleric, Sheikh Abdul Aziz Sheikh, charged that Wadud had "violated God's law" and condemned her as an "enemy of Islam."

Although Wadud was then over fifty years old and a grandmother of three, several Muslim scholars criticized her on grounds that a woman is a sexual distraction to a man's ability to concentrate on prayers. Sheikh Mohammed Tantawi, the head of Egypt's Al Azhar University, said women could only lead other females in prayer because a woman's body is "lewdness" and should not be thrust in front of men during religious services. Al Jazeera's televangelist Sheikh Yusuf al Qaradawi attacked Wadud for heresy and potentially arousing men.

"Leadership in prayer in Islam is reserved for men only," he said in a scathing fatwa. "Prayer in Islam is not like prayer in Christianity, in which . . . people perform their supplication while standing. In Islam, worship has movements: standing, sitting, bending, and bowing. She will bow her body before the men—and who says that man is an angel and that nothing will arise in his mind? These matters are unacceptable."[34]

With her usual bluntness, Wadud dismissed the reaction as sexist. "Personally," she said, "I worry what that says about Muslim men, if even in worship they cannot keep their minds on Allah and away from their lust."[35]

None of the criticism deterred Wadud. Seven months later, she led another mixed-gender prayer service in Barcelona, Spain, shortly after she gave a lecture at the International Congress on Islamic Feminism. Over the next four years, she also led prayers in Britain, Italy, and Indonesia. A few other women scholars have dared to follow suit, albeit with much lower profiles.

A few months later, I asked Wadud how long she thought it might take for women to be widely embraced as preachers and prayer leaders in mixed congregations, one of the ultimate symbols of the feminists' success.

"Are you asking just about Islam?" she replied, with a chuckle. Orthodox Judaism has many of the same customs and restrictions, dating back many millennia before Islam. And the Catholic Church has not budged on female priests in two thousand years. Wadud paused to consider her answer.

"Actually," she replied, peering over her reading glasses, "I believe the Koran adapts to the situation of modern women as smoothly as it was adapted to the original Muslim community fourteen centuries ago. It's just a matter of getting men—and some women—to see it that way. So, fifty years, maybe longer.

"But it will happen," she said. "The movement has evolved too far to back down."

7.

The Living Poets Society

Gender justice is essential to the divine order of the universe.

—Islamic feminist Amina Wadud[1]

Hissa Hilal hardly looked the rebel. Whenever the mother of four from Saudi Arabia walked onto the glitzy television set, she was always engulfed in black—floor-length robe, head covering that draped down her back and over her bosom, and a veil over her face. The only openings were two tiny slits for her eyes. The ensemble, known as *niqab,* is the most conservative Muslim dress. Women are supposed to be protected by niqab. But to outsiders, they often appear to be prisoners of their clothing.

The setting was not traditional political turf either. *The Million's Poet* contest is the most popular reality show in the Persian Gulf. It is a local version of *American Idol,* only in verse. In the Islamic world's most conservative corner, poetry has historically been more permissible than song. The competition is broadcast from Abu Dhabi TV to some 300 million people throughout the Middle East. A three-man panel judges the performances. Viewers vote by text message. Both the first and second prizes are worth more than a million dollars.

Poetic themes for the contest are usually safe subjects, such as life in the desert, a flower's sweet scent, the passions of sport, or the richness of coffee. So Hilal's words, in a strong and rhythmic Arabic, shocked the audience.

From behind her enveloping black veil, she railed against Muslim rad-

icals and ideologues. She assailed clerics' intolerant fatwas. And she condemned extreme versions of Islam.

I have seen evil from the eyes
Of the subversive fatwas,
In a time when what is permitted
Is confused with what is forbidden.

Before she could continue, the segregated audience—men on the
right, women on the left—interrupted loudly with applause.

For the spring 2010 contest, thousands of applicants had been whittled
down to forty-eight poets from twelve countries. They competed for the
best verse of *nabati*, a form of simple and direct poetry about everyday
life that originated with nomadic Bedouin tribes in the Arabian Peninsula. Arabs often know many verses of *nabati* by heart; it is a popular
form of oral history. The attachment is also strong because the Koran's
rich Arabic is poetic. Reciting its verses and other poetry, popular among
both the literate and illiterate, is an equalizer in society.

Hilal's raging poem broke new ground on many fronts. Coming from
a country defined and ruled by religious code, her poetry was political
commentary. It was scathing in both content and tone. And a woman
was delivering the condemnation.

Encouraged by the reaction, Hilal's voice grew stronger. Her right
hand rose, then waved in the air, as if conducting the words.

When I unveil the truth,
A monster appears from his hiding place;
Barbaric in thinking and action,
Angry and blind;
Wearing death as a dress
And covering it with a suicide belt.

Again, the crowd erupted with applause. A camera panned around the
room to catch nodding endorsements.

Hilal's poem, entitled "The Chaos of Fatwas," was an attack not only
on extremist groups. She was also going after established clerics—a
long-standing taboo, especially in her homeland. Saudi Arabia was
formed in a merger between the al Saud tribe and Wahhabi clerics from

the most conservative brand of Sunni Islam. The country was named after the tribe; its belief system was named after an eighteenth-century cleric. Religious sheikhs often had the last word on how Saudis should lead their lives.

Shortly before the poetry contest, a hard-line Wahhabi cleric had issued a fatwa imposing the death sentence on anyone who allowed mingling between the sexes.

"Whoever allows mixing," ruled Sheikh Abdulrahman al Barrak, "allows forbidden things and is an infidel. And this means defection from Islam . . . Either he retracts or he must be killed . . . Anyone who accepts that his daughter, sister, or wife works with men or attends mixed-gender schooling cares little about his honor, and this is a type of pimping."[2]

Al Barrak had also endorsed rulings that Christians and Jews were unbelievers and that Shiite Muslims were infidels. Although these were not official Saudi policy, the state rarely reined in its clergy, even though they were on the state payroll.

Hilal, however, showed no hesitancy.

He speaks from an official
Powerful platform,
Terrorizing people
And preying on everyone seeking peace.

The audience cheered even louder. Simply by speaking, Hilal was violating extremist views on *awrah*—an Arabic word that generally translates as "nakedness," "private," "shame," or "vulnerable." It usually refers to women. It most often connotes the body. A woman wears niqab or hejab to cover her *awrah*. Extremists take the concept even further: a woman's voice is also *awrah*—and should never be exposed in public. Hilal's bold poem had crossed both a political and a social threshold.

But the audience was by then captivated with the formless black shape seated in a lone chair, red and plushly overstuffed, on the otherwise empty stage.

She launched into the last verse—this time directed at her audience.

The voice of courage ran away
And the truth is cornered and silent,

When self-interest prevented one
From speaking the truth.

It was a chilling rebuke of her brethren for not doing enough to isolate religious hard-liners and militants.

"My message," she told me later, "was enough—to both the extremist minority and the silent majority. Extremist fatwas represent subversive thinking, terrifying thinking, and everyone should stand against them.

"One should not kill or call for the killing of people only because they do not belong to their system of thought or to their religion," Hilal explained. "There is something very wrong with people who embrace this way of thinking."

The simple verse made Hilal an instant sensation—with the judges, the audience, and the television public. Scoring forty-seven of fifty points, she was the judges' favorite for the night. They praised her for tackling such a controversial subject. The public vote put her over the top.

She became the first woman in the competition's history to advance to the finals.

Poetry is so much a part of Arab life that Osama bin Laden often used his own verses in jihadist propaganda. The al Qaeda chief even referred to himself as a "warrior-poet."

In the 1990s, his poems were actually in demand at wedding banquets and other feasts. Some of his performances were recorded. In early 2001, he threw a lavish wedding reception for his son Mohammed in Afghanistan. The guests included senior Taliban officials as well as al Qaeda operatives. Instead of toasting the bride and groom, bin Laden burst into verse about the al Qaeda attack on the USS *Cole*. In 2000, a small dinghy carrying two suicide bombers had rammed into the giant US destroyer moored off Yemen's coast. Seventeen American sailors had been killed.[3] Bin Laden wrote an ode in honor of the operation that he recited at the wedding.

A destroyer: even the brave fear its might.
It inspires horror in the harbor and in the open sea.
She sails into the waves,
Flanked by arrogance, haughtiness and false might.

To her doom she moves slowly, clothed in a huge illusion.
A dinghy awaits her, bobbing in the waves.[4]

After the US invasion of Afghanistan in 2001, several of bin Laden's recorded poems were found among more than 1,500 audiotapes at his abandoned headquarters. His poems, which romanticized death by weaving together mystical references with jihadist images, were popular on jihadist websites.

In what may be the last poem written before he fled his Afghan headquarters, bin Laden outlined al Qaeda's mission—in verse. The full version, coauthored with one of his lieutenants, ran three pages. It appears to have been written after the American bombardment of Afghanistan began in late 2001. It raged at the United States, Israel, and his Arab brethren.[5]

Why, father, have they sent these missiles, thick as rain,
Showing mercy neither to a child,
Nor to a man shattered by old age?
It is a world of criminality, my son,
Where children are, like cattle, slaughtered.
Zion is murdering my brothers
And the Arabs hold a congress!
They are America's henchmen,
Blinded and devoid of vision.
This, by your Lord, is a major brand
Of shame to be recorded,
A treachery being pieced together.
Is our best defense to come from traitors?
I swear by God the great
That I shall fight the infidel!

Bin Laden's jihadist poetry made Hissa Hilal's courageous verse all the more striking. After she made the finals, newspapers around the world ran stories about her audacious poem. YouTube videos of Hilal's performance, with translations in several languages streaming across the bottom, were viewed by tens of thousands of people on the Internet. In the United States, ABC News picked her as the "Person of the Week."

"Most people agree with her. She is part of a movement, especially among young people, who refuse to listen to extremists," said Hassan Hassan, a reporter in Abu Dhabi who covered the competition.

"The movement has always been there. But it's increasing because extremists now have powerful TV channels, and they comment on almost every contemporary issue. People watch their programs and get angry. They say these people don't represent me, these people say all these crazy things. And someone has to say no, this is wrong," he told me after the contest ended.

"And Hissa is one of them. She said, 'I stand up because I believe in peace. These people are evil and we should stand up against them.' Voices like Hissa's are coming to the fore because people are more and more disillusioned."

In authoritarian countries, those voices are also being heard as new reality television programs provide an outlet for the public to counter rigid religious sentiment.

Not everyone is on board. The show provoked a bit of a backlash against Hilal, including a death threat on an Internet forum. The larger issue was simply a female speaking publicly for the movement. Other critics condemned her for "entertaining" in public. A few dismissed her as a whore. Hilal said she was concerned by the denunciations, but they were not enough to send her into hiding.

"Most people on the streets were very happy that I spoke so openly," she told me later. "Many said they agreed with what I said. But when you talk about these issues, you can expect the worst." Her primary concern was the danger to her four children, all girls, all under the age of twelve. The youngest was autistic.

Hilal, whose nom de plume is Remia, had been writing poetry for eighteen years. She once had a part-time job as poetry editor at an Arab newspaper. But she had never spoken in public. She chose such a sensitive subject, she explained, because fatwas were the way for extremism "to creep into our society." The idea was also sparked by the foreign reaction to her Islamic garb. Niqab was part of ancient culture among Arabian tribes and it was her choice to wear it, she said. During her travels, however, she realized outsiders associated Muslim women's modesty with terrorism.

"Western people looked at me suspiciously because I was wearing the niqab," she explained. "But they would not do the same when they see an Indian Sikh wearing the turban. Who is responsible for this suspicious look? Who made it happen?

"It was this kind of people—extremists—who have given us a bad name," she said. "Muslims, instead of being respected, are a source of fear and suspicion because of these people."[6]

Hilal was widely touted as the favorite to win the competition. For the final round, her poem was a defense of freedom of thought—another controversial idea in one of the world's most controlled societies. Of the six finalists, the judges again gave her the highest scores. Once public votes were counted, however, she came in third out of five. The winning poem was about helping others. Hilal still walked away with more than $815,000—and far more fame than the winner.

"My poetry has always been provocative," she told me a few weeks after the competition. "I always write what I think and feel regardless of society's opinion. It's a way to express myself and give voice to Arab women, silenced by those who have hijacked our culture and our religion."

Among the 650 million Muslim women spread across the globe, some of the most outspoken are in societies that have produced the vilest forms of extremism. Osama bin Laden's homeland may be the worst offender, not only because the oil-rich welfare state pretends to take care of all its people.

The problem in Saudi Arabia is that only men are people. Women are, legally, all minors. Merely appearing in public defies authority—and carries a penalty.

In 2008, a Saudi financial consultant working for a reputable company in Jeddah went to Starbucks with a male colleague after the power in their office went out. Married for twenty-seven years and the mother of three children, she was hardly a seductive young female. The two of them sat in the "family section," the area of Saudi restaurants where women can sit with men, preferably relatives. Her laptop was open and they were talking business—specifically brand equity and sovereign wealth funds—when members of the vice police swooped in. The squad is formally called the Committee for the Promotion of Virtue and the Prevention of Vice. She was taken to Malaz Prison, fingerprinted, questioned for hours, refused permission to call her husband or a lawyer, lectured on sinning, and eventually ordered to sign a confession that she was in a state of *khulwa*—seclusion with an unrelated man.[7]

Saudi women often bear the brunt of guilt for other crimes carried out against them. In 2009, after she was raped by five men, a twenty-three-year-old Saudi woman was sentenced to one year in jail and one hundred lashes for fornication and seeking an abortion. A few months later, a Saudi man shot his two sisters in "honor killings" after they simply "fraternized" with men who were not relatives. Their father absolved him of both murders.[8]

Saudi religious rulings on women can also border on the bizarre. In 2010, a Saudi judge ruled that a man could slap his wife for lavish spending, even if the money was used to purchase Islamic dress.[9] A few months later, a Saudi cleric said all foreign maids allowed into the kingdom should be Muslim—and even then segregated from men by employers to prevent illicit mixing between the sexes. Hard-line cleric Sheikh Yousuf Ahmad also ruled that maids should be required to wear hejab and forbidden to serve food to men. Ahmad had earlier called for the Grand Mosque to be destroyed and rebuilt in a way that would segregate the sexes.[10]

Yet, against overwhelming odds, women have been increasingly creative, even in Saudi Arabia. Hissa Hilal is no longer unique in deeply religious societies.

Across the Islamic world, women in the early twenty-first century have become one of the two leading engines of change. From Morocco to Malaysia, Iran to Indonesia, they are leading street protests, mobilizing millions of signatures on petitions to change laws, energetically building civil society, and creating the first generation of women to run for public office.

After little Kuwait became one of the last countries to give women the vote in 2005, nineteen women ran for parliament in 2009. Four were elected, despite a fatwa that declared voting for women was a sin.

Even in restrictive Saudi Arabia, a 2007 Gallup poll found that almost 70 percent of women said they should be able to vote—and "without influence." More than three of out four said they should be able to work at any job they were qualified to hold. Women had even convinced men. In the survey, almost 60 percent of Saudi men said women should be granted the franchise.[11]

"In my poetry, I'm trying to tell people that it's time to revise many of our ideas," Hissa Hilal told me. "Many things are wrong and will destroy our religion if we don't change. Everyone must stop listening to extremists."

After the contest, the public still had no idea what Hissa Hilal looked like. But they did know her voice.

O N A SCORCHING August day in 2006, Wajeha al Huwaider abandoned her enveloping *abaya*, a black cloth that covers body and hair but not the face. She instead donned a calf-length pink shirt, loose pink trousers, and a matching pink scarf. Then she took a taxi from the island of Bahrain across the sixteen-mile bridge to a signpost marking the frontier of Saudi Arabia. She got out in desert heat and, in her bright pink clothing, marched the rest of the way on foot—holding up a large poster for all other motorists to see.

The placard said, simply, "Give Women Their Rights."

She lasted about twenty minutes before Saudi security forces picked her up.

For the next several hours, al Huwaider was interrogated by Saudi religious police. She is a spirited woman. Even her long dark bangs, which curl over her forehead and eyebrows, make a defiant statement; a Saudi woman's hair is supposed to be neatly and completely tucked under her head cover.

"Control this," an intelligence officer told her, pointing at her mouth, "and we won't have a problem."

Al Huwaider has never been easily silenced. "In what way are we different from prisoners at Guantánamo Bay?" she said in a noticeably audible voice, in a room full of men, when I went to see her in Dhahran. She works at the headquarters of Aramco, the world's largest oil corporation, on the Persian Gulf.

"At least many of the Guantánamo prisoners have been released, while we are still in this prison—and nobody ever hears of us," she said. "When will we be freed?"

Al Huwaider became a social revolutionary, in a Saudi context, courtesy of the new media. She posted so many scathing comments on newspaper websites that the editor of *Al Watan*, Saudi Arabia's leading daily, invited her to write a column in 2000. The English-language *Arab News* picked up her pieces. Then the newspaper *Al Youm,* or "Today," did too. She was not a logical choice. Saudi Arabia is an overwhelmingly Sunni country. She is from the Shiite minority.

Al Huwaider proved to be equally merciless in her columns. In one piece, she condemned the entire Muslim world for giving "rise to pygmies afflicted with narcissism and the desire for a monopoly over power and money [who] repressed, apostatized, exiled, chased, and assassinated those who didn't toe the line." [12] She drew both Arab and outside attention. For her writing on human rights and the plight of Saudi women, she won the Freedom of Expression Award from International PEN, the global writers' group.

But she also soon went too far for Saudi sensibilities. She was abruptly banned from publishing in 2003.

"The authorities never communicated this to me directly, but I got the word through a friend," she told me, with her usual rapid-fire intensity. "And then, one by one, the editors of each publication rejected my pieces. And when you're banned in Saudi Arabia, none of the Arabic television channels or satellite stations will invite you on. So it was an attempt to silence me."

That's when she launched her one-woman acts.

On International Women's Day in 2008, al Huwaider went out into the Saudi desert and broke the law. She drove. Only men can drive in the desert kingdom. Women usually sit in the backseat, even if the front passenger seat is empty.

The Saudis take the driving issue quite seriously. Women had tried to defy the religious ruling once before.

In 1990, forty-seven heavily veiled women rendezvoused in a Safeway parking lot in Riyadh, the Saudi capital. Since women are not allowed to drive, they were chauffeured to the supermarket. Once there, they dismissed their drivers. Fifteen of the women, who had international driver's licenses from traveling abroad, then got behind the wheels of their cars. The rest piled in as passengers.

In orderly single file, the women then drove their fifteen cars through downtown Riyadh. [13] "I loved the double takes the men did when they saw us," Nora al Sowayan recalled in 2008. [14]

The women had tried to get permission before their adventure. They petitioned the Riyadh governor. They pointed out that there was no prohibition in the Koran against women driving any form of transportation.

Indeed, the Prophet Mohammed's first wife owned a camel caravan business between Arabia and Jerusalem and Damascus. And in Saudi Arabia's remote desert areas, contemporary Bedouin women were allowed to drive cars, even trucks.

Women also drove in all other Gulf countries. The Saudi women acted after Iraq's 1990 invasion of neighboring Kuwait over oil rights on their common border. Tens of thousands of Kuwaitis fled to Saudi Arabia; many of the cars were driven by Kuwaiti women. Then, under a United Nations mandate, tens of thousands of foreign troops—from three dozen countries—massed in Saudi Arabia to protect the kingdom and liberate Kuwait. Again, many of the soldiers were female.

"In Saudi Arabia and the Gulf states, men watched as foreign militaries came in to rescue them. Even Western women were being brought in to free them," al Huwaider told me when we met in the Saudi oil capital of Dhahran.

"You could sense the loss of confidence, self-respect, and even of manhood. There were lots of stories at the time about Saudi men being unable to perform in bed," she added, with a chuckle. "But the exposure to what other women were doing was a game changer for a lot of Saudi women. They began to ask a lot of questions."

The driving escapade, however, triggered a national scandal, even though the ban was a cultural rather than a legal taboo. The women were taken to jail and held in a cell so small they all had to stand. The passports of all forty-seven women, as well as their husbands, were confiscated for a year. Several women, including six who taught at King Saud University, lost their jobs. Powerful clerics condemned them as harlots. Leaflets distributed at mosques charged the women with advocating "American secularism." Their names, addresses, and phone numbers were published—in a country with phone directories that do not list a single female. Several women received menacing calls. And both the government and the chief cleric issued sweeping bans to ensure the women did not take over their family cars again.

"Driving by women contradicts Islamic traditions followed by Saudi citizens," ruled Sheikh Abdul Aziz ibn Baz, a former Saudi grand mufti.[15]

The Gulf War to liberate Kuwait—code-named Operation Desert Storm—ended up hurting women's rights. The presence of "infidel" foreign forces in the birthplace of Islam enraged bin Laden. "The Saudi regime is but a branch or an agent of the United States," he told CNN. "It has stopped ruling people according to what God revealed."[16]

He vented most of his rage at the Saudi royal family. "Since Allah spread out the Arabian Peninsula, created its desert and drew its seas, no such disaster has ever struck as when those Christian legions spread like pest, crowded its land, ate its resources, eradicated its nature, and humiliated its leaders," bin Laden later wrote.[17]

The royal family, which had enriched the bin Laden family through hundreds of construction projects, expelled bin Laden in 1991 and eventually stripped him of his citizenship. But the government also recognized the dangers of bin Laden's message. After Kuwait was liberated and foreign troops withdrew, the monarchy responded by reinforcing religiosity.

Saudi women bore a disproportionate share of the burden. "The government put more religious police on the streets," al Huwaider recalled. "Women were watched more. They were prevented from being exposed to other societies, even in the Gulf. There were new restrictions on schools."

Many of the same limits are still in place a generation later, despite repeated promises of reforms. Women can own cars but they cannot drive them. A Saudi woman won a car race in Dubai but could not drive even at normal speeds at home. Another woman got a pilot's license but she could not drive herself to and from the airport. Women could also become lawyers but could not appear in courts.

In the early twenty-first century, the majority of Saudi university graduates are young women, yet the female workforce is under 15 percent—one of the lowest in the Islamic world. Saudi women are also legally minors throughout their lives. Every woman has a male guardian related by blood or marriage—usually her father, husband, or son—who must provide written permission for her to attend school, open bank accounts, work, and travel. Men who divorce their wives, as in al Huwaider's case, often refuse to transfer their ex-wives' guardianship to another man in her family. It is a way to punish her or have leverage over her future. With twenty-first-century technology, a man no longer has to be in his wife's presence to pronounce "I divorce thee" three times, the legal means of divorce in the kingdom. A Saudi court ruled that a husband can text-message his wife with the news of his split.

Women have little recourse. Human Rights Watch cited the case of a woman who refused to file a complaint against her husband after he shot her—on two separate occasions—because her male guardian would have to be present in any legal action. The guardian, of course, was her husband. The third time he shot her, she died.[18]

Trying to challenge the system has been costly. A Saudi woman filed a petition to the king after years of harassment by a judicial official. A local judge had repeatedly urged Sawsan Salim to divorce her husband after he was jailed for debt. She repeatedly refused—to the point of filing 118 complaints against the judge and others for abuse of power between 2004 and 2008. Instead of helping her, the local court charged her with "spurious complaints"—and appearing in court without a male guardian. In 2010, she was convicted in a trial before two judges, one of whom was the justice who originally harassed her.

Salim was sentenced to three hundred lashings and eighteen months in jail.[19]

So al Huwaider's decision to drive in 2008—a full generation after the Gulf War and bin Laden's denunciation of the royal family—was still daringly defiant. She also had no significant mass of women to literally drive home the point. But she did take along a friend to film her. As she drove, al Huwaider appealed to the government to allow women to enter the twenty-first century.

"For women, driving is *not* a political issue. It is *not* a religious issue. It is a *social* issue," she insisted, as the car bumped along the road. "We know that many women of Arab societies are capable of driving cars. We also know that many families will allow their women to drive."

Al Huwaider turned to what was then a relatively new tool to get attention for her one-woman act—YouTube.[20] Her driving video was viewed by more than 250,000 people. Her challenge to the government was also picked up by media around the world, including some programs that beamed back into the kingdom. All by herself, one woman had circumvented the world's most rigid restrictions on women.

She took some heat from Saudi women who argued that driving was not a top priority.

"Wealthy, educated, or liberal Saudi women don't care a lot about less fortunate women. They have chauffeurs," she told me. "But for working-class and poor women, driving is a genuine priority. Otherwise, they have to pay drivers to shop for food or go to work. And if we can't get this basic freedom of movement, however small it may seem, then we can't get or use the more vital rights." More than 60 percent of Saudi women surveyed in a Gallup poll in 2008 also said Saudi women should be able to drive—and without their male guardians.

Al Huwaider took her campaign with her when she traveled. During a trip to the United States, she staged a one-woman demonstration at a car dealership in a Virginia suburb of Washington, DC.

"I addressed my message to American automakers," she explained. "Saudi women *want* to buy your cars—and many can afford to buy the best brands. But first, you must support *our* fight for the right to drive."

Again, she put her demonstration on YouTube.

She too turned to poetry to reach an audience more attached to verse than newspaper prose. Her sweeping poetic commentaries ridiculed both extremist dogma and rigid Wahhabi rule. With stunning candor and bitterness, she was scathing about all patriarchal politics, as in her poem "When."

> *When religion has control over science—you can be sure that you*
> *are in an Arab country ...*
> *When you hear the clerics saying that democracy is heresy, but*
> *seize every opportunity provided by democracy to grab high*
> *positions—do not be surprised, you are in an Arab country ...*
> *When you discover that a woman is worth half of what a man is*
> *worth, or less—do not be surprised, you are in an Arab country.*

In her expanding repertoire of women's rights issues, al Huwaider devoted special attention to a woman's worth. The issue is personal for al Huwaider. After twenty-five years together, al Huwaider's husband divorced her when she became a social activist. Yet he remained her guardian.

"He couldn't stand the publicity and fame," she told me. After the divorce, however, he refused to transfer his authority over her life to their two sons—in part because he later wanted her back, this time as a second wife after he remarried. She refused.

"I have the divorce papers, but I'm still registered with the government as his first wife. When I leave the country, my ex-husband still has to sign permission. And if he's angry, he won't finish the papers," she told me. "Some men simply disappear from their ex-wives' lives without transferring guardianship, and women are stranded."

In her epic poem "When," the anger steadily builds on other issues too.

> *When you see that the authorities chop off a man's hand for*
> *stealing a loaf of bread or a penny, but praise and glorify those*
> *who steal billions—do not be too surprised, you are in an Arab*
> *country . . .*
> *When you are forced to worship the Creator in school and your*
> *teachers grade you for it—you can be sure that you are in an*
> *Arab country . . .*
> *When young women students are publicly flogged merely for*
> *exposing their eyes—you are in an Arab country.*

Al Huwaider often campaigned on behalf of child brides in Saudi Arabia, a common problem that prevented many females from going out in public or even exposing their faces. Al Huwaider was especially preoccupied with the case of a nine-year-old girl basically sold by her father for $4,000 into marriage with a seventy-year-old man.

To highlight the issue, she organized another video for YouTube of Saudi girls and teenagers pledging never to be child brides. It too was picked up by CNN and other international media—and, in turn, beamed back home courtesy of satellite dishes and Internet sites.

With unusual bluntness, she once advised women that it was "a thousand times" better to be an old maid than to marry an Arab man— particularly men in Gulf countries.[21]

The final lines from "When" reflected on women's rights as the essence of Arab problems across the Middle East.

> *When covering the woman's head is more important than*
> *financial and administrative corruption—do not be astonished,*
> *you are in an Arab country . . .*
> *When women are house ornaments which can be replaced at any*
> *time—bemoan your fate, you are in an Arab country . . .*
> *When fear constantly lives in the eyes of the people—you can be*
> *certain that you are in an Arab country.*

An Arabic reform website compared al Huwaider to Rosa Parks, the American civil rights pioneer from the 1950s.[22] In a Saudi context, she was certainly as outspoken.

On a popular Internet site, she warned Muslim leaders that they were "digging their graves with their own hands" for repressing their people. "The day will come when these graves will swallow you and your thrones, without mercy, if you persist in repression," she wrote in 2006.[23] By 2011, she looked almost prophetic.

"We have raised a generation on the belief that we are a special people, that we are the cradle of Islam, that the truth is ours and ours alone, that we are the Saved Sect of Islam," she said in 2008, on a television station beamed to the entire Arab world. "People have begun to believe all these lies.[24]"

She was always up to something. For years, I have gotten emails every few weeks with some new campaign, new video, new issue, or new zinger against the political or religious establishment.

"For Saudi women, every day is a new battle," al Huwaider told me. "It's about constantly finding ways to live without colliding with the law, with men, with society, with the religious clerics, or with the political establishment.

"But the important thing," she said, "is that we're now willing to do battle."

8.

Satellite Sheikhs and YouTube Imams

**Radicals learned long ago the power
of trying to interpret the Koran in their favor.
Moderates are now rushing to do the same.
This battle gets down to the very essence
of what it means to be Muslim.**

—AZZAM TAMINI, DIRECTOR OF THE
INSTITUTE OF ISLAMIC POLITICAL THOUGHT.[1]

In Saudi Arabia, Ahmad al Shugairi is the closest thing to Elvis. His personal appearances elicit teary adulation. The young cheer him in standing ovations. His first television show, a five-minute program filler, was so popular that it grew by five minutes every year. By 2010, a beefed-up version ranked among the top ten programs on the largest of five hundred Arab satellite channels.

Somewhat uncomfortably, al Shugairi acknowledged the comparison. In 2008, he had to be bundled out the back door of a packed concert hall to escape the adoring crowd.

"Elvis has left the building," he joked with a *New York Times* reporter.[2]

Al Shugairi is one of a new generation of satellite sheikhs and YouTube imams who have taken to the airwaves across the Islamic world. They are not real preachers; they are unschooled in theology and have not produced serious scholarship. They use unconventional media to spread their message. But their popularity has produced a gentler genre of Islamism. They sell feel-good Islam instead of suicide bombs. Among women, they encourage the "pink hejab"—being both observant and fashionably female. Many now have followings that rival—and deeply irritate—Islam's traditional clergy, whose strict fatwas have long dominated Muslim life.

The young televangelists have energized the counter-jihad. They have set the tone for young Muslim activists.

Born in 1973, al Shugairi is the antithesis of the ponderous Muslim preacher. He is as comfortable in faux-bleached jeans and T-shirts as in a flowing white *thobe* and *ghutra* headdress. He has worn both on his shows. Instead of a beard, he sports a neat mustache and light stubble that makes him look more like a movie star than a scholar. He is tall and has the build of a soccer player or swimmer. His face is long and lean; his eyebrows are a bit bushy.

Al Shugairi actually uses Elvis in his sermonettes about happiness.

"Let's have a look at someone who had all kinds of enjoyments," he began one of his first shows, which is still available and widely viewed on YouTube. "A handsome guy who was pleasured by good health and a lively body! He was extremely rich, had as many women as he wanted and a wife from among the most beautiful women of the era. Elvis Presley, my sisters and brothers, owned the world and what's in it!

"Even though he had all these enjoyments, do you know how he died?" he asked, then paused. "Elvis Presley died in the toilet of his house from an overdose of drugs! And everyone who reads his biography knows that he was sad and depressed. The problem of Elvis Presley, my brothers and sisters, and the problem of a lot of us is that we look for happiness in the wrong places!"

In his public appearances, al Shugairi concedes that he is not a trained sheikh. He is self-taught. His easygoing energy is more motivational speaker than classical Islamic scholar, more Tony Robbins than Sheikh Yusuf al Qaradawi, an elderly Egyptian cleric with a long-running religious show on Al Jazeera. Al Shugairi does not lead Friday Prayers or work in a mosque. On his latest television show, *Khawater*, or "Thoughts," he dispenses everyday morality rather than Islamic jurisprudence.

But satellite sheikhs have become so popular across the Islamic world that Malaysia launched its own reality show in 2010 modeled on *The Next Top Model*—only for the next top imam. The show—*Imam Muda*, or "Young Imam"—put ten aspiring clerics (whittled down from 1,000 applicants) through several tasks to test their Islamic aptitude. Contestants counseled couples with marital problems. They supervised the slaughter of animals to ensure the work conformed with Muslim practices. They advised troubled teenagers. They recited verses from the Koran. They consoled the elderly. They even washed an unclaimed corpse for burial in accordance with Muslim tradition.

The twenty-seven-year-old winner received cash, a new car, a laptop computer, and a scholarship to study in Saudi Arabia. After the show, he said he planned to set up a young imams club. *Imam Muda* was the highest-rated show on Astro Oasis, a Malaysian cable channel.[3]

The rise of the satellite sheikhs is largely a by-product of 9/11.

"I remember it still," al Shugairi told me when I met him at the Andalusia café in Jeddah. He opened the café as a meeting place for Saudi Arabia's young, who have few public places for socializing.

"I was having coffee with friends, and we saw it on TV. I was shocked. Only a few people in the crowd were against it. Everyone was happy, even people who were moderates," he said. "I had many debates with friends over the next three weeks."

Al Shugairi had already gone through his own flirtation with militancy, a reaction to teenage excesses. "From ninth grade until my third year in college, I had a wild time, a blast," he recalled. He studied information management systems at California State University at Long Beach, where he partied heavily, womanized, drank, and smoked instead of prayed.

In the mid-1990s, however, he started to drift toward the other extreme. "For the next five years, I tried to make up for the lost years," he told me. "I was very extremist. It was intellectual, not physical extremism."

In 2000, he began to study Islam more seriously. He soon settled into what he called a "more tolerant" understanding of the faith that allowed for "diversity and flexibility." Several of the satellite sheikhs went through personal crises and epiphanies. Most of them emerged from other professions, from business to banking, farming to teaching. Al Shugairi inherited and still ran his family's import business, which specialized in cleaning products. The satellite sheikhs' confessional storytelling—about their journeys and experimentation, whether with strict secularism or extremism—is a big part of their appeal.

The common turning point was the impact of 9/11 on Islam. "It forced me to clarify things in my mind," al Shugairi told me.

For al Shugairi, the evolution into Islamic televangelism was a fluke. Friends asked him to help manage a new television project called *Yalla Shabab*, or "Hello Youth." They went to Cairo to shoot the pilot.

"We don't have a lot of young television presenters in Saudi Arabia, so we looked at each other and said, 'Who can do the talking?' They chose me," he recalled, smiling and shaking his head. "I said, 'No, sorry, I'm just not into this. I've never been in front of a camera.' But they said, 'Please, just for this episode.'

"I was so scared the night before," he recalled, with a laugh. "I had dreams of snakes coming out of the camera and eating me. Thankfully, it wasn't live, and it never aired."

But he did end up hosting *Yalla Shabab* for three years. It became a big hit on Middle East Broadcasting (MBC), the region's leading news and entertainment satellite channel. The show tried to navigate a middle ground between extremism and secularism. It also tried to steer young Muslims toward cultural tolerance.

Al Shugairi and his team shot one season in Europe to explore Islam's relations with the West. They went to Spain to illustrate a high point of Islamic history, when Andalusia—or Al Andalus in Arabic—was the center of power and achievement in the Middle Ages. (It also inspired the name of al Shugairi's café.) The show then went to London and interviewed Muslims in Britain's House of Lords. It went to France to shoot at its oldest mosque. Throughout the season, al Shugairi interviewed American Muslim convert Sheikh Hamza Yusuf about Islam and the West. Yusuf was born Mark Hanson in Walla Walla, Washington.

The next season was shot in the United States—in New York, Philadelphia, Chicago, and California. The show went to Ground Zero in New York. It also interviewed a Jewish lawyer who was defending Muslim prisoners in Guantánamo Bay.

"It was a kind of reality television," al Shugairi told me. "Everywhere we went, we talked to people. We met all kinds—Christians, Muslims, Jews, even rabbis." The series was educational, not religious. The format was largely interviews, not lectures.

Al Shugairi became known as a satellite sheikh when MBC launched his second series. *Khawater* began in 2005, at the tail end of the terrorist wave in the kingdom. The public mood had begun to shift in 2003 when suicide bombers hit Riyadh, he told me. By 2005, Saudis—particularly the young—were ready for a different message.

In the new show, al Shugairi focused on basic life lessons. One series had the feel of Jay Leno's "Jaywalking" street interviews. In one episode, al Shugairi wandered around Jeddah asking if anyone knew where the public library was. They didn't.

The issue resonated, he explained, because *iqraa* was the first word of God to the Prophet Mohammed, as recorded in the Koran. It means "read" in Arabic. *Iqraa* is widely interpreted to be a command to learn of God's wisdom and mercy. (Iqraa was also the first specialized religious satellite station in the Islamic world. It is owned by a wealthy Saudi businessman.)

In the 2009 season, al Shugairi launched another series with a title meaning *What If He Were among Us?* He set up *Candid Camera* situations, taped the reaction, and then emerged from a hiding place to ask what the Prophet Mohammed would have done in the same situation. In one episode, he planted a wallet on the ground. In another, he left a banana peel on the floor. In a third, he watched what people did after a simple act of kindness.

"We put the Prophet in context of our simple daily situations to make people understand," he told me. "Religion is not just about memorizing the Koran or the hadith. It's about living Islam's principles in all we do."

During a taping in Cairo, the unsuspecting subjects turned out to be Christian Copts, who account for some 10 percent of Egypt's 85 million people. "So I asked them, 'If Jesus were among us, what would he have done?'" al Shugairi said, chuckling. "And we kept it in the show."

Al Shugairi's shows are often Islam lite. His topics have ranged from dirty bathrooms in mosques to double-parking, littering to feeding animals popcorn in a zoo. He did one show on smoking from the perspective of economics, human rights, and charity as well as religion. Investing the price of a daily pack of cigarettes for twenty-five years, with interest, he told viewers, would yield 1 million riyals.

"So it's up to you, my brothers and sisters," he said. "Either you become a millionaire or decide on burning your money every day."

The Saudi government spent 5 billion riyals on health care because of diseases related to smoking, he pointed out. The same amount would sponsor 4 million orphans around the world. Smoking is a serious issue among Saudi youth. The flashing factoids on al Shugairi's show claimed that 41 percent of Saudi high school students were smokers.

He closed the show by quoting the Prophet Mohammed: "Don't be harmed and don't cause harm to others."

Al Shugairi's favorite themes revolve around justice, education, and freedom. He often encourages civic engagement and environmental activism. In 2010, he volunteered to become the spokesman for water conservation in a country with the third-highest use of water per capita in the world, after the United States and Canada, but less than 2 percent arable land. He urged Saudis to take the Water Savers pledge—and to apply it even when they did the ritual washing before daily prayers.

"You can easily save five to six liters of water during ablution if you don't keep the tap open all the time," he said in the campaign. "The same applies to other household tasks." [4]

Al Shugairi has also taken on tough topics, including the controversy about a cartoon of the Prophet Mohammed published in a Danish newspaper. The cartoon sparked protests across the Islamic world and death threats against the cartoonist. Al Shugairi urged calm and a more reasoned response. The Prophet's message, al Shugairi told his audience, was to build, not destroy.

"We will affirm for once in our contemporary history that we are a people who are civilized," he said. The goal should instead be "transforming this person from the biggest attacker to the biggest defender" of Islam.

Al Shugairi's programs are distinctive from the shows of other satellite sheikhs because they invite critical self-examination. In the fifth season of *Thoughts*, he wanted to emphasize Muslim potential—so he went to Japan. Impressed with Japanese humility, hard work, manners, cleanliness, and punctuality, he told viewers that the Japanese followed the ethics of Islam without being Muslims. [5]

"These commandments are universal, so you don't have to believe in the Prophet Mohammed to be clean," he told a radio program. He then laughed. "I'm just trying to make the Arab world jealous about the Japanese streets. I mean, I ask the Arab world, if the Prophet Mohammed came today, who will he see implementing his teachings more—the Japanese or the Muslim world?

"And I say that, by the way, also about the United States," he added.

"Most of the prophetic teachings are practiced in the US much more than they are in the Islamic world."[6]

For the sixth season in 2010, al Shugairi and his crew shot in Córdoba, Damascus, Baghdad, and Cairo, once among the world's most enlightened cities. "Those cities were the Tokyo and New York of the Middle Ages," he told the *Saudi Gazette*. "They were the places where everyone dreamed of living: the biggest, cleanest, most advanced cities with the most universities and best education."[7]

Al Shugairi's version of Islam is an ethical guidebook. It does not punish or threaten apostasy. It is populist Islam versus jihadist Islam. He urges the young to volunteer, especially during the holy month of Ramadan, and to avoid violence. He promotes religious identity but in a real-world context that blends seventh-century values with twenty-first-century technology, the Koran with the Internet. (By 2010, al Shugairi had more than 220,000 fans on Facebook.)

Speaking in folksy, colloquial Arabic, he tells Muslims that they can aspire to heaven but also enjoy life on earth. They can be believers but also have fun.

His café reflects al Shugairi's attempt to help the young navigate the modern world while still being loyal to the values of their faith. The Andalusia is divided into separate front and back spaces by three grand Moorish arches. Moroccan-style lanterns hang from cathedral ceilings. In the front, velvet couches and settees are grouped around tables; they are accented by pillows with maxims like "Fall seven times, stand up eight" and "Trust a few, wrong no one." Shelves along the walls offer books for reading. A large flat-screen television was showing sports events on the day I visited. The back room has high-backed chairs and tables. An upper room, above a balcony, is for men only. The menu offers cheesecake shakes as well as Andalusian tea.

Both Islamic purists and Muslim liberals have criticized the satellite sheikhs and YouTube imams. Purists contend they preach "yuppie Islam" or "easy Islam" or "Western Islam" that appeals only to middle- and upper-class Muslims who watch their sermons on YouTube rather than attend mosque services.

Liberals allege they are a flashier version of classic fundamentalists like the Muslim Brotherhood. The satellite sheikhs, liberal critics contend, are just the starting point for a slow slide into extremism. The new pseudo-imams may insist that women have equal rights, but most also urge women to wear headscarves.

The satellite sheikhs' appeal may well prove to be a political or social fad. Over its fourteen centuries, Islam has witnessed many cycles—as have other religions. Osama bin Laden's extremism is one of them. The satellite sheikhs and YouTube imams certainly address the same kind of alienation, identity crisis, or drifting that has led the young to join al Qaeda and other extremist groups.

Yet their shows provide one thing that al Qaeda does not—basic solutions to the problems of everyday life.

JAMAL KHASHOGGI IS one of the kingdom's most outspoken analysts. He has angered both sides of the political divide. As editor of the newspaper *Al Watan,* he ran a series of articles disparaging Saudi Arabia's notorious religious police—formally known as the Committee for the Promotion of Virtue and the Prevention of Vice—that infuriated the government. He also ran articles on women's rights and political reforms that outraged Islamists. Khashoggi was eventually fired for a scathing editorial after Saudi Arabia's first big suicide bombing in 2003. The editorial criticized a fourteenth-century cleric named Ibn Tamiyya, a leading figure during the second wave of Salafism. Ibn Tamiyya inspired the clerics who founded Wahhabism in the eighteenth century.

Wahhabism is so central to the identity of the Saudi state that a twenty-first-century editor could get fired for criticizing a sheikh who lived seven hundred years earlier. In the long editorial, Khashoggi wrote of the Saudi bombers,

> Why did they wave the banner of jihad . . . ? The answer is this: Ibn Tamiyya said . . . that if the ruler does not observe the commandment to promote virtue and prevent vice, the clerics are obliged to do it. It is these words that are the real problem. We must stop cajoling and say: These words are a mistake and a true disaster that lead to anarchy . . . because anyone who thinks himself a cleric will then try to remove everything he considers vice. Anyone who thinks music is forbidden will blow up stores that sell tapes. Anyone who thinks smoking a *narghile* [hookah water pipe] is forbidden will blow up shops offering them for sale, and so on.

This is no exaggeration. The day is not far off when they open fire on satellite dishes.

Khashoggi was reinstated as editor in 2007, only to get fired again in 2010 after the paper ran an article by a Saudi poet again critical of Salafism. (Khashoggi was later hired by a Saudi media baron to run a new twenty-four-hour news channel.) Born in 1959, he has a salt-and-pepper goatee and mustache and wears wire-rimmed glasses. He grew up with the Islamic revival and witnessed both the loosening and tightening of religious restrictions. He was also intrigued by the satellite sheikhs.

"In the 1970s, there were very few young people who prayed in public," he told me when we met in Jeddah. "Then in the 1980s, we got caught up with the rise of Islamic sentiment throughout the Muslim world. A stream of activities began, linked largely to the Muslim Brotherhood in Egypt.

"A few years later, the Salafis—our Taliban, the people of religion—caught up with it," he said. "The Salafis created an image of Islam as very conservative, very rigid. You were either religious or corrupt and evil. The Salafis gave the public a hard time, and they eventually took over the university campuses."

After the wave of bombings between 2003 and 2005, however, a more relaxed form of religion emerged in the kingdom. He called it the reconciliation movement.

"Shugairi and others have tapped into people who want to be Islamic but don't accept the hard Salafi doctrine," Khashoggi said.

"It's a movement of young people who defy an important principle of being religious the old-fashioned way, where men and women don't mix together. Yet they see themselves as religious. They carry out religious duties and some social political responsibilities, such as gathering donations for Palestinians in Gaza. They're quite active. It's reconciliation with fundamentalism."

But the reconciliation movement did not necessarily mean any less anger at the West, particularly the United States, Khashoggi noted.

If a public opinion poll asked whether Saudis liked what bin Laden had said about the United States, he predicted that up to 80 percent would say yes. But if the poll asked whether they would have wanted bin Laden as their leader, he predicted, 99 percent would say no.

"This admiration of radicalism is okay when it is against someone else," he explained. "People are angry at America. But there is no infatuation with fanaticism as a solution to their everyday problems. Radicalism doesn't have a policy for education or health or the economy. Nobody wants another Taliban state."

The reconciliation, or emergence of a middle ground, was facilitated by public access to satellite technology and the Internet. Since the mid-1990s, both created alternatives to state-controlled media. Iqraa, the first satellite channel to specialize exclusively in Islamic programming, was launched in 1998. Satellite dishes have since transformed cityscapes throughout the Islamic world. I saw them even in the so-called City of the Dead, a massive Cairo cemetery where tens of thousands of homeless live among the mausoleums. They had illegally tapped into electricity lines and set up satellite dishes for televisions on the tombs.

The introduction of satellite television was a huge step for Saudi Arabia. For decades, the Saudi clergy had resisted it. King Faisal finally convinced the clergy to allow the first channel in 1965 on grounds that television could be used to promote Islam.

Television remained controversial for years, even within the royal family and even though the state tightly controlled all programming. King Faisal's decision also came at a high personal cost. Shortly after the new television headquarters opened in 1966, a young zealot attacked the facility; he was killed by security guards.

Nine years later, in 1975, the zealot's brother attended a public meeting hosted by King Faisal. When it came time to meet the king, he pulled out a gun and fired several times at the monarch. The assassination was linked to the controversy over Saudi Arabia's first television station.

The zealous young brothers were both nephews of the king.

In the early twenty-first century, however, the new Islamic media is a booming business—with a far wider audience than al Qaeda's periodic videos. Bin Laden issued about two dozen video messages in the decade between 9/11 and his death. His lieutenant Ayman al Zawahiri issued around forty. Together, their tapes ran less than a few days of television time.

In contrast, satellite television has transformed how Muslims follow their faith. Since 9/11, the number of Arab satellite stations devoted only to religion has soared from one to more than eighty.[8]

Many stations now run New Age Islamic televangelists. Amr Khaled, an Egyptian, has had programs on four separate networks. Often dressed in jeans or tailored suits and speaking slangy Arabic, he tells folksy tales of the Prophet Mohammed adapted to modern life. He is ridiculed by real clerics for having trained as an accountant. But the media has compared his preaching on hard work, good works, and good manners to telemegastars Joel Osteen and Dr. Phil. Hundreds of his sermons have been loaded on YouTube. And his website—in eighteen languages, including English, Hebrew, Russian, Turkish, and even Danish—has had tens of millions of hits. He was selected as one of *Time's* one hundred most influential people in 2007—he was sixty-second—and *Newsweek's* fifty global elite in 2008.

At the height of Egypt's upheaval in 2011, the number of Facebook users soared to 5 million. In just two weeks alone, Facebook users created 32,000 new groups and 14,000 new pages. The most popular Egyptian Facebook page belonged to Khaled, who had 2.5 million fans. [9]

Islam's new religious media also feature far more than just sermons. In 2010, Khaled launched a new series modeled on *The Apprentice* on Dubai TV. More than 25,000 people applied to be on the show. Sixteen young Muslims—eight females, all wearing hejab, and eight males from nine countries—competed by doing charitable and community projects in several Middle Eastern countries.[10] They helped build an orphanage, found jobs for the unemployed, and worked with ex-convicts. One of the toughest assignments was in war-torn Sudan, where they had to form kids' soccer teams, transform rural land into soccer fields, compete for the largest audience, and generate a message that teams were a means to foster unity—all in three days. The winner won 100,000 euros to support a development project in his own country.[11]

On the show, Khaled played the role of Donald Trump. The final scene each week—when one contestant was fired—replicated Trump's boardroom. The show was entitled *Mujaddidun*, which means "Renovators" or "Renewers."

Other religious programs borrow from Western models. In an Islamic version of *The Great Race*, three Muslim youths travel the Middle East. An Islamic quiz show features trivia questions on religion. Several stations carry talk-show variations on *Oprah*. On talent shows, Muslim pop stars sing the equivalent of Christian gospel music, with themes about religion, family, or the Prophet Mohammed's life.

Al Resalah, which means "The Message," is typical of the new media.

It vows to present "the true Islam." Critics charge that it has run anti-Western and anti-Israeli content. It has also run al Shugairi's programs. Its shows have state-of-the-art sets; its staff is coed. Men and women—including females who are not veiled—have appeared together on shows. Its programs cite fatwas from senior clerics that approve of music, SMS chatting, and unveiled women. Its subjects range from polygamy to extremism.

Al Resalah was launched in 2006 by Saudi billionaire Prince Alwaleed bin Talal, one of the biggest donors to Harvard and Georgetown universities and a stakeholder in EuroDisney. The channel is now beamed from Europe across the Middle East to South Asia. Its general manager is Sheikh Tarek Swidan, a popular Kuwaiti motivational speaker who spent seventeen years in the United States.

"We are directing the channel to be in clash . . . with terrorist ideas," he said in 2006. "We are going head-to-head." [12]

The new airwaves are still a battlefield between the past and the future. In 2008, the head of Saudi Arabia's supreme judicial court, Sheikh Saleh al Lohaidan, issued a fatwa sanctioning the killing of anyone who produced or broadcast immoral programs on television. Reminiscent of Iran's 1989 fatwa against *Satanic Verses* author Salman Rushdie, the fatwa sparked an uproar. Al Lohaidan appeared on state television to clarify his ruling but only increased the controversy. He said anyone charged with indecent programming—what the Middle East press dubbed "celluloid crimes"—would, of course, be tried first.

King Abdullah sacked al Lohaidan as well as the head of the notorious Saudi religious police a few months later—at the same time he appointed the first woman to his cabinet. But the clash was far from over.

"The next decade will be a tussle between Shugairi and the Wahhabis. The clergy have a hold on the people and they don't want to let go," Khaled al Maeena, the Saudi editor of *Arab News,* told me. "But there's now a younger generation who are sick and tired of violence, and they don't want to be labeled terrorist and carry that collective guilt. They get very upset when they hear the term 'Muslim terrorists.' "

A decade after 9/11, al Shugairi seemed as intent on his television counter-jihad as the various al Qaeda franchises were on their militant jihad. "Today is our dark ages," he conceded. But Islam, he claimed, was still the best answer to extremism.

"I haven't come up with something new," he told me. "The message is the same as the prophets and philosophers, from Plato and Aristotle on. It's to live a balanced life. Do good. Respect others, including other religions. Perfect your work."

He laughed again. "I'm just packaging it in a way that young people can understand and accept."

9.

The Axis of Evil Comedy Tour

We're converting people, one laugh at a time.

—COMEDIAN DEAN OBEIDALLAH[1]

The counter-jihad can, literally, be quite funny.

Maz Jobrani is one of a new breed—the Muslim stand-up comedians—waging their own often quirky campaigns against extremism. They ridicule terrorists. "You know, one guy can really mess it up for the rest of us," the Iranian-born comic often laments onstage, shaking his shaved head as he paces the floor. "Look at the Christmas bomber, the guy who tried to blow up the Northwest flight from Amsterdam to Detroit, this Abu Abu Moustafa Boo Boo, or whatever his name is. I say this guy was crazy! Come on—any man would back me up.

"After all, *where* was the bomb?" Jobrani looks out, incredulously, at the audience. "Yeah, right, in his *un-der-wear*! I mean, really! Any *normal* man would surely question that instruction."

Switching to a Middle East accent, Jobrani assumes the role of a "normal" hijacker in a final discussion with his terror-masters. "Ah, excuse me. I have one, ah, one last question for you. You say my reward in heaven will be seventy-two virgins. So do you think, maybe, we could put the bomb somewhere else? I mean, I *really* think I'm going to need my penis."

The crowd roars.

Comedy is the most unusual tool in the cultural revolution sweeping the Islamic world. A decade after 9/11, an edgy blend of humor and mockery has become a popular means of rejecting extremism and reaching out to heal the cultural chasm with non-Muslims. Laughter is the new antidote to the militants' exhortations, from al Qaeda's jihadist rants to Iran's stern remonstrations against fun.[2]

Comedy as counterterrorism originated among American Muslims, whose identities and loyalties have been most challenged since 9/11. Hundreds of young Muslims—mainly from the latest generation of immigrants still transiting between their heritage and their new homeland—are now using comedic shtick as a weapon against militant ideologies, autocratic politics, and outdated social practices. They are also now taking comedy back to the region, teaching the candid voice of stand-up to help develop skepticism, sarcasm, and open questioning.

The two-way traffic is, in turn, helping to bridge the cultural divide.

Humor is hardly new to the Islamic world. The Prophet Mohammed is widely reputed to have enjoyed a playful story. He was supposedly a bit of a punster.[3] Islamic history is littered with celebrated humorists. Mullah Nasruddin was a thirteenth-century Sufi cleric whose humorous anecdotes, often followed by morals, are still told eight centuries later. From secular Egypt and Islamic Iran to religion-lite Indonesia, some of the cleverest, silliest, and most cynical humor comes from contemporary Muslim societies.

But extremism, particularly the 9/11 attacks, spawned a whole new genre of humor with a distinct agenda. "I make jokes about terrorists," Jobrani told me, "because comedy sneaks the bigger message across."

Jobrani was born in Iran in 1972 but moved to San Francisco shortly before the 1979 revolution. He still identifies with his ethnic roots. "I'm Perrrrsian," he likes to tell audiences. "And I keep telling people I'm not dangerous. I'm Perrrrrsian, like the cat. You know. Meowwww."

He looks the part too. His dark mustache is long and curves down around the sides of his mouth to join a tiny goatee that curls under his chin. Yet he also grew up very American. He loved performing, he told me, ever since he won the lead in an eighth-grade production of *Li'l Abner.*

When he was working on his doctorate in political science at the University of California, Los Angeles in the mid-1990s, Jobrani decided it was boring and gave it up to go back onstage. He got bit parts in movies—Jennifer Garner's *13 Going on 30, The Interpreter* with Sean Penn and Nicole Kidman, Kevin Costner's *Dragonfly,* and Ice Cube's *Friday after Next.* He did guest shots on television shows ranging from

The West Wing to *Malcolm in the Middle*, and including *24, NYPD Blue, ER, Curb Your Enthusiasm,* and *Law & Order.* In 2008, he played an Indian taxi driver, one of several misfits plotting to rob Mick Jagger, in Fox's short-lived *Knights of Prosperity.* But his first love had always been comedy.

In the late 1990s, Jobrani first banded with three other comedians as the Arabian Knights. But the 9/11 attacks gave the troupe new relevance—and urgency. They revamped their act of ethnic jokes and instead began ridiculing the pomposity of extremist ideologies and the foolishness of terrorists as well as the outside world's stereotypes of Muslims generally.

In 2005, they took their name from President George W. Bush's 2002 State of the Union address. They dubbed the show *The Axis of Evil Comedy Tour.* It was an instant hit. The first show sold out the 1,400-seat auditorium at George Washington University in Washington, DC, just a few blocks away from the White House. The four comics toured coast to coast for the next three years, then in Europe, the Middle East, and Australia. A Los Angeles production company taped the show to run on Comedy Central; Jobrani served as executive producer.

The Axis of Evil Comedy Tour was the first program with a purely Middle East cast ever to show on American television.

"It shows how suited comedy is to introducing a group that mass culture has stereotyped, literally, as walking time bombs," *Time* magazine said in its review. "Stand-up comedy is warfare by humorous means."[4]

The show is biting and brash. *Playboy* dubbed it the "shock and guffaw" tour. Each segment of the show begins with a comedian walking through a metal detector onstage, getting frisked and then grilled by a mock airport security guard, a Rubenesque African American woman. The sequence frames many of the initial jokes.

"Remember Jose Padilla?" Jobrani asks the audience, pacing the stage as he nurses the mike. Padilla was the Brooklyn-born Muslim convert convicted of conspiring to fund and support overseas terrorism. Although never charged, he was also suspected of plotting a radioactive "dirty bomb" attack.

"The biggest piece of incriminating evidence on Padilla," Jobrani continues, "was that his fingerprints were found on an application to go to an al Qaeda training camp. I never knew al Qaeda had applications! Can you just imagine what they ask—and the answers. Like, what are your goals?

" 'To blow myself up.'

"And what are your lifetime ambitions?

" 'To blow myself up.'

"Do you have any references?

" 'They blew themselves up.' "

Terrorism as inanity.

Jobrani usually does his show dressed in jeans, sneakers, a dark sports coat, and a tie—the latter a taboo in strictly Islamic and anti-Western Iran. Both sides of his dual identity are at the center of his routine. He digs at his American audience even as he ridicules Islamic extremists.

"Just because I'm from the Middle East, people who want to travel abroad often come to me and ask what I've heard."

" 'Heard where?' I ask.

" 'You know,' they say, 'on the street.'

" 'What street?' I ask. 'What are you talking about?'

" 'You know what I mean,' they say, as if just because I'm Muslim I'll know when the next terrorist hit is coming down."

"Besides, it's not always us," Jobrani tells his audience, then hesitates and shrugs. "Well, okay, quite often it is—but not *always*. There was a blackout in New York not too long ago. The TV newscaster warned that it might be a terrorist attack. 'Whoops, sorry,' he admitted later, 'it was just *Enron*.'

"And the other day there was a traffic jam on the Ninety-Five," he says. "Again, the news speculated about terrorism. 'Oops, no. It was just *cars*.'

"They even blamed the anthrax attacks on us at first. I *knew* it wasn't a Middle Easterner. That's not the way they work. A Middle Easterner would have been like"—Jobrani assumes the accent again—" 'What! All you want me to do is put anthrax in an envelope? And put a stamp on the envelope? And then simply mail it? No, no, no, no. That's *not* how I do it. Can't I wrap the anthrax around myself and run into somebody?' "

The new Muslim comics are now taking the same route used by other minorities. For decades, humor has been a tool to integrate and bridge cultural differences. Minority comedians making fun of themselves—and showing that their lives, loves, flaws, foibles, and mothers-in-law varied little from anyone else's—broke the ice for their racial, ethnic, or religious group generally. Humor humanized.

The Yiddish-accented parodies of Fanny Brice, the bawdy jokes of Lenny Bruce, and the political humor of Mort Sahl helped bring American Jews into the mainstream from the margins. The gentle prodding of Bill Cosby, the angry satire of Dick Gregory, and the confrontational humor of Richard Pryor helped African Americans move beyond the racial divide of segregation. By stepping forward, taking the mike, and sounding off in ways that engage and entertain, George Lopez has done the same for Latinos.

"For us," Jobrani explained, shortly after I'd seen the show, "the goal is not simply to make people laugh. It's also to have people, when they leave the show, go, 'Wow, that guy was funny, and he was Middle Eastern, and he didn't try to kidnap or hijack us.'

"That's why the Christmas Day bomber—he would have to pick Christmas Day, wouldn't he—was going against everything I'm trying to counter. It affected our whole community. Here I am trying to show that we're not all nutty," Jobrani said. "He's only one guy and there are so many of us, proportionately, who disagree profoundly with everything he did. But it just takes one or two to ruin everything for the rest of us."

A HMED AHMED, a burly Egyptian-born comic, is another member of the Axis of Evil Comedy Tour. His name is also on the FBI's Most Wanted list. "Twice!" he tells audiences. Ahmed has been detained in London and Montreal; he spent twelve hours in a Las Vegas jail on the eve of the 2004 presidential vote. Someone with the same name was a bin Laden cohort wanted for conspiracy to murder Americans and destroy U.S. defense facilities.

"Now I have to get to the airport *six weeks* before any flight," he jokes. "Getting through airport security is so tough, I now wear a G-string. Hey, it cuts the search time in half!"

The media has not helped. In 2006, the *New York Post* reviewed Ahmed's routine at a local comedy festival. The caption under his picture read, "Egyptian-born Ahmed Ahmed trying not to suicide bomb during his set."[5]

Ahmed still devotes his biggest jokes, however, to extremism and its envoys.

"There are so many terrorist organizations out there," he cracks, "how do you know which one is the best to join? Are there recruiters? I always picture these guys like standing outside a mosque recruiting little Muslim boys. '*Habibi* [Arabic for "dear"], come here, I want to talk to you. Don't go to al Qaeda. Come to Hamas. They only promise you seventy-two virgins. We'll give you seventy-two virgins—plus one whore and a goat!' "

Ahmed is sanguine about being a Muslim in the post-9/11 world. "We can't define who we are on a serious note, because nobody will listen," he told a PBS documentary. "So the only way to do it is to be funny about it." [6]

After 9/11, one of the biggest adjustments for Muslim comedians—and the broader community—was abruptly becoming "the other." Many had considered themselves a minority only in context of their nation of origin, such as Lebanese Americans or Iranian Americans. Suddenly, all Muslim immigrants in the United States—coming from dozens of different countries on diverse continents—were lumped together based purely on their faith.

"On September tenth, I went to bed and I was white," cracks Dean Obeidallah onstage in Axis of Evil. "But I woke up the next morning and, suddenly, I was Arab."

Obeidallah was actually born in the United States. There's no hint of Middle Eastern heritage in either his voice or his appearance. His short haircut looks like it's from a Middle American barber, and his clothes—pin-striped shirt, untucked over jeans—from the Gap. He roughly resembles the slightly nerdy chiropractor brother Alan Harper, played by Jon Cryer, on *Two and a Half Men*. His father is a Palestinian Muslim, his mother a Sicilian Catholic.

"I come from eastern Palestine," he tells audiences. "That's also known as New Jersey."

He jokes about his father's attempt to integrate. "My dad, he would go to church on Christmas and Easter to be part of my mother's family," Obeidallah recalls. "He took communion one time. When he came back, I asked him what he thought of communion, and he goes, 'It needs more salt.' "

Obeidallah worked for several years as a lawyer but quit—"It was extinguishing the spark in my soul"—to try entertainment.[7] He took a huge pay cut to become a page at NBC, making only ten dollars an hour. His first break was a job as a video researcher on *Saturday Night Live*, where he spent seven years before going out on his own.

After 9/11, however, Obeidallah felt his name made him conspicuous. It translates from Arabic as "little servant of Allah." So he started doing his routines as Dean Joseph, using his middle name instead. To end the sense of being under siege, Obeidallah joined with Jobrani and two others to launch the Axis of Evil Comedy Tour in 2005.

As with most of the new breed, Obeidallah's most poignant humor is about the struggle to be accepted and move beyond stereotypes.

"I really wish that a drug company in America would come out with a medication for us, like our own Paxil or Zoloft," Obeidallah tells the audience. "Like you could turn on the TV and it's 'Hello, are you depressed because no one wants to fly on the same plane with you? Are you anxious because you resemble several people on the government's Most Wanted list? Are you angry because every time you go to the airport, you're randomly selected for extra screening? Then you need Arab-be-gone! Just days later, your chest hair will begin to fall out. You'll stop using words like *habibi* and instead call everyone "pal." And it comes in flavors you'll love—like hummus!'"

Obeidallah often refers to the need to confront extremism, but he also uses humor to warn against hysteria.

"As a person of Middle East heritage, I think it's really important that we catch terrorists," he begins in a serious moment onstage. "But did you know that, under the Patriot Act, the government can get the name of any book you take out from the public library? Do they *really* think the guys from al Qaeda are going to public libraries to check out books?"

Adopting an accent, Obeidallah imagines the conversations of two terrorists.

"Okay, Omar," says terrorist one, "we've been planning this attack for years, but to pull it off we're missing the one thing we really need—a book. So your mission is to go to the library. And try not to look suspicious!"

Then, imagining Omar entering an American library, he continues as terrorist two: "Oh, hello, Miss Librarian. I'm looking for, ah, a book. Do you have anything on how to wage war against the infidel dogs? And can you please direct me to the holy war section?"

This one gets a big laugh too.

To reach a larger audience, Obeidallah occasionally pens op-ed pieces. He offered a tongue-in-cheek formula for peace in an op-ed for the *Huffington Post* after the announcement of indirect Middle East peace talks in 2010. Since Israel and the Palestinians could not agree on either a one-state or a two-state solution, he proposed a three-state solution: one state each for the Palestinians and Israelis who want to live in peace, and a third state for the people on both sides who want to keep on fighting. His piece envisioned producing a reality television show featuring the confrontations and clashes in the third state.

"Maybe," he wrote, "we can turn it into a pay-per-view special or even a reality show called 'Last Semite Standing.' By the way," he quickly added, "Arabs and Jews are both Semites." Through humor, he admonished both sides to take peace efforts more seriously.

To give other new Muslim comedians a shot onstage, Obeidallah co-founded the Arab-American Comedy Festival in New York with Palestinian comedienne Maysoon Zayid, who splits her time between the United States and the Middle East. It quickly became an annual event. By 2009, it featured fifty acts. The two of them then took six acts on tour in "Arabs Gone Wild." I saw one of the first shows in early 2010. Despite a blizzard that shut down most of Washington, DC, the show was sold out—and almost everyone showed up.

As a female, Zayid stands out in the show for her blunt, even bawdy humor. Born in 1976, she is a handsome woman with glamorous eyes and long brown hair parted down the middle. For that show, she wore it braided down the back. She makes no pretense of observing Islamic modesty, even though her father, a Palestinian refugee from the 1967 war, is a devout Muslim who performed the pilgrimage to Mecca. She was dressed in Western casual; in summer performances she's gone sleeveless, her arms fully exposed. She used to wear a green T-shirt with a revealing neckline that advertised her one-woman show *Little American Whore*.[8]

"I believe in Allah, I really do, but I'm very sparkly," she cracks, "so I want my Allah to be bling-bling." Her raunchy jokes cover everything from the hassles of menstruation to her father's resemblance to Saddam Hussein.

Trained as a classical actor, Zayid won small roles on *As the World Turns* and *Law & Order*. But she realized that her life would be limited to bit parts because she was born with cerebral palsy. So she switched to comedy.

"For those of you who don't know me, I'm a Palestinian Muslim virgin with cerebral palsy from New Jersey," she begins her routine, after wobbling onstage and resting on a tall stool.

Her routines center on her own limitations. During her early shows, she joked about the struggle to find a mate. "I'm really disappointed in you," she teased the Arab men in the audience. "I give you one year, just one more year, and if after that none of you bitches has put me away, then I'm going to marry an Israeli soldier!"

She was engaged when I saw her perform. "Yeah, I finally found a guy," she joked. "He was in Gaza. He had no way of getting away from me."

Female comedians may go the furthest in shattering stereotypes. Tissa Hami does her comedic shtick in full Islamic dress—black headscarf, formless black coat over her full figure, and black trousers underneath. The coat, however, stops above the knees. "To be honest," she notes at the top of her act, "I should be wearing a long coat, but I was feeling a little *slutty* today." The line is an instant icebreaker.

Born in Iran, reared in Boston, and now living in San Francisco, Hami is reverent about her faith. "I don't pray five times a day. During Ramadan I start out right, but halfway through I'm only skipping lunch," she told me, referring to the holy month of fasting from dawn to dusk. "I guess I'm the equivalent of a Christmas-Easter Christian. But culture and religion are also so intertwined in Iran that it's hard to know where one starts and the other ends. So I do identify as a Muslim."

As a comic, however, she is thoroughly irreverent. Onstage, her scarf covers all but her face, yet she jokes about the full array of Muslim traditions.

"I've noticed that Americans have a lot of misconceptions about Islam," she begins. "For example, in a mosque the men pray in the front and the women pray in the back. Americans look at that and they think, Oh, that's so sexist, those women are so oppressed, they have to go *behind* the men even just to pray.

"But we're not in the back because we're oppressed—we just like the *view*!" she says, beaming naughtily. "We're praying for a piece of that. Oh, *thank you*, Allah!"

When she started out as a comedian, Hami told me, her first joke was often followed by a moment of silence as audiences absorbed the different cultural context of her jokes. The seconds were anguishing. But when the laughter finally erupted, she knew she had bridged the gap.

"I understand that there are Muslim customs that Americans find strange," Hami continues onstage, with a knowing nod. "Like harems. Harems *are* strange. Because there's, like, one hundred women and only one man. But what's *really* strange is that this one man, he never stops to ask himself *why* a bunch of women would want to live together with only one man around. He's just there, typical guy, going, 'Yeah, yeah, I'm a stud, they *all* want me.'

"The thing is, only one type of Muslim women join harems—*lesbians!*" she jabs. "Check out what's going on in the other ninety-nine bedrooms, pal."

Born in a small town near the Caspian Sea in 1973, Hami had no intention of going into comedy even though she started cracking jokes in the eighth grade. After graduating from Brown University, she went into investment banking in Boston. But it did not hold her interest. The 2001 attacks on the World Trade Center and the Pentagon nudged her in a different direction.

"I don't think I would ever have gone into stand-up comedy if it hadn't been for 9/11," she told me. "It gave me a reason to finally get onstage and use my voice."

It took her a year to get up the nerve. She enrolled in a Boston adult education class on stand-up comedy. There were only six sessions; graduation was performing on the "sacrificing virgins" night for new comics in a local club.

"I had the idea of going onstage as a veiled woman and giving people the thing they least expected," she explained. Hami normally does not wear hejab. Offstage, her dark hair falls in large curls over her shoulders. "I was so determined to change the image that Americans had of Muslims, especially women," she said. "My life is not like that."

Many of the Muslim comedians actually talk about their career changes as a post-9/11 calling. What struck many of them one decade later was how many had the same idea.

"When I decided to do this after 9/11, I was at first just trying to survive onstage. But as I grew into it, I realized that other people were growing into this as well—poets, writers, and playwrights as well as comedians," Hami told me.

"It's interesting that all of us, in a kind of collective consciousness, came up with similar ideas at the same time."

I N THE POST-9/11 world, the bridge furthest built may be with the American Jewish community. Many Muslim comedians got their breaks through alliances with Jews in the entertainment industry. The genesis of the Axis of Evil Comedy Tour can be traced to Mitzi Shore, the Jewish founder of the Comedy Store in Los Angeles and mother of comedian Pauly Shore. Shore was famous for pulling together groups of comedians for a night of black, Jewish, or other ethnic humor. In the late 1990s, she recognized an appetite—and a need—to hear from emerging Muslim comedians. The Arabian Knights group was launched under her tutelage.

Obeidallah and his friend Max Brooks, son of Jewish comedian Mel Brooks, cocreated *The Watch List*, a series with an all-Muslim cast launched in 2007 on Comedy Central's Internet channel Motherload. "*The Watch List* for me is also important because, in a strange way, I feel like we're heading off potential terrorism at home," Brooks said in 2008.

"When you grow up in your home country that doesn't want you, of course you're going to turn to something radical," Brooks added. "The only way to head that off in this country is to embrace everyone, and give everyone as much a piece of the pie, and give everyone something to lose."[9]

The oddest couple of comedy, however, may be Rabbi Bob Alper and Azhar Usman. Alper is a white-haired reform rabbi from rural Vermont who, in a dapper sports coat, pin-striped shirt, and tortoise-shell glasses, looks like a preppy senior citizen.

"I'm the world's only practicing clergyman doing stand-up comedy— intentionally," he often begins his act. Alper became a part-time comedian in 1986 after coming in third in a Jewish Comic of the Year contest, behind a chiropractor and a lawyer. Being a rabbi, he told me, was a great warm-up. "It's all those years of performing in front of a hostile audience!"

Usman is a fullback-sized young Muslim of Indian descent with a bushy beard who occasionally leads Muslim prayers at a Chicago mosque. He often wears a Muslim prayer cap over his shoulder-length black hair, and he prefers sweatshirts to suits when he performs. Nicknamed "the ayatollah of comedy" and "Osama bin Laugh-in," Usman often opens his act before reticent crowds by telling them what it's like to board a plane.

"When people see me, they turn to each other and say, 'Oh, my God, I'm gonna die! Honey, I love you. He's soooo hairy! He smells like donut-kabob. And he keeps staring at me!' " Usman pauses and grins.

"Hey, can I be honest with you? I really don't understand what people are so scared of," he continues. "If I was a crazy Muslim fundamentalist terrorist about to hijack a plane, this is probably *not* the disguise I'd go with."

Together, Alper and Usman are the Laugh in Peace Comedy Tour. Their most frequent sponsors are synagogues and young Muslim groups.

Alper's publicist first suggested the combo after 9/11. "At first I said, 'What other ideas do you have?' " Alper told me. "The issue wasn't working with a Muslim comedian. It was just any comedian, because we tend to be neurotic." The publicist pressed anyway and found Ahmed Ahmed, the Egyptian American comic. The two comedians exchanged tapes.

"I still remember what I think of as a magical moment," Alper told me. "It was Valentine's Day, 2002. My wife was supposed to go to Dartmouth Hospital the next day for tests for a rather hideous form of cancer. We were anxiously counting the hours. So I told her about the tape, and we sat down to watch it. And here was this guy out of left field who made us laugh out loud. It offered such relief.

"I'm not a mystic at all, but I took it as a sign that this was a good thing. So I called him and said, 'Let's try it.' "

Their first show was at a synagogue in suburban Philadelphia. "Ahmed was sweating bullets," Alper recalled. Muslim colleagues had told Ahmed that he faced physical danger performing before a Jewish crowd so soon after 9/11. He was, instead, a hit.

"I can still see what happened afterwards, when twelve middle-aged Jewish mothers crowded around him trying to fix him up with their daughters," Alper told me, only partly in jest.

The two performed more than one hundred shows together, until Ahmed went off in 2005 to join the Axis of Evil tour and make movies. To replace him, Alper Googled "Muslim comedian" and came up with Usman, who had graduated from the University of Minnesota Law School. Usman had given up his legal practice after three years to try comedy.

For synagogue crowds, Usman likes to tell the audience he's more Jewish than any of them. "After all, I have the full beard," he says, pulling on the abundant facial hair that almost hits his chest. "And I keep *strictly* kosher," since Muslims and Jews share the same dietary prohibitions. "Plus"—he smiles broadly—"I'm a *lawyer*!" A videotape of their performance shows the Jewish crowd erupting in laughter, then applauding.

"He was no longer an alien," Alper said. "They saw him as friendly, even affable. It's a mind changer."

Usman also draws on their common bond in his routine. "I was in the UK recently," he told the synagogue crowds when George W. Bush was president. "It's a *totally* different vibe over there. It was actually kind of refreshing because in America I'm just so used to people hating me for being a Muslim. It was nice to finally be hated just for being an American."

The two comedians often cross cultures for each other—and occasionally into the Christian world as well. In 2008, "Rabbi Bob," as Alper is known, performed with Usman at a fund-raiser for an African American Muslim women's group held at the Episcopal Church of the Holy Apostles in New York City. The two performed a few weeks later on Christmas Eve at the Prince of Peace Lutheran Church in Schaumburg, Illinois, in an event jointly sponsored by a synagogue and a mosque. On the day we talked in 2010, Alper had just booked one gig at the University of Delaware through Hillel, and a second performance at George Washington University sponsored jointly by the Muslim Students Association, the Jewish Students Association, the Afghan Students Association, the Saudi Students Association, Students for Justice in Palestine, and the Arab Students Association.

Alper later wrote me in an email, "This event is part of Islam Awareness Week, and if, as a baby rabbi, anybody told me that at age sixty-five I'd be doing stand-up comedy, at a college, as part of Islam Awareness Week, I'd no doubt have referred them to my wife, a psychotherapist."

The two comics are not just colleagues. Their families have become friends, visiting each other and sharing meals. Still, they avoid the Arab-Israeli dispute in their routine. Neither uses profanity or sexual material either. And they close the G-rated show with a humorous quasi-sermonette on peace.

"We realize there are tensions between our peoples," says Alper, standing close to Usman.

Adds Usman, "We're not political scientists or pundits, but we have one idea that we think might work."

"We think," Alper interjects, "that there would be peace between us all if only we could all—"

And then the two shout together, "just learn Irish dancing!" And on cue, to a blast of Celtic music, the two launch into finely coordinated, Riverdance-style Irish step dancing.

"The dance," Alper told me later, "was the only hard part to do together."

THE NEW MUSLIM comedians' biggest impact, however, may be on Muslims themselves. Usman got his big break with *Allah Made Me Funny*, a trio of comedians who joined forces in 2004. Their show was modeled on *The Original Kings of Comedy*, the Spike Lee film that brought together black comedians Bernie Mac, D. L. Hughley, Steve Harvey, and Cedric the Entertainer.

The Allah Made Me Funny tour included Usman, Palestinian-born Mo Amer from Houston, and Preacher Moss, an American convert from Washington, DC. They performed more than fifty shows across the United States and Canada in the first year alone. In 2008, *Allah Made Me Funny* came out as a documentary following the comedians around as they wrote, anguished over, and performed their material. I went to the premiere in Washington.

The candid humor in *Allah Made Me Funny* plays off on the hassles and fears of life for Muslims after 9/11. Mo Amer, the Palestinian, re-counts the dilemma of watching his nine-year-old nephew run down the aisle during a trip to Walmart.

"Like, I can't shout after him or have him paged. I mean, look, his name is Osama," he tells the crowd. "Do you know how many people who go to Walmart also hunt? You know exactly what will happen if I call out *OSAMA!* I can just see Dick Cheney coming out of aisle six with his shotgun loaded."

But *Allah Made Me Funny* also goes deeper, holding a mirror up to Muslims and urging them to look back at themselves—and laugh. Usman admits he has gone through a change in his own life after flirting with a fundamentalist phase. "I was a purist, you know—religion shouldn't be mixed with culture, which is an absurdity," he told interviewers for a PBS documentary.

> Then when I heard that Muslims were responsible for 9/11, I felt that they have actually hijacked Islam itself . . . My view is that religion is something transcendent . . . It should make you a better moral, ethical human being. If religion fails to do that, then what good is it? [10]

At a meeting with his Chicago prayer congregation, the burly comedian once discussed what it was like to be "utterly Muslim and at the same time utterly American," utterly loyal to religious tenets from the seventh century and at the same time utterly engaged in a modern globalizing world. [11]

The conflicts are at the heart of *Allah Made Me Funny* in ways both playful and painful. It's comedy as therapy.

"What's wrong with us?" Usman says, shaking his head teasingly in front of a predominantly Muslim crowd. "We can never be on time, even though we speed all the time. We're the fastest drivers out there. So how can you speed everywhere but *always, always, always* be late for *everything*?" The joke produces a huge laugh. Anyone who has ever been in the Middle East particularly knows that the time Arabs live by bears almost no resemblance to the hands on the clock.

His jokes also confront religious pretenses in daily life. "This weird hypocrisy emerges among Muslim men and women—like when they're just in their normal lives, when they go to work and school, and it's pretty normal, right?" Usman continues. "When a guy's at work, you know, he says to his female colleague, 'Hey, what's going on, Jennifer? Hey, let's high-five! Come over here and give me a hug.'

"But then the same guy walks into a mosque, and he says to the woman, 'Get away from me, sister, get away, *get away*, you stupid!' "

The audience laughs again. Many women nod knowingly.

The diverse identities of the three comedians in *Allah Made Me Funny* are also at the heart of the show's more subtle message. The outside world tends to lump the world's 1.57 billion Muslims together—as the notorious "them"—but they are actually widely diverse and divided, even in the United States. Tensions among Muslims can be deeper than their tensions with the outside world.

American Muslims are fragmented by racism and an unspoken caste system, especially between blacks and South Asians. They also belong to different branches of the faith. The majority of Arab Americans are Sunnis, while the majority of Iranian Americans and some Pakistanis are Shiite. The rigid ideas of Salafi and Wahhabi Islam have made significant inroads in the black community, about one-third of American Muslims.

Differences are reflected in how the various communities came to the United States. The ancestors of many black Muslims arrived centuries ago as slaves, without choice or financial means. Most recent Arab, Persian, and South Asian immigrants gained entry because they had financial means, advanced professions, or powerful connections. Many blacks resent the superior airs of immigrant Muslims, some of whom seem to imply that the African American experience as Muslims is not valid. As a result, the diverse communities tend to live far apart, worship in separate mosques, and even avoid each other.

Allah Made Me Funny deliberately includes an African American, an Arab American, and an Indian American, the three largest Muslim blocs in the United States. "Clearly there is a problem, a major and deep-rooted problem of racism within the American Muslim community," Usman reflected. "People in that audience may have been living in that city for years, but they have never been in the same room."[12]

The trio of comedians have been trying to end the rancor among Muslims as well as ease the divide with non-Muslims.

A decade after 9/11, most of the Muslim comedians were sufficiently successful to tour in solo shows. Jobrani was on the road performing *Brown and Friendly*, a one-man show that premiered on Showtime in 2009. Ahmed Ahmed shot a new video, *Just Like Us: A Modern Generation Coming of Age*, that premiered at the 2010 TriBeCa Film Festival. Usman was the opening act for noted mainstream comedians like Dave Chapelle. Tissa Hami's one-woman show was called *Veiled Humor*. And Dean Obeidallah was touring with his one-man show *I Come in Peace*.

After the success of the Arab-American Comedy Festival, Obeidallah and Zayid decided to take their humor back to their homelands. The Middle East has a long history of comedic theater, but stand-up has been largely a Western art form. To introduce comedy as a tool of sociopolitical change, they launched the Arab Comedy Festival in Jordan in 2008. It's now an annual event.

"When I started, no one in the audience knew what I was doing," Zayid told me. Her stand-up soon became widely popular, especially as her routine focused on the political challenges in the Islamic world.

"I do jokes about the Palestinian Authority being criminal and Hamas being the worst thing that happened to us," the young Palestinian American said. "These are the things they need to talk about. And in many of these places, comedy is the best—or only—way to do it."

The two comics also started workshops for aspiring comedians in Jordan. "At the first one, we had to teach them the basics, like a one-liner, and how to get a joke to work onstage," she said. The classes became sufficiently popular that other workshops followed in Cairo, Doha, Amman, Beirut, and Ramallah. YouTube helped, as a means both to watch other comics perform and to give new Middle Eastern comedians exposure.

The Middle East now has an up-and-coming cadre of comedians. They perform regular shows in Jordan, and a club in Egypt holds open-mike nights once a week. In 2009, Jordanian Stand-up Comedians launched their own page on Facebook "to show the world Jordanian people laugh all the time and get that stereotype out of the way!" Within days, more than seven hundred people signed up.

Muslim comedy has even crossed the toughest threshold. In 2010, Obeidallah mobilized young Saudi comedians to perform with the Arabs Gone Wild crew in the desert kingdom, the birthplace of Islam and the most intolerant Muslim society. One of the budding Saudi stars is Fahad Albutairi, who calls himself the Jerry Seinfeld of Saudi Arabia. He tells jokes about the inanities of local life—like Saudis who go grocery shopping by parking their cars outside stores and honking for food to be delivered or Saudis who work out on expensive treadmills as they puff away on cigarettes.[13]

Under the cover of laughter, comedy created new space for candor and self-criticism—and even political challenges. "Comedy in the Middle East," Zayid reflected, "is just as much about giving people a voice as giving the audience a laugh."

* * *

THE 99 ARE a collection of merry young Muslims who combat evil across the globe. Each comes from a different country. Each has a different power to generate good in a violent world. And each reflects one of God's ninety-nine virtues, from wisdom and love to generosity.

And all ninety-nine are comic book superheroes.

A decade after 9/11, The 99 have become alternative role models to al Qaeda's killers. The characters are all anti-jihadis. The themes are all about nonviolence. And their do-good adventures are the fastest-selling comic books from Morocco to Indonesia.

The 99 superheroes include Jabbar the Powerful, an Arab version of the Incredible Hulk. The towering man-mountain weighs more than four hundred pounds; as he struts, muscles bulge across an outsized chest and arms. His touch can shatter a brick wall; his sneeze can level a building. The young Saudi uses his physical powers to thwart evil.

Widad the Loving is a glamorous young Muslim with flowing black locks and sultry hazel eyes. She delivers humanitarian supplies to danger zones. Born in the teeming Philippines, she has the power to induce compassion and happiness in others.

Bari the Healer has miraculous powers to diagnose and heal wounds, mend broken bones, even treat a plague. Of Muslim Indian descent, he grew up on a struggling South African farm, where he learned to tap into other people's energy to help them heal.

Noora the Light has the power to manipulate the sun's rays to help people see the truth. Born to a wealthy family in glitzy Dubai, the pretty Arab teenager discovered her powers after being kidnapped and held hostage in a deep hole.

The comic books even include an American. Darr the Afflicter is a young blond Muslim from St. Louis. He's been confined to a wheelchair since a drunk driver hit his car, killing the rest of his family and leaving him paralyzed from the waist down. He has the ability to punish villains by making them feel the pain they inflict on others.

Islam's new superheroes are the brainchild of Kuwaiti psychologist Naif al Mutawa, who is also the father of five young sons. In the age of al Qaeda, he wanted to fill a void. The region has the world's youngest population but limited literature that is both contemporary and Islamic.

"The 99 is part of a fundamental effort to expand and refine the ways in which jihad can be performed," he said, when we met for lunch in palm-fringed Kuwait City. "It's about not letting a certain minority force their definition on everyone else. That version of jihad is now valueless."

Mutawa and Osama bin Laden had similar roots in Kuwait and Saudi Arabia, both conservative Gulf sheikhdoms. Both boys were shy, self-conscious, and often reclusive growing up. Bin Laden was the only child of his father's tenth wife; they divorced when he was young and his mother remarried. Bin Laden was something of an outsider in both halves of his family. Mutawa was a pudgy child, deeply insecure about his weight, an issue that still bothered him decades later.

Both men had fathers with modest backgrounds who made fortunes after oil prices soared in 1973. Bin Laden's father came from Yemen, the poorest Gulf country; he made billions from construction in Saudi Arabia. Mutawa's father had been in the Kuwaiti police; after the oil boom, he went into business and investments.

Both fathers wanted their boys to get modern educations. Bin Laden attended Al Thagher, a comparatively secular school in cosmopolitan Jeddah where boys wore charcoal blazers, button-down shirts, and ties instead of the traditional white *thobe*. The school taught sciences as well as religious tenets. English-language classes were taught by British and Irish instructors.[14] Mutawa went to Bayan in Kuwait City, also a private bilingual school where students wore Western dress. At Bayan, he developed a taste for children's literature from the West. He particularly liked the Hardy Boys and Nancy Drew mysteries.

Both bin Laden and Mutawa were exposed to Western ideas; both traveled abroad. In a family that toured the world and had its own plane, the young bin Laden reportedly went to London, on a big-game safari in East Africa, and even made a brief trip to the United States.[15] Like many Kuwaiti families, Mutawa's parents sent their young son out of the desert during the searing summers. He went to Camp Robin Hood—located in Sherwood Forest, no less—in New Hampshire.

"This is the camp where I picked up my first comic book in 1979," Mutawa told me. Thirty years later, he still remembered reading about Casper the good ghost and Richie Rich, the charitable rich kid.

Both bin Laden and Mutawa also went on to prominent universities where they studied the same subjects—the sciences and business administration. Both considered themselves devout Muslims who prayed regularly and fasted during the holy month of Ramadan. Both wore the flowing *ghutra* headdress and white-cotton *thobe* common in the conservative Arabian Peninsula. Faith defined their vision and goals.

Yet, when both were in their twenties, similar circumstances produced vastly different understandings of Islam and distinctly different practices of jihad. Bin Laden went to South Asia, became engrossed in the Mujahadeen campaign against the Soviet Union, and used his wealth to support foreign fighters in Afghanistan. The experience produced the seeds of what grew into al Qaeda and a generation of global jihadis.

Mutawa went to the United States to study clinical psychology. In New York, he worked with survivors of political torture at Bellevue Hospital. When he returned home, he worked with Iraqi prisoners of war. "That's when I decided," he said, "that I needed to create a different idea of a hero."

He turned to his early love of children's literature as a medium. His first attempt was a kids' book about Bouncyland, where all the characters are round and all are judged by how high they can bounce and how far they can roll. His protagonist was Bouncy Junior, who was born a half-circle and scorned for his inability to bounce at all. He had other less appreciated talents, however, that end up helping save society.

To Bounce or Not to Bounce won a 1997 United Nations award for children's literature tackling intolerance.

The Kuwaiti psychologist wrote two other children's books set in fictional worlds with other forms of social injustice. *What's in a Color?* takes place in Rainbowland, where society is divided into colors. The reds are superior to the oranges, which are in turn superior to the yellows, which are better than the blues, and on down the color spectrum. At the bottom, the violets are the untouchables. Crossing the color divide is forbidden. Intermarriage between reds and blues, for example, is banned. The young protagonist helps to literally turn things around when he shows inhabitants the rainbow's colors reflected in a lake—where their order is inverted. Violets are suddenly on top.

The third book, *Get Your Ties Out of Your Eyes,* takes place in the island nation of Tieland, where all sons must wear the ties handed down through many generations of men, even when the ties are outdated, don't fit, or are too ragged to tie well. Anyone who dares to remove his tie is banished. Writing it on the day his first son was born, Mutawa wanted to address adapting ways of the past to the present. Bouncy eventually convinces tailors to make new ties for all the Tielanders.

Get Your Ties Out of Your Eyes was the most innocent of Mutawa's three books. But it was also the first one banned in Saudi Arabia.

"The book spoke about the need to reconcile tradition with modernity," Mutawa explained. "But the censors felt that I was advocating a reinterpretation of Islam's holy texts."

Few ideas are more contentious in Saudi Arabia, guardian of Islam's holiest sites and home to Islam's most rigid practices. With the kingdom's wealth and power, any ban can kill a project. So, discouraged, the Kuwaiti psychologist stopped writing and went back to medicine.

In 2003, five years later, Mutawa's sister prodded him to write again. "With all the degrees I had earned, I told her that any idea would have to have the potential impact of a Pokémon to be worth my time," he recalled. "Then I began thinking about what the religious authorities might have against Pokémon," the Japanese cartoon that had also been banned in Saudi Arabia.

"Then I thought, my God, what has happened to Muslims?" he said. "What has happened to the tolerance from the times of the great libraries in Baghdad and Alexandria and the times of great knowledge and discoveries in science, medicine, and architecture in the Islamic world?

"I thought how disappointed Allah must be. And I thought how ridiculous [is this state of affairs], especially since one of God's ninety-nine attributes is tolerance," he told me. "So that took me from the idea of creating a lead character as captivating as Pokémon to a new idea for The 99 superheroes and -heroines, each of which would be distinguished by one of God's attributes."

The 99's central storyline draws on history to create twenty-first-century adventures. Under the Islamic Empire, the greatest repository of knowledge was the House of Wisdom, or Dar al Hikma, in Baghdad. It was destroyed during the Mongol invasion in the thirteenth century. The Mongols threw the library's books—at that time all handwritten—into the Tigris River. The ink temporarily turned the great river black. The Mongol invasion marked the end of Islam's golden age of great literature, scientific discoveries, innovative architecture, and rich arts.

Then the comic book fiction begins. To preserve the library's knowledge from oblivion, Mutawa's storyline has the fictional Guardians of Wisdom dropping ninety-nine stones in the Tigris to absorb the knowledge of the discarded books. The "stones of enlightenment" were then scattered by the winds. Eight centuries later, The 99 superheroes are each separately empowered by acquiring one of the stones. In each issue, The 99 solve a crisis using their new special powers.

The comic's subplot is that The 99 must keep the stones away from Rughal, their common nemesis. Rughal schemes and manipulates to amass all ninety-nine stones for himself so he will have invincible power over all mankind. Rughal is the symbolic equivalent of Osama bin Laden, a destructive force willing to use any form of violence.

"Rughal wants to play God. And that's what people like bin Laden have done," Mutawa told me.

"The central no-no in Islam is *shirq*, which is claiming to be a partner of God or speaking for God," he explained. "These are people who end up telling you what is right and wrong, and what is kosher. They effectively claim they have all the attributes of God. And they believe there is only one truth—theirs. This is something strictly forbidden in Islam.

"I don't define the message as specifically anti–bin Laden," he added. "I chose not to fight that fight. That's a zero-sum game. I decided instead to create an alternative universe. But I do have a message that's different from his. My message is that there's more than one truth, and no one person can dictate belief."

The idea of imbuing comic book characters with religious values is not new. Most comic superheroes are openly or implicitly based on religious archetypes, from Baptists to Buddhists, Jews to Jains, Shintos and Scientologists to Sikhs, according to a study of over 20,000 comic book characters. It deduced that Superman was a Methodist, Batman an Episcopalian, the Hulk a lapsed Catholic, and Spider-Man and Captain America unspecified Protestants.[16]

"When Superman's father sends him to Earth, he says, 'I have sent to you my only son.' That's Jesus from the Bible," Mutawa explained.

The 99 have implied links to religious values, but like Western superheroes, they never declare or proselytize their creed. None of the storylines mention God, or Allah. "I used an Islamic archetype, but no one is praying," Mutawa said. "Nobody is reading the Koran.

"I want The 99 to serve the one-quarter of the world's population that subscribes to Islamic beliefs. But the characters intentionally transcend all language and cultural barriers. I told the writers that The 99 will only be successful if Jews think the characters are Jewish, Christians think The 99 are Christian, and Hindus think they're Hindu," he added. "The

99 are based on values that we all share—generosity, strength, wisdom, and mercy."

Before creating his characters, Mutawa studied Western superheroes with the intensity of a doctoral candidate. Most were initially orphaned or poor or confronted overwhelming challenges, he discovered. As they grew up, they gradually recognized their unusual powers—and the great responsibility that came with them. Superman's parents dispatched their newborn into space moments before the dying planet Krypton exploded. As reporter Clark Kent, Superman was a bumbler; the Man of Steel emerged when called upon to face a crisis. As a child, Bruce Wayne saw his father and mother gunned down in front of him; the industrialist playboy became Batman, the Caped Crusader, when summoned to combat sensational crimes. The orphaned Peter Parker was reared by his aunt and uncle; he was transformed from lonely nerd to Spider-Man when evil threatened society.

So too Mutawa's ninety-nine superheroes emerged from poverty, illness, obscurity, or other adversities to help conquer evil—sometimes with unique twists that shatter stereotypes in the Islamic world.

The 99 superheroes include Mumbita the Destroyer, a runaway teen who lived a hard life on the streets, traveled as a stowaway, and learned to fight to survive. Mumbita was briefly a "bone-breaker" in an illegal fight competition before acquiring one of the ninety-nine gemstones, which allowed the young Portuguese Moor to use martial arts skills such as agility, speed, strength, and fast reflexes to save others. Mumbita is especially unusual because the character is female.

Half of The 99 are female. Reflecting the diversity within Islam, some wear Islamic dress, while others look more like glamorous Batwoman.

The 99 are the first characters in comics to portray Muslims as heroes rather than villains. Since the advent of DC Comics' Superman in 1938, the vast majority of Muslim characters have been men like Abdul the Thief and assorted other sorcerers, pirates, evil sheikhs, or more recently, extremists. Captain America's nemesis was Faysal al Tariq, an Iraqi terrorist. The Black Knight faced threats from the Arabian Wizard, while Team America had to thwart Achmed the Egyptian. Even Aladdin's genie, who first appeared in Marvel's Black Panther comics in 1977, is portrayed as a thief.[17] Most reflect stereotypes from the Middle Ages rather than modern times.

The 99, in contrast, have a distinctly global, twenty-first-century feel.

Sami the Listener was born in Sudan but he grew up in France. Hadya the Guide is of Pakistani descent but lives in London. Musawwira the Organizer was born in Ghana, but she moved to the United States. Their identities address issues of diversity and plurality, tolerance and commonality that are now at the heart of Islam's internal stirrings.

The characters are too groundbreaking for some Muslim countries. Saudi Arabia initially banned, then unbanned, then rebanned the comic books for appearing to mock Islam—by personifying God, interpreting Allah's virtues, and depicting his attributes in the form of young women with flowing locks uncovered. In Saudi Arabia, many women still wear up to four layers of veils to cover their faces. Most schools and workplaces are segregated by gender, while men and women are not supposed to touch each other unless related by blood or marriage. Although The 99 are fictional, the heroic operations by male and female superheroes together cross many red lines. To accommodate conservative traditions, The 99 characters always team up—in groups of at least three—so an unrelated male and female are not working together alone.

Mutawa has otherwise refused to surrender to conservatives. In 2008, The 99 was the centerpiece of a university course in Kuwait on "The Superhero in the Arab World." The students' final coursework included creation of their own superheroes. During a guest lecture, Mutawa was challenged by a female student who expressed astonishment that his heroines were shown going off to pray without veils.

"Do you think only people who wear the hejab ask God for help?" Mutawa replied.[18]

"Osama bin Laden's message was that there's only one way to be a Muslim," he later told me when we met in Kuwait City on an old dhow that had been converted into a restaurant. "My goal is to teach children that there are ninety-nine ways to solve a problem. And there are also at least ninety-nine ways to be Muslim."

For all the obstacles, his Muslim superheroes have sold plenty of comic books. By 2010, more than three million copies had been distributed in eight languages, including Arabic, English, Turkish, Bahasa Indonesian, and Chinese, with licensing rights sold in seven other languages. Mutawa also found backers to build six new Disneylike parks, with The 99 characters as centerpieces, in the Middle East. The first one opened in Kuwait in 2009. Mutawa then inked a deal to put The 99 into animation for children's cartoons.

In a joint venture, Matawa worked out a deal with DC Comics, the American publishing giant, for six special crossover issues in 2010. The storylines had The 99 superheroes fighting evil alongside Superman and Batman. Crossovers are virtually unprecedented in the intensely competitive world of superheroes.[19]

Even the White House took note. In April 2010, President Obama invited Muslim innovators to Washington. He singled out Mutawa in his opening address as "the most innovative" person in the crowd. "His comic books have captured the imagination of so many young people with superheroes who embody the teachings and tolerance of Islam," Obama said. "In his comic books, Superman and Batman reached out to their Muslim counterparts."

Then with a wry chuckle, Obama added, "And I hear they are making progress."

A decade after 9/11, Mutawa ran an entertainment empire that bridged East and West. His staff included a former *Rolling Stone* publisher, a writer for the Power Rangers and X-Men series, and Marvel Comics' former marketing chief. Many of the artists came from the West and knew nothing about Islam. One of his coproducers was a Hindu from India, the other a British Christian. Forbes named The 99 one of the world's top twenty new trends.[20]

"I'm trying to help take back Islam from the extremists," Mutawa told me under a warm Kuwaiti sun. "We need to move on."

Jihad Jones and the Kalashnikov Babes

The main arena for jihad today is culture, not combat.

—Playwright Yussef El Guindi[1]

For most Muslims today, the real jihad is simply rescuing the moral struggle at the heart of the faith from extremists. A new generation of Muslim playwrights and filmmakers is turning it into an art form. Using stage and screen, they have created a new counter-jihad culture that bridges East and West.

Yussef El Guindi—which rhymes with "windy"—is an Egyptian-born playwright out to prove that the pen is mightier than the suicide bomb. "After the comedians come the playwrights," he told me with a chuckle. El Guindi is a slightly stocky man with black hair cropped stubble-short. He has a neat mustache-goatee that surrounds his mouth, and a mole at the top of his right cheek. He has an impish sense of humor. *Jihad Jones and the Kalashnikov Babes* is his best-known work. I read the script in the quiet car of an Amtrak train. I laughed so often and so loudly that other passengers darted dirty looks at me. The play is both poignant and hilarious. I ached, in many ways, at the end.

Jihad literally means "to strive in the path of God's goodness." It is primarily about the inner personal struggle to be a decent human being; it is not supposed to be about acts of angry revenge or war against non-believers, except in self-defense. Muslims name their children Jihad with the same reverence that Spanish-speaking Catholics name their children Jesus.

The new theater of counter-jihad is trying to restore the original meaning. In the process, the new genre takes audiences deep into the hearts and minds of Muslim life.

El Guindi's *Jihad Jones and the Kalashnikov Babes* is a dark comedy about Ashraf, a talented young Egyptian-born actor fresh off rave reviews in a local theater version of *Hamlet*. The pay was too paltry to cover the bills, so he is looking for a break when his agent lands him a starring role in a blockbuster action film. The director is his idol. The female costar is a Hollywood bombshell famous for falling in love with her leading men. And he would be paid big bucks.

The only glitch is that Ashraf's part is a lecherous, bath-deprived terrorist who takes an American family hostage on Thanksgiving, pisses on their family photos, dangles their four-year-old toddler out the window, rifle-butts the mother, threatens to rape the eighteen-year-old daughter, considers buggering the seventeen-year-old son, snaps the grandmother's neck, then sticks his hand inside the Thanksgiving turkey, scoops out all the dressing, and throws it on the floor.

In one exchange with the nubile daughter, the character leers, "Allah be praised. You have great tits. They are like dates. They remind me of home."

During a script reading with the director, Ashraf stops at that line to protest.

"Another fruit then instead of dates?" the oblivious director responds. "Oranges perhaps?"

Ashraf insists that he would rather not take the role than prostitute himself for a paycheck. "This is bad English, wrapped around bad writing, wrapped around a hideous plot filled with enough cheese to put me off dairy for the rest of my life," he wails.

His agent tries to encourage him because of the million-dollar paycheck. "Do you realize the worst film of last year was seen by more people worldwide than the absolute best play ever staged in the past five hundred years?" interjects the agent, anxious for his own cut.

Ashraf reluctantly agrees to a reading with the starlet. But the script only gets more offensive. At one point, his terrorist character says to her, "I am big for women too. Want to see how big?"

Ashraf stops again. He begs the director not to make the film. "There are enough stereotypes here to create a whole new cartoon network," he says. "It blows a hole in the minds of the audience until they actually think this garbage is true—that people of my ethnic persuasion are naturally violent and prone to blow up at the slightest thing, that we're vicious and a menace to decent people everywhere. Why punish everyone for the few assholes?"

As he pleads, Ashraf waves the gun he was using as a prop around the room for emphasis. The director, starlet, and agent all scramble for cover. They assume he intends to turn the prop gun on them.

"Jesus God, we're hostages!" his own agent shouts.

Ashraf clearly rejects extremism as much as the American director. But with a prop gun in his hand, nothing he says will convince them that he is not a real version of the character in the script.

"Why isn't my dream director asking me to do a romantic comedy?" he laments. "You know—a visiting Arab dignitary discovers the joys of windsurfing when he visits Hawaii and falls for the scuba-diving instructor. And then has to persuade his parents that a life on the beach won't undermine his religious obligations. Or how about an action sci-fi where a muscled Arab in a Marine uniform fights off a horde of creepy aliens who've come to suck our bone marrow because that's like oil in their world. And there's a showdown in the mosque where he uses the minaret to spear their leader's spaceship."

Jihad Jones and the Kalashnikov Babes—which performed sold-out shows in San Francisco, Philadelphia, Seattle, New Orleans, and Dallas— was Yussef El Guindi's response to 9/11. He was an aspiring playwright with new American citizenship when al Qaeda destroyed the World Trade Center and struck the Pentagon. He was initially stunned into silence because of fear about his own history. Mohamed Atta, the hijacker pilot who flew American Airlines Flight 11 into the first World Trade Center tower, was also Egyptian. Both men were born in the 1960s. Both grew up in upper-middle-class families; both came from Cairo. Both men were Western-educated. Both were Arabs. And both were Sunni Muslims.

El Guindi withdrew because of public hysteria about Islam, followed by passage of the Patriot Act and a disproportionate number of airport searches when he traveled.

"Suddenly you weren't sure what your rights were," he told me. "You heard stories of people being stopped for books they were reading at airports or the FBI going to galleries and questioning artists. I worried about what I might have in my apartment if an FBI agent showed up, because I have a Koran, books on Islam, and research materials on assassins and guns. In my paranoia, I imagined all kinds of things that might happen."

Fear turned to alienation as he watched the widespread portrayal of Muslims as extremists in the news media, television, and movies.

"Negative portrayals have gone on a long time. And tensions between Islam and the West go back to the Crusades. But what happened after 9/11 shook me," he said. "I was really proud when I became an American. I thought I had permanently become part of this country's history. But without being aware at first, I was being unplugged from the country I had adopted as my own."

The welling anger—at extremism and, then in reaction, at Western perceptions of Islam—eventually prodded El Guindi to start writing again. Over the next eight years, he crafted a series of hauntingly provocative plays from a base in Seattle. He has been heavily influenced by George Bernard Shaw, whom he reveres for wit and theatricality in tackling serious subjects.

El Guindi is drawn to absurdist comedy, he told me during one of several discussions as I read the trilogy of plays that launched his career. "Fear for me elicits a nervous laughter—laughter then being a way of tackling that fear. Taming it. Turning it from this thing that might swallow you whole into a more manageable force," he explained.

"Humor becomes the element most needed to clear the air and balance things out," he added. "Besides, one has to laugh sometimes just to get through it all!"

Back of the Throat is another in the trilogy. It is a one-act play about Khaled, a mild-mannered Arab American writer. He is visited by two FBI agents tracking suspects after a terrorist attack in the United States. Khaled welcomes them and says he had actually thought about offering his services after the attack, but he hesitated because his rusty Arabic might not be good enough for the agency's needs.

The title comes from Khaled's efforts throughout the play to get the agents to pronounce his name correctly—*Kha*-led, not Haa-led or Kay-lid. The guttural sound of Arabic words comes from the "back of the throat." The FBI agents' failure to ever get it right symbolizes the American failure to understand either the individual or his cultural roots. The abyss only deepens as the play unfolds.

The FBI agents begin noting items in his small apartment. One agent asks Khaled to translate a word on a picture frame.

"A present from my mother," he responds. "It says, er, God." Then he hastily adds, "I'm not religious myself."

The agent picks up a book in Arabic. "It's, um, the Koran," Khaled says. "Another present from my mother. Her idea of a subtle hint."

The agents ask Khaled how to sum up the Koran's message in a couple of lines. "Er, the usual," he says, "Be good. Or else." The agent says it sounds like good advice and asks, then, why Khaled is not religious.

"I was never comfortable with the 'or else' part," Khaled responds. "I'd like to think God isn't as small-minded as we are."

The probing becomes Kafkaesque as the FBI visit turns into an interrogation covering everything from Khaled's library visits and sexual habits to his chance encounters with other Muslims. Based on his books—all from major American publishers—one agent concludes that Khaled must be "a left-leaning subversive with Maoist tendencies who has a thing for bestiality and militant Islam. Throw in your research on guns and assassins and I could have you inside a jail cell reading about yourself on the front page of every newspaper before the week is out."

Khaled tries to convince the FBI that he is innocent—of what, he is not even sure. But happenstance—often so ridiculous it is funny—condemns Khaled to guilt by suspicious association.

The often chilling performance is infused with a stream of comedic twists. After intensive questioning, one of the FBI agents asks Khaled to fill out a questionnaire evaluating the agents' performance as interrogators.

"We're trying to get direct feedback from the public," the agent explains, "especially from our target audience."

Back of the Throat—which opened in 2005 and has since been performed in New York, London, San Francisco, Chicago, Seattle, San Diego, St. Louis, and several smaller cities—was nominated for an American Theatre Critics Association New Play award.

In each play, El Guindi also evolves through his characters, who take progressively bolder positions. In *Back of the Throat*, the protagonist is nervous and defensive, a victim. He lives on the margins. He allows the outside world's perceptions of his religion and ethnicity to determine his fate.

In *Jihad Jones*, the protagonist is assertive, challenges conventional wisdom, and tries to navigate a normal place in society in a mainstream career. His faith is private and irrelevant to his public life—except to others who fail to see that he stands against extremism even more than they do.

"Creating plays becomes a political act," El Guindi told me, "as you're stepping out from the political shadows and for the first time presenting your humanity in three dimensions. In the past, you'd get an Arab voice but it'd be from one of two extremes—a conservative or a radical—who didn't represent the majority.

"The struggle of my life, my jihad," he said, "is to write and have my voice and the others like mine heard to counter the negative narratives."

His third play is *Ten Acrobats in an Amazing Leap of Faith*. It is a rich dramedy about the Fawzis, an immigrant family who try to balance the American dream with adherence to their Islamic faith. Each character also represents a different challenge in the personal jihad to be a true and decent Muslim. Each confronts an issue pitting traditional values against twenty-first-century mores, pitting rigid religious laws against flexible secular freedoms, to determine what is *halal* (allowed) and what is *haram* (forbidden) in a Muslim's life.

The play explores three of the most controversial issues for Muslims in the twenty-first century—women's rights, sexuality, and the loss of belief itself. The dramatic dilemmas—each filled with comedic twists—play out in the struggles of the Fawzis' three children, all young adults.

Huwaida is the college-educated daughter who voluntarily donned conservative hejab yet has a recurring dream about appearing in the Miss America bathing suit competition. In the dream, she wears a bathing suit revealing every bodily curve but also a scarf covering every hair on her head. In the pageant's interview portion, she dreams about commenting,

It's time we Muslims stepped out into the light and made a big splash. For too long we have let others misrepresent us, mock our ways and call us everything under the sun. Well, I say, enough of that. We're here. We're proud. And by golly we can kick ass along with the best of them! . . . And to all my Muslim brothers, I say *assalam alaykum* (peace be upon you), and please hold off on your objections until after you see me in the talent competition.

After detailing her dream to a therapist, Huwaida confesses, "I'm mortified. But a part of me also takes note of, wow, I'm not bad. That diet really worked."

Tawfiq is the son who struggles with his faith in an era of reason and science. He argues that God is all merciful and compassionate only as long as a believer plays by God's rules. "After that, it's burn, baby, burn," he laments. "I'd rather live without God and have some compassion than have God and use him to punish anything I don't like."

Tawfiq says he stopped believing "when I did what God commands all of us to do: to open our eyes and look around us. Investigate, question. I took those commands very seriously. I questioned, I looked. Unfortunately, I questioned him right out of the equation."

Hamza, the third child, is a college student and musician who faces his first homosexual temptation during a chance encounter with another student. "Muslims don't do this," he tells Kevin, a Catholic law student, as he initially resists.

"What, you think God's straight?" Kevin counters. "Isn't that just as dumb as thinking God is gay? I don't think he gives a damn. I don't think he has sex. I don't think he's as sex-obsessed as the people who speak on his behalf are." The two students are later caught by police having sex in the bushes.

The children's parents reflect the rival approaches to personal struggles in the twenty-first century. The family matriarch reacts to her children's challenges with common sense. "I just hope he used a condom," she muses about her gay son. She has created a practical space that embraces both sacred religion and human reality.

But the family patriarch treats each of his children's struggles as a shameful scandal. He has no tolerance for freedom of choice or deviations from a single long-standing tradition. Freedom compromises religion, he insists.

"Your thinking offers nothing but chaos to do anything you want," he admonishes the son who questions his faith. "No family could survive for a day with your ideas. There is a reason this book [the Koran] and our beliefs have lasted through wars, famine—and even America."

The generational rift mirrors the divide in contemporary Islam. For both generations, the central personal struggle—or jihad—is navigating what is arguably the most complex social minefield since the faith was founded in the seventh century.

Extremists and fundamentalists—from al Qaeda's Sunni ideologues to Iran's Shiite theocrats—contend that Muslim life is dictated by one unwavering truth fourteen centuries after the faith was revealed. Attempts to adapt it to different times and conditions are *haram*—forbidden and punishable. But reformers and a growing number of young Muslims now reject authoritarian versions of their faith.

In the third play of his trilogy, El Guindi evolves beyond the pitfalls in relations between Muslims and non-Muslims—the issues that have defined much of the decade since 9/11. He instead invites non-Muslims deep inside the anguishing trials and traumas of contemporary Muslim life—what jihad really means to the ordinary Muslim. It is the ultimate response to 9/11.

Culture, El Guindi told me, is the public forum most accessible for Muslims who abhor violence to declare themselves—and be taken seriously. It is also the best place for public therapy.

"Culture is a creative place for dialogue, a meeting place to exchange ideas, a public square, like Hyde Park Corner, to get up on a box and speak," he said. "Muslim participation in culture worldwide has been lacking.

"The struggle for us now is to step up and voice up—to say we are like you," he added. "We are part of the same thing you are."

The theater of counter-jihad has even turned to romantic comedies to redefine jihad. The new generation of playwrights is using slapstick farce to disparage—and parody—religious fanaticism.

Til Jihad Do Us Part was written by Shai Hussain, a Muslim of Indian descent who lives in London. The story centers on a young couple looking for love. Meena is a Muslim version of Bridget Jones with a love life full of romantic flops and lying boyfriends. Sarwar claims to be a chef, but he is really a senior Indian spy on the run from the forty-second-most-dangerous terrorist group in the world. The young couple is paired in an arranged marriage that gets caught up—beginning at the wedding reception—with Sarwar's secret mission. The script mixes *True Lies, So I Married an Axe Murderer,* and Hitchcock's *Suspicion* with the flamboyant satire of a Bollywood film.

The play, which was performed on BBC radio in 2010, dismissively pokes fun at the militants' hapless antics, which play out in the background of a love story. After terrorists capture and tie up the couple, Sarwar has to reveal his true identity to Meena. He quietly explains to her that his secret mission is to bring down the terrorist group "Bloody Monday" by winning a high-stakes poker game they are planning to finance their latest terrorist plot. (Extremist groups, from al Qaeda and the Taliban to Hezbollah, are notorious for using ill-gotten gains acquired—directly or indirectly—from narcotics, smuggling, and other criminal activity.[2]) The dialogue exposes the hypocrisy of ideologues.

"Islamists playing poker?" she retorts, still suspicious of him. "It's against the religion to gamble!"

"Meena, everybody follows religion," he counters, "in their own hypocritical, pick-'n-mix kind of way!"

Hussain initially wrote *Til Jihad Do Us Part* out of guilt and embarrassment about being Muslim after the 9/11 attacks. "The world had reached such a disturbing level of Islamophobia," Hussain wrote on his blog, "that even Muslims were afraid to be around other Muslims, in case their reputations were tarnished by hanging around with the scarved or bearded ones."

The real plot of *Til Jihad Do Us Part*, however, centers on the couple's relationship and their personal struggles—hers to trust a man again and his to build a personal life beyond his profession.

"I wanted to show that there's more to Muslims than religion," Hussain told me. "It's basically a script about a man and a woman trying to make their marriage work without the essential ingredient of trust.

"The point is that each person's internal jihad—the struggle to come to peace with oneself—will differ from the next," he said. "A few extremists may not be able to fully come to peace with themselves until 'all infidels burn in hell.' But for the majority of Muslims, this is more likely to mean the struggle to achieve fulfillment in love, family, and everyday personal life."

THE NEW COUNTER-JIHAD theater is also grippingly candid about what it is like to be an ordinary Muslim in an era of Islamic extremism. It exposes the personal pain better than any other art form.

The Truth about Your Father was performed by a Muslim theater company in London. It is set in 2015—a decade after four suicide bombers simultaneously attacked three London subway trains and a double-decker bus. Fifty-six people were killed; seven hundred were wounded. For the British, the attacks on July 7—known as 7/7—are as defining as 9/11 was for Americans.

The true story of one of the suicide bombers, who left behind a pregnant wife, inspired the idea for the fictional play. *The Truth about Your Father* follows the widow as she explains to her ten-year-old son that the father he never knew had been a suicide bomber—and why his father had been wrong. As in El Guindi's comedies, the cathartic drama by Luqman Ali explores the idea of jihad—and the deep personal grief among Muslims when it is hijacked by their brethren, including members of their own families. The son's name is Jihad.

Sitting at a kitchen table, a laundry basket in front of her, the mother uses a series of classic Muslim fables to frame the father's mistakes for her son. One is about the wind and the sun. In the Muslim fable, the wind uses its force to blow off a man's coat, while the sun uses its warm rays to persuade the man that it is time to take it off.

"Your father chose to be the wind or—rather—a mercilessly violent storm taking people's lives and limbs rather than their coats," she tells him.

She tries to steer her son on a different course. "Your father fled the real jihad, of making peace between the two sides of himself and living by the principles of Islam," she tells the young boy. "Like the prophets said, the greatest jihad is against the enemy within."

In the culture of counter-jihad, Parvez Sharma may have produced the most daring project. A Muslim of Indian descent, he spent six years secretly filming *A Jihad for Love* in Iran, Afghanistan, Pakistan, and nine other countries. The documentary tells the true personal stories of Muslims tenaciously committed to a faith that would reject them—and, in some places, sentence them to death—if they revealed their true identities. His subjects are all gays or lesbians.

A Jihad for Love gives voice to the most silent minority within Islam. Theirs is quite literally a struggle for love. The film begins with Imam Muhsin Hendricks, a plucky South African cleric who announced on national radio, "I am Muslim, I'm an imam, and I'm gay."

It was an extraordinary step for a man whose father and grandfather had been the spiritual leaders of Cape Town's orthodox Muslim community. Hendricks had carried on the family tradition, memorizing the entire Koran at an early age. "God is everything to me," Hendricks explains in the film. "He's the source of my strength. He's the center of my life." As a young man, he had agreed to an arranged marriage and sired three children in hopes that it would help him conform. But his wife figured out his secret and left him.

In Islamic law, any case alleging homosexuality technically requires four eyewitnesses to the act, the same rule as for adultery, although it is not systematically observed. Modern laws vary widely. Homosexuality is not a specific crime in countries like Turkey and Jordan, while religious governments in Saudi Arabia and Iran strictly forbid it. Of the fifty-seven predominantly Muslim countries, three dozen outlaw homosexual acts or "behavior." Ten can impose the death sentence.

Hendricks actually lives in the country with the world's most liberal laws on gender. South Africa's constitution, which was passed in 1996 after the apartheid era ended, outlaws discrimination on the basis of sexual orientation as well as race, religion, and gender. But when he decided to go public, Hendricks was cast out by his own community. He was expelled from the two religious schools where he taught. And a senior cleric declared him an apostate, an excommunication so sweeping that it bans burial in a Muslim cemetery.

In a moving scene, Hendricks asks one of his daughters what she would do if other Muslims came after him. Specific punishments for homosexuality also vary, but in some Muslim societies they can include beheading and stoning to death.

"I would look them in the eye," the little girl replies, "and say, 'Oh, don't let my daddy feel this, and just let him die with the first stone.' "

Iran's government has been the most aggressive in prosecuting homosexuality. It has executed dozens of gays and lesbians since the 1979 revolution.[3] Iran's former judiciary chief, Grand Ayatollah Abdolkarim Mousavi-Ardebili, called for particularly cruel punishments.

"They should seize him, they should keep him standing, and they should split him in two with a sword," he told a group of Tehran students. "Or they should dig a hole, make a fire in the hole, and throw him alive into the fire. There cannot be the slightest degree of mercy or compassion."[4]

In a speech at Columbia University, Iranian President Mahmoud Ahmadinejad actually boasted in 2007 that Iran had no homosexuals—a claim *A Jihad for Love* distinctly disproves. Sharma's film also follows the story of Amir, an Iranian who was sentenced to one hundred lashes for crimes of "sexual preference, sexual contact, illicit speech, illicit dress, makeup, and mannerism."

But *A Jihad for Love* is not just about the struggle to love openly or without persecution. It is not just about marginalized Muslims or victims. The documentary also embodies the spirit of the counter-jihad. It reflects the proactive effort to find a more nuanced understanding of Islam on all subjects relevant to contemporary life, including sexuality.

Ijtihad means "interpretation." In Islam, it allows scholars to explore the essence of the faith—through the Koran and the hadith traditions of the Prophet Mohammed—for new interpretations. *Ijtihad* is a tool to adapt Muslim practices based on new understandings or new circumstances. It is the tool that can make the faith organic and flexible. *Ijtihad* is derived from the word *jihad.* Both are forms of the same struggle.

In the twenty-first century, *ijtihad* is the heart of the struggle within Islam. Both radical extremists and fundamentalist ideologues believe that Islam's truths were revealed in the seventh century—and that there is no space for reinterpretation. Reformers contend that the understanding of God's revelations was not meant to be fixed to one moment or one culture for the rest of time.

A Jihad for Love is ultimately about the call for *ijtihad*— on the issue of sexual orientation specifically but generally also on all issues affecting all believers.

Historically, Muslim clerics outlawed homosexuality on the basis of God's wrath against the people of Sodom and Gomorrah, an Old Testament story repeated with variations in the Koran. According to both Hebrew and Muslim legend, two angels disguised in human form visited Sodom and Gomorrah. They were offered shelter by Lot, the nephew of Abraham. During the night, men from Sodom surrounded the house and demanded that Lot bring the two visitors outside so the Sodomites could have sex with them. Lot tried to put them off by offering his two virgin daughters instead of his guests, but the men of the city refused. The angels prevented the sexual assault by striking the Sodomites blind.

As part of *ijtihad*, Hendricks reinterprets the central issue. The Sodomites' offense was intent to forcibly rape, to do bodily harm, and to violate basic human rights. But the Koran, Hendricks contends, does not directly deal with the act of consensual male-to-male sex between lovers.

In his counseling of gay Muslims in South Africa on a radio talk show, *A Jihad for Love* films Hendricks telling them "to accept Islam for the goodness it comes with. Let Allah be the judge."

Several callers condemned Hendricks on the air, suggesting that he be thrown off a mountain, burned to death, or have his genitals cut off.

"This is a battle for Islam within Islam," said Sharma, the director. "Greater reform needs to come from within, and it is only the believers who will bring that reform. The debate began before 9/11, but there has been a far greater urgency since then to go back to the text and apply it to current situations."

Despite its controversial subject, *A Jihad for Love* was shown in almost fifty countries; it was selected for several international film festivals.

"Jihad represents a life struggle, and I call myself a jihadi with pride, as do all the others in this film. Our struggle is one of faith and understanding," Sharma said. "There's a whole set of culture warriors in Islam today."

PART THREE

A Wild Ride

The Beginning of the Beginning

**I have lost too much during this revolution.
I won't let anyone steal it from me now.**

—Banner at a protest after
Mubarak's ouster[1]

One week after the uprising erupted in Benghazi, Libya's second city, volunteers rushed to fill the political vacuum as Moammar Qaddafi's troops withdrew. Lawyers, judges, doctors, and academics set up ad hoc committees in the local courthouse, a stopgap government in a country that had been an absolute dictatorship for over forty years and an absolute monarchy before that. The first foreign reporters to get into Benghazi described the scramble, including the sighting of a berobed judge on the street commanding drivers to fasten their seat belts.[2]

"They are in charge," said Iman Bugaighis, an orthodontist and new spokeswoman. Then she hastily added, "Nobody is in charge."[3]

And so another awkward transition began.

The rage and rebellions rocking the Islamic world are only the beginning of the beginning. The new political mix—the Arab revolts against autocrats, the counter-jihad against violence, and the rejection of Islamist theology—has created a different and dynamic energy across the region. The new cultural rhythm—in the arts, literature, film, and music—reflects its depth.

Muslim communities worldwide are showing they have more constructive human capital than they are given credit for. Change has already been seismic. There is much to commend.

But there is still a wild ride ahead. And the day after is going to be traumatic, disorienting, and divisive, as the once-united opposition breaks into rival parts. Pity the inheritors.

For all the protesters' courage and imagination, the rebellions were led largely by amateurs pumped up by adrenaline and a sense of making history. They were raw. They lacked experience in running a party, a country, an economy, or even in knowing how to protect their young movements. They all learned on the job—or while trying to get it.

In Libya, most of the protesters who picked up arms—after Colonel Qaddafi's security forces opened fire with machine guns on peaceful demonstrations—knew little about weaponry. One admitted that he figured out how to use an AK-47 rifle "from what I saw in the movies—and also from PlayStation."[4]

Even as the old authoritarian order is imploding, the new order has yet to take form. The emerging diversity is almost overwhelming. In Tunisia, one party monopolized politics for sixty years; after the uprising, more than fifty parties registered to run for parliament.

Uprisings, by nature, are also impatient. But transitions will take significant time to play out, even as publics want instant change and rewards for their courage. New governments will face conflicting demands for both social justice and economic growth. Social justice means affordable or subsidized food, adequate health care, access to education, and a large public sector that guarantees jobs—all of which could deepen already sizable debts. But economic growth in a globalizing world means privatization, competition, efficiency, and personnel cutbacks that may most hurt the young whose unemployment and outrage at political abuse flamed the unrest.

No new governments will be able to accommodate expectations of either jobs or social justice anytime soon—and probably for years to come.

So the early euphoria and momentum will be hard to sustain. The postrebellion letdown may stir up further public discontent. Many countries may face a second round of crises, maybe even a series of them. The next decade will be tough.

Political predators—from illiberal leaders to Islamist extremists—will certainly try to take advantage of fragile transitions. Modern history is replete with new autocrats replacing old autocrats after uprisings. The three most original upheavals of the past 250 years—in introducing new ideologies that redefined the world's political spectrum—were the French, Soviet, and Iranian revolutions. In each, the democratic spirit was soon devoured by ruthless and unsavory authoritarians.

Extremists will also try to find a foothold in the new political scenes. They have already tried to psych their brethren and the world on their supposed progress.

After the Tunisian and Egyptian uprisings, Anwar al Awlaki wrote an essay in *Inspire*, an English-language online magazine. "The mujahedeen around the world are going through a moment of elation," wrote the American-born leader of al Qaeda in the Arabian Peninsula, now based in Yemen.

"I wonder whether the West is aware of the upsurge of mujahedeen activity in Egypt, Tunisia, Libya, Yemen, Arabia, Algeria and Morocco. The outcome doesn't have to be an Islamic government for us to consider what is happening to be a step in the right direction." [5]

The world was also dazzled by another set of political transformations just a generation ago. I witnessed many of them—and the aftermaths. The Islamic world could face the same type of hurdles and setbacks on the long road ahead.

I have a small mounted piece of the Berlin Wall from covering communism's collapse in Eastern Europe in 1989, and I was in the Soviet Union as it imploded in 1991. Yet almost two decades later, I traveled with an American secretary of state to Moscow for her talks with Russian leader Vladimir Putin. A former communist and KGB spy still ruled in Moscow. More than half of the Russians had wanted democracy in 1991. By 2009, a generation later, only about one in four Russians still preferred democracy over a "strong" leader, according to the Pew Research Center. [6]

I was also in Soweto, the segregated black township outside Johannesburg, when South African schoolchildren launched the first mass black uprising on June 16, 1976. The niece of the first child to die, Hector Pieterson, is my goddaughter and namesake. He was only twelve. It was one of the most inspiring protest movements of my lifetime. I then went back to watch Nelson Mandela walk to freedom in 1990. Yet a generation after South Africa abandoned apartheid, many blacks were no better off economically than they were under white minority rule. Unemployment in 2011 was a staggering 24 percent. [7] Corruption was politically corrosive. And the president was a man tried for rape who admitted having unprotected sex with a friend's HIV-positive daughter. He was acquitted. In court, Jacob Zuma said that he had reduced the risk of contracting the disease by showering afterwards, a claim that appalled AIDS experts. Because one out of every five South African adults was infected with HIV, life expectancy had dropped from sixty years when Mandela was freed in 1990 to forty-one years when Zuma was elected in 2009.[8]

Fragile democracies also slip back. In 1990, I went to Venezuela, South America's first democracy, to write about the end of military dictatorships across that continent. But Venezuelans subsequently elected Hugo Chavez, a former military officer, to the presidency to confront chronic political and economic instability as the twentieth century ended. Chavez had been imprisoned in the 1990s for a failed coup attempt against a democratically elected president. Once elected, Chavez successfully pressed to abolish constitutional term limits so he could keep running for office.

The Middle East already has an inkling of the obstacles. Lebanon's Cedar Revolution erupted after the assassination of popular politician Rafiq Hariri in 2005. More than one-quarter of its 4 million people poured onto the streets of Beirut to demand the government's resignation and the withdrawal of Syrian troops, who had occupied Lebanon for almost three decades. Protesters promised to stay until they prevailed. It took six weeks.

In getting Syria to withdraw, the Lebanese people won a concession that neither the United Nations nor the United States had been able to achieve for decades. It was a huge triumph for a country smaller than Connecticut over its much mightier neighbor. But over the next six years, Lebanon experienced repeated political crises that included the brink of civil war, the rise of Hezbollah, and a war with Israel. By the time uprisings erupted in other Arab countries in 2011, Syria had also restored some of its political influence in Lebanon, if not its military forces.

The outcome of elections may also produce surprises. In 2006, under intense American pressure, the Palestinians held the most democratic elections ever conducted in the Arab world. Residents of the West Bank and Gaza elected Hamas, an Islamist movement. The outcome reflected several problems. Fatah, the long-ruling faction of the Palestine Liberation Organization, had failed to improve life or achieve independence. Its political tactics were thuggish. And it ran too many candidates, splitting its own vote.

But Palestinians, more fundamentally, were rejecting the corrupt and autocratic status quo. It was a rebellion taken to the polls. The outcome was nonetheless deeply unsettling to the West and Israel. It split the Palestinians over different visions of their future. And it set back peace efforts.

Other uprisings will also not play out with the breathtaking speed of Tunisia and Egypt. Iran's opposition Green Movement boldly challenged the regime for six arduous months in 2009 but lost the first round to the theocracy's thugs. Iran is where political Islam first seized power. It may prove the toughest to change.

Aᴛᴀ Tᴜɴɪꜱɪᴀ's Jᴀꜱᴍɪɴᴇ Revolution, the epicenter of the Arab rebellions was renamed.

The downtown plaza in rural Sidi Bouzid was dubbed "Martyr Mohamed Bouazizi Square" for the street vendor who set himself on fire to protest government abuse—and in turn ignited unrest across the region. After the Tunisian president fled, a massive portrait of Bouazizi was draped from a makeshift memorial in the square where he often sold seasonal fruit from a portable cart.

"Stand up for your rights" was spray-painted in Arabic, French, and English on a nearby wall.

"The man is a symbol for eternity, for all the world," Tunisian movie director Mohamed Zran told CNN, as he planned a film on Bouazizi. "For me, he's more important than Mandela or Gandhi or Martin Luther King Jr. Really. Because with his act we are seeing, watching everywhere revolution . . . And it's coming from this little town."[9]

Yet the Jasmine Revolution did not improve the lives of Sidi Bouzid's poor. Roughly one in three workers in the rural town was unemployed when Bouazizi died. Little had changed months later. In hopes of new opportunities, hundreds of young men lined up daily at the governor's office—the same site where Bouazizi had doused himself with paint thinner—to apply for nonexistent jobs. The new government responded by putting up a new fence for fear of further unrest because it could not deliver.[10]

Nationwide, the uprising crippled tourism, which plummeted 40 percent. Tunisia was a favorite European vacation spot, famed for its whitewashed buildings and warm Mediterranean beachfronts; tourism had accounted for some 400,000 jobs—out of 3.3 million in the labor force. Tunisia's credit rating also dropped to junk status; investments took a nosedive.[11]

Politically, little changed for many Tunisians except the head of state—and the ability to gripe in public. A trade unionist tweeted: "Tunisia has got rid of the dictator but hasn't got rid of the dictatorship yet."[12]

Tunisia's interim government tried to placate the protest movement. It promised reforms. It pledged new elections and ended restrictions on political parties and civil society, including communist and Islamic groups. It abolished the ministry of information in charge of media censorship. It released political prisoners. And it vowed to end corruption and repression.

But change increasingly seemed incomplete. Most of the exiled president's cronies still held high offices. Secretive security forces still had dark powers. The changes involved more promises than action.

As discontent deepened, thousands of Tunisians again took to the streets. Part two of the Jasmine Revolution began on February 20, five weeks after the president's ouster, with a sit-in at Casbah Square. The large plaza of whitewashed buildings is in the capital's old quarter; it borders both the government center and the medieval cobblestoned bazaar.

Part two was far more ambitious and, in a haphazard way, better organized. The sit-in evolved into a squatters' camp-in, complete with its own security committee and volunteers taking down the names and hometowns of people in each tent.[13] Protesters posted a long list of demands—written out neatly in black ink on a giant red and white Tunisia flag—on a Casbah wall. They stipulated that they would not leave the square until the prime minister and leftover cabinet ministers resigned. They demanded dissolution of the ruling party and the state security police. And they called for a whole new constitution—from scratch.

The government initially stalled. "I have stressed that we do not have a magic wand to change twenty-three years of accumulated problems in a matter of weeks," Prime Minister Mohammed Ghannouchi plaintively told the nation.[14]

Once again, however, the opposition had the momentum. Protests spread to other parts of the capital. So did tensions. Security forces opened fire; protesters threw stones. Several protesters died—bringing the toll to over two hundred since Mohamed Bouazizi's death. "We will not give up till victory," boasted one of several slogans spray-painted on the Casbah's white walls.

Within a week of renewed protests, the prime minister resigned. So did other holdovers in the cabinet. Within two weeks, the interim government capitulated to every demand, including a new constitution. A day later, the protesters at Casbah Square packed up and went home.

Yet two unprecedented political victories did not end Tunisia's instability or economic woes.

In the first two months after President Ben Ali resigned, some 15,000 Tunisians bribed owners of old fishing boats to smuggle them to the tiny Italian island of Lampedusa in search of jobs or a future, the United Nations reported. Lampedusa's refugee center was built to hold only eight hundred, leading more than 6,000 people to camp out in makeshift camps. Lampedusa was so overwhelmed that the islanders launched protests at their own town hall against the former Tunisian protesters.[15]

Egypt also reveled in its rebellion, only to soon confront similar setbacks. It faced both the best of times and the worst of times.

Unprecedented millions turned out for a referendum on nine constitutional amendments six weeks after President Mubarak's ouster. Many women and young opposition leaders actually opposed the changes as too modest; they wanted a whole new constitution. They feared the rushed amendments gave an edge to the old ruling party and the Muslim Brotherhood rather than the forces of change. But there was a spirit of tolerance about the outcome.

"It was amazing to see such great people there," said Dalia Ziada, the young Egyptian activist who had translated the Martin Luther King Jr. comic book. "Families were coming together to the poll. I really knew what democracy tastes like today. I voted no and my mother voted yes, but at the end of the day I do not really care what the result would be. I am 100 percent confident that it was fair, and whatever my people want, I am with them.

"Democracy," she emailed me, "is delicious." Then she added a ☺.

But Egypt's uprising also spawned a culture of protests that escalated after Mubarak's resignation. Pent-up rage was unleashed at new demonstrations in front of parliament, businesses, banks, industries, state television, government ministries, even a department store. Their initial demands were for better pay or more jobs. Labor strikes rallied pharmacists, pensioners, lawyers, railway workers, doctors, journalists, students, and in an incongruous twist, the police once charged with putting down protests.

Egypt's population had doubled from 40 million to over 82 million during Mubarak's three decades in power.[16] The most populous Arab country is not oil-rich. By 2011, one in five Egyptians lived below the poverty line. They expected more once Mubarak resigned. And they were willing to use their new voice to demand it.

The cycle produced an instability that undermined the uprising's initial purpose. At least short-term, the plight of the average Egyptian worsened.

To commemorate Mubarak's ouster, street vendors at Liberation Square started selling uprising T-shirts, trinkets, posters, and face paints in the colors of the Egyptian flag. But they had few takers. Tourism plummeted by 75 percent. One million foreigners had been evacuated during the eighteen-day uprising.[17] Tour companies predicted foreigners would not return in large numbers until a sense of stability was reestablished. The shrinking tourism market rippled across other industries.

The Egyptian stock market, which closed for almost two months during and after the uprising, dropped 10 percent in the first minute after it reopened. The initial loss totaled $6.8 billion.[18] The market bounced back a bit, unsteadily. But the price of oil—soaring above $110 per barrel, partly due to global unease about the region-wide upheavals—in turn affected everything in Egypt that used petroleum products, including agriculture. As times got tougher, crime also soared.

Uncertainty further fueled the cycle.

As protests spread, the ruling military council cracked down. One month after Mubarak fled, on March 9, soldiers moved in to clear Cairo's Liberation Square. Many protesters were detained, Amnesty International reported. At least eighteen women were beaten, subjected to electric shock, strip-searched and photographed nude by male soldiers, then given "virginity tests." Anyone who failed the test, they were warned, faced prosecution for prostitution.[19]

After originally pledging to stand with the Egyptian people, the military then outlawed protests altogether. The interim government announced any demonstration that would "harm societal peace" or "obstruct" the work of public institutions was a crime. New penalties were stiff. For inciting, writing, or advertising protests, protesters could face one-year prison terms and fines of up to $16,000.[20]

In a particularly ironic twist, the military council took to issuing communiqués on its own new Facebook page.

Anxious and angry Egyptians responded with more protests.[21] On April 1, seven weeks after President Mubarak stepped down, thousands turned out again at Liberation Square for a "Save the Revolution" rally. A week later, Cairo witnessed the biggest demonstration since Mubarak's ouster in a bold challenge to the military and especially its chief, Field Marshal Mohamed Hussein Tantawi. "Dictator, dictator, Tantawi is next," they chanted.[22]

Over the next decade, the toughest challenge for all Muslim societies undergoing change will be finding a viable balance between political and economic rights while also ensuring basic security. The same challenge confronts other countries after longer struggles to transform, from Russia and South Africa to Venezuela. But the balance is especially pivotal in a region where odious ideologies and extremists still try to seduce followers—and where the momentum had been moving in the other direction.

Yemen represented the perfect storm, the potentially catastrophic confluence of crises: A turbulent political revolt challenged President Ali Abdullah Saleh, who had ruled ruthlessly since 1978. Months of turmoil traumatized the nation. Yemen's economy was already the poorest in the Arab world. Almost half the population lived under the poverty line, with unemployment over 35 percent. Annual per capita income was a mere $2,600. And it was the most insecure country in the region. A decade after 9/11, al Qaeda cells were most active out of covert bases in picturesque, chaotic Yemen.

A country of harsh mountains and harsher deserts, Yemen reflected how long-ruling leaders had lingering impact even after they left office. Saleh's rule was based on "a system of grand corruption" involving the military, politicians, tribal leaders, and business elites, the US Agency for International Development reported. Allies were rewarded and elites pacified "by grand patronage payoffs in exchange for political quiescence," it said.[23]

The regime's response to a popular uprising pushed an already fragile economy to the cusp of collapse. During months of unrest, it reportedly paid tens of thousands of Yemenis ten dollars a day—more than most people would otherwise earn—to attend pro-government rallies or not join protests against the president. It also halved taxes and increased the salaries of government employees, none of which it could afford. The government printed more money to deal with expenditures during the crisis. Tapping into its reserves undermined the value of its currency.[24]

More than any other country, Yemen had a lot of damage to undo.

"We are going to face the legacy which Saleh has left," said Nadia al Sakkaf, the young editor of the *Yemen Times*. "He is going to leave us with no money. And there will be dwindling oil resources. There will be resentment among the youth. The common enemy that united them will be gone. And so they will turn around and see that there's nothing left to fight for.

"The jobs that they wanted, they are not going to be created overnight," she said. "So, we're going to be facing a lot of disappointed youth waiting for opportunities to happen."[25]

For vastly diverse governments, the pivotal challenge will be creating new social contracts that no longer take their people for granted or assume their political silence is for sale. Even oil-rich countries will have trouble finding viable formulas. Bahrain, Iraq, Kuwait, Oman, and Saudi Arabia offered increased aid, cash payouts, financial perks, pay raises, or new subsidies to preempt protests. Most were unsuccessful in either beating back revolts or appeasing dissidents with money alone. Problems ran far deeper.

Shortly after Mubarak resigned in Egypt, Saudi Arabia's aged and ailing King Abdullah returned home from three months of medical treatments abroad to announce more than $100 billion in emergency economic measures. It was a defensive strike to address unemployment, which hovered between 10 and 12 percent in 2011. Saudi citizens also accounted for only one in ten people in the private sector; the rest were foreigners.[26] The new grants included support for unemployed and lower-class youth, more overseas scholarships, debt forgiveness and pardons for jailed debtors, home loans, a 15 percent pay hike for government employees, and even funds for literary and sports clubs.[27]

But the king's handouts included no significant political reforms. Discontent continued to fester over corruption, women's rights, discrimination against the Shiite minority, and fissures between an aging

leadership and its young people. Two-thirds of the 20 million Saudis*
were under the age of thirty, while the average age of cabinet ministers was sixty-five.[28] The king was eighty-six and the next two princes
in line to the throne were over eighty. As in other oil-rich states, the
long-standing social contract—granting financial largesse in exchange
for support of tribe-based monarchies—was no longer enough.

Saudi Arabia had no equivalent, politically or physically, of Liberation Square. So the kingdom's young—including many of its females—
turned to the Internet as a virtual protest site.[29]

"We don't want money," tweeted a young woman in Jeddah. "I want
to know that I'll be protected under a written constitution for the rest of
my short life."[30]

A MID CONVULSIVE POLITICAL upheaval in the Islamic world, the
most contentious issue is the role of Islam in the new political
lineup.

After the Jasmine Revolution, Tunisia's cosmopolitan capital witnessed disparate protests in the same week. At one demonstration, thousands marched through the streets of Tunis to demand the separation of
mosque and state in the new political system. "Politics ruins religion and
religion ruins politics," one banner declared.

At the other demonstration, a procession of Islamists paraded through
the alleyways housing Tunis's bordellos. They demanded an end to legally sanctioned prostitution. "No to brothels in a Muslim country,"
they shouted.[31]

Islam will almost certainly play a major role in transitions. In most
Muslim countries, large numbers share conservative values, even as they
push for democratic freedoms of speech, press, politics, and public assem-
bly. The right to human dignity, Muslims believe, is God-given. The values of their religion are a starting point for all other aspects of life.

Two months after President Ben Ali resigned, a public opinion poll
showed that 48 percent of Tunisians preferred a new political system
that was based "strongly or somewhat" on religion. Just slightly fewer,
44 percent, preferred a "strongly or somewhat" secular system, according to the International Republican Institute survey.[32]

---

* Saudi Arabia is also home to some 5.5 million "nonnationals."

Politics and piety are not necessarily contradictions, even for the nonobservant.

Egyptians shared similar sentiments. In 2010, a year before their uprising, almost 60 percent of Egyptians surveyed said they wanted democracy. But 48 percent also said Islam played a "large role" in their nation's political life, reported the Pew Global Attitudes Project. (That sentiment was even larger in Indonesia, Turkey, and Nigeria, three predominantly Muslim and democratic countries continents apart.)

Among Egyptians, 85 percent viewed Islam's role in politics favorably—compared to 2 percent who viewed Islam's role unfavorably.[33] Under Hosni Mubarak, Egyptian laws had to be compatible with Sharia, or Islamic law, a rule not likely to change anytime soon.

The new spectrum will take a long time to shake out. Movements that initially emerged from the uprisings disavowed extremist violence. They reflected the broader counter-jihad. But each had a different place for Islam in its political agenda.

The new parties will generally fall into three broad categories.

One group will come from the dregs of the old regimes. Tunisia's Constitutional Democratic Rally party was legally disbanded, while the hierarchy of Egypt's National Democratic Party resigned in droves. But members of the old ruling parties have the organizational know-how, campaign savvy, connections, and resources to put up candidates to preserve their interests. They may try to reconfigure old parties or morph into more than one new party. Most will try to find younger members and candidates as part of a political makeover. Somewhat disingenuously, they will also almost certainly invoke conservative Islamic values to tap into the public's cultural comfort zone.

The second group will come from popular movements that inspired and led the uprisings. They will often be the most secular politically, even though many of their female followers wear hejab. They will most symbolize the counter-jihad.

In Egypt, they generated civil disobedience demonstrations that defied overwhelming odds to oust autocrats. Their democratic goals and communication tools were very twenty-first-century. They generally endorsed religious tolerance, both within and among faiths. But many also did not want to strip religious sensibilities from politics—any more than Western societies have abandoned Judeo-Christian values after centuries of democracy.

At least in the initial rounds, the popular movements may be the weakest of the three categories. In Egypt and Tunisia, several scrambled to form new parties. But they lacked experience, resources, and the time requisite to evolve into well-organized political groups before the first elections. They also tended to be young, many still students—old enough to vote, organize, and campaign, but in some places not old or seasoned enough to run for office even if they had platforms, political bases, or funds.

Leaders of the opposition movements often split once their revolts succeeded.

Wael Ghonim, a Google marketing director for the Middle East, was one of the young masterminds of Egypt's uprising. In 2010, he started the Facebook page for a fellow blogger who died in police custody, and then called for protests in his honor. Both were seeds for the most important Arab revolt. After his twelve-day imprisonment in 2011, his teary interview on a popular satellite station channel revived Egypt's flagging uprising. But after Mubarak resigned, Ghonim broke with other activists over the critical next steps and party affiliation. It was a bitter break. Former allies launched three Facebook pages against Ghonim within a week. One was entitled "Ghonim Traitor." [34]

"It's all changing so fast, movements and parties are being born and disappearing and dividing and uniting and changing faster than anyone can keep track of it all," human rights activist Sally Sami told the *Wall Street Journal*. [35]

The third group will be made up of Islamic parties, some of which were the most organized opposition even in countries where they had long been illegal. They will usually be determined, disciplined, resourceful, and fairly well funded. Not to be confused with extremists, they may be savvier politically than the Facebook generation, although most will have their own bloggers too.

But they are a full spectrum unto themselves. And even within a party, they do not always share a common agenda.

In Egypt, the Muslim Brotherhood, the grandfather of modern Islamic movements worldwide, is the largest Islamist group. It was formed in 1928 by a twenty-two-year-old schoolteacher who mobilized disgruntled workers in the Suez Canal Company. Initially a utopian grassroots movement, it sought to create stronger Muslim societies as the seeds for a different kind of state. It has since spawned eighty-six affiliates in dozens of countries across Asia, Europe, and Africa.

Egypt's uprising might not have succeeded without the eventual buy-in of the Brotherhood, which kept its distance until the protests proved their staying power. Indeed, the movement was as surprised as the Mubarak government at the young protesters' early resolve—and rapid impact. But when the uprising reached a lull midstream, the Brotherhood's mobilization of its own followers filled many tents at Liberation Square for the final push.

The uprising both helped and hurt the movement. As Egyptian politics opened up, the Brotherhood launched the Freedom and Justice Party to run candidates under its own legal mantle for the first time. The uprising, however, also exposed a long-simmering divide among its three factions—ideologues, pragmatic conservatives, and reformers. New freedoms inspired deeper internal debate.[36]

The young had already started drifting away from the Brotherhood gerontocracy over its autocratic and outdated ideas. One controversial plank decreed that Christians and women were "unsuitable" for the presidency. Another called for all legislation to be approved by a panel of Islamic scholars before a parliamentary vote. The Brotherhood lost further ground after the uprising when it decreed that no member could join any party other than Freedom and Justice.[37]

An Egyptian analyst dubbed it "Brother-tarianism."[38]

Ibrahim Houdaiby symbolized the alienation. Both his grandfather and his great-grandfather were supreme leaders of the Brotherhood. Born in 1983, he started working on the movement's English language website in 2005 and became its best-known blogger. But he also emerged as a leading advocate of pragmatism, internal democracy, less secrecy, greater religious tolerance, and women's rights.

"One day before my grandfather's death I was at the hospital with him," he told me. "I had lots of debate with my grandfather. When he finished his argument, I would often say, 'I'm not convinced.' He would say, 'I'm not trying to convince you. You're a different generation, and if you stop where we stopped, then we're getting nowhere.'

"One of our debates was over which comes first: freedom or Sharia. My grandfather said Sharia leads to freedom. My argument came from the Koran, which says, 'Let there be no compulsion in religion.' I said freedom comes first."

Houdaiby eventually resigned from the movement. From the out-side, he challenged the movement to redefine its political mission and goals. Other young activists who stayed demanded the right to form and join their own political parties separate from the religious movement. In a country with over one-quarter of the Arab world's 300 million people, the most powerful Islamic party cracked into multiple parts. Its evolution—like its creation—may set a precedent for other countries.

Among Islamists, the wild cards are the Salafis, the ultraconserva-tive radicals inspired by Saudi Arabia's puritan Wahhabi sect. They are often a hybrid. In Egypt, many renounced violence. Some even crusaded against the jihadist tactics they had once endorsed.[39] But their willing-ness to share power long-term was not always convincing. Their cred-ibility as part of the counter-jihad has yet to be proven.

As a young intelligence officer, Abdoud al Zomor provided the bullets used to assassinate President Anwar Sadat in 1981. He spent three de-cades in prison for aiding and abetting terrorists. He was released shortly after Mubarak's ouster. He was repentant over extremism but not over the goal of creating an Islamic state.

"The ballot boxes will decide who will win at the end of the day," he told the *New York Times.* "There is no longer any need for me to use violence against those who gave us our freedom and allowed us to be part of political life."[40]

Such was the danger, as well as the promise, at the beginning of the beginning.

12.

The Diplomatic Pas de Deux

**Those countries that respect the universal rights
of their people are stronger and more successful
than those that do not.**

—PRESIDENT BARACK OBAMA[1]

The old authoritarian order in the Middle East is being shattered,
but so is American foreign policy. An epic policy swing—after six
decades of rock-solid relations with impervious monarchies and
sclerotic autocrats—played out publicly over the first eleven days of February 2011.

The shift started on February 1, when President Obama stepped before a microphone in the White House's cavernous Grand Foyer. It was
6:44 p.m.

Obama had been delayed waiting for President Mubarak's speech to
his own people. The Egyptian uprising had spread rapidly across the
country in only a week. Protesters demanding the president's ouster
were camping out around the clock at Liberation Square. Mubarak, looking haggard, finally appeared on national television at 11 p.m. Egyptian
time. Obama watched it on the big screen in the Situation Room, the
wood-paneled conference center in the West Wing basement equipped to
monitor crises at home or abroad.

Mubarak's ten-minute address was both emotional and unequivo-
cal. He announced that he would not run for a sixth term. After ruling
Egypt longer than all but three early pharaohs, he pledged to step aside
after scheduled elections in September. But unlike his Tunisian counterpart, he vowed not to leave office early—or leave Egypt.

"The Hosni Mubarak who speaks to you today is proud of the long years he spent in the service of Egypt and its people," he said firmly. "Here I have lived and fought for its sake and defended its land, sovereignty, and interests. And on this land I will die."

Afterward, Obama called Mubarak. They spent a half hour on the telephone. It was, aides said, a tough conversation. Mubarak had been the closest Arab ally through five American presidencies.

Then it was Obama's turn. He walked down the Grand Foyer's red carpet to speak to a small pool of television cameras and White House correspondents.

Egypt had reached the tipping point, Obama told them. "We've borne witness to the beginning of a new chapter in the history of a great country," he said.

"Over the last few days, the passion and the dignity that has been demonstrated by the people of Egypt has been an inspiration to people around the world," Obama said. "Particularly to the young people of Egypt, I want to be clear: We hear your voices. I have an unyielding belief that you will determine your own destiny and seize the promise of a better future for your children and your grandchildren."

Obama then publicly abandoned a stalwart of US policy.

"What is clear—and what I indicated tonight to President Mubarak—is my belief that an orderly transition must be meaningful, it must be peaceful, and it must begin *now*," he said.

Obama's pronouncement would have been unthinkable just one week earlier. Since most Muslim countries gained independence after World War II, both Democratic and Republican administrations have enabled autocrats to survive in the name of oil, stability, anticommunism, or counterterrorism.

The most egregious example was Iran. In 1953, the Eisenhower administration co-orchestrated a coup, with Britain, that forced a democratically elected government from power and put Shah Mohammad Reza Pahlavi back on the Peacock Throne. The next five administrations only increased diplomatic ties, aid, military sales, and intelligence links to an increasingly unpopular regime. American strategic and economic interests took precedence. Iran was one of the world's largest oil exporters; it also shared a long border with the then Soviet Union. Washington trained and equipped Iranian intelligence and security forces who carried out the shah's repressive policies.

In 1977, just weeks before the year-long revolution erupted, President Carter extolled the shah for his "sound judgment," wisdom, and sensitivity.

"We have no other nation with whom we have closer consultation on regional problems that concern us both," he said in a New Year's Eve toast in Tehran. "And there is no leader with whom I have a deeper sense of personal gratitude and personal friendship."[2] Just over a year later, the shah and his empress flew into exile.

Under twelve presidents since World War II, the United States has given little but lip service to democracy in the Arab world. In 2003, President Bush admitted as much.

> Sixty years of Western nations excusing and accommodating the lack of freedom in the Middle East did nothing to make us safe—because in the long run, stability cannot be purchased at the expense of liberty. As long as the Middle East remains a place where freedom does not flourish, it will remain a place of stagnation, resentment, and violence ready for export. And with the spread of weapons that can bring catastrophic harm to our country and to our friends, it would be reckless to accept the status quo.[3]

Yet President Bush was no better. He once publicly prodded America's two closest allies—Egypt and Saudi Arabia—to embrace reform, then effusively embraced their leaders. He was even photographed holding hands with the Saudi king during his visit to the Bush family's ranch in Texas. At a time of unprecedented US power, Bush did little to tangibly push any of Washington's other allies.

As a result, the Arab Spring of 2004 and 2005 collapsed largely because leaders initially nervous about American pressure realized Washington's words were empty. Fledgling democrats felt abandoned. By the time he left office, Bush was also widely seen in the Islamic world as having discredited democracy. The US wars in Iraq and Afghanistan had only produced greater unemployment, crime, corruption, and political uncertainty.

The United States also consistently misread public sentiment in the Islamic world. In 2008, shortly before a visit by Secretary of State Condoleezza Rice, a US Embassy cable heralded Tunisia as "a country that works."

"While Tunisians grumble privately about corruption by the first lady's family," the cable concluded, "there is an abiding appreciation for [President] Ben Ali's success in steering his country clear of the instability and violence that plagued Tunisia's neighbors."[4]

During his first two years in office, President Obama did little as well, despite stirring speeches about freedom in Turkey, Egypt, and Indonesia. In his 2009 Cairo speech, he acknowledged past US mistakes in treating Muslim countries as "proxies without regard to their own aspirations." He said no strategy should be based "only upon what comes out of the ground [oil], nor can it be sustained while young people are out of work." He warned that "suppressing ideas never succeeds in making them go away."

Yet in December 2010, the United States was caught "totally flat-footed," a senior White House official told me, when Mohamed Bouazizi's self-immolation ignited a chain reaction of rebellions in more than half of the Arab world's twenty-two countries.

For weeks afterward, Washington seemed to be constantly playing catch-up. It basically just watched as Tunisians forced their president from power in January 2011. During the first week of Egypt's uprising, the White House only called for meaningful reform—under President Mubarak. On January 27, Vice President Joe Biden was asked on *PBS NewsHour* if the time had come for the Egyptian leader to step down.

"No," he replied, "I think the time has come for President Mubarak to begin . . . to be more responsive to some of the needs of the people out there. A lot of the people out there protesting are middle-class folks who are looking for a little more access and a little more opportunity."[5]

Biden also said he did not foresee the kind of domino effect that rippled across Eastern Europe and felled communist regimes from 1989 to 1991.

The very next day, January 28, tens of thousands of peaceful protesters held their own against well-armed Egyptian security forces on Lovers' Bridge in Cairo. They eventually made it to Liberation Square to start their decisive vigil. Demonstrations had also erupted in Yemen and Algeria, with growing signs of political unease elsewhere.

So on Saturday, January 29—four days into Egypt's protests and six weeks after the Arab revolts began—Obama huddled with his foreign policy team in the Situation Room to figure out what to do. They concluded that the Mubarak dynasty, the president and the son he was grooming to succeed him, was no longer viable long-term. When Obama made his remarks on February 1, however, the White House envisioned reforms, a gradual transition, and elections seven months later.

But the accelerating pace of protests across Egypt pushed the administration to move faster. By Friday, February 4, the United States had switched to managing a speedier, if unspecified transition. US officials kept using the word "orderly."

The policy leap, still unfolding, was not easy. It met serious resistance from Arab allies. President Obama had to rebuff pressure from Saudi Arabia's King Abdullah to permit Mubarak the final dignity of staying in office until scheduled elections in the fall. After Obama's telephone conversation with the king on February 9, the White House issued an unusually candid statement. It was an outright rejection of the Saudi appeal.

"The President emphasized the importance of taking immediate steps," it said, "toward an orderly transition that is meaningful, lasting, legitimate, and responsive to the aspirations of the Egyptian people."

It was the type of blunt talk that would make any Middle Eastern leader think twice about his own future too.

In the background, US officials held a flurry of consultations with their own Egyptian counterparts. They nudged them to talk frankly with Mubarak. They prodded them to consider the country's future. But no one talked about timing.

In the end, the protest at Liberation Square had the momentum. As in Tunisia, Egypt's military decided it was unwilling to fire on millions in cities throughout Egypt who had basically closed down parts of the country. Many of its own conscripts were openly sympathetic to the uprising and cheered it on.

It was all over by February 11. Without his army, Mubarak had little choice. He and his family quietly slipped off to their villa in the Red Sea resort of Sharm el Sheikh. His recently appointed vice president made a terse three-sentence announcement on television, then faded away too. An interim military command took over.

In Washington, Obama signaled the full turn in American policy later that day. He appeared again in the Grand Foyer. It was 3:06 p.m. He was buoyant.

"There are very few moments in our lives where we have the privilege to witness history taking place," he said. "This is one of those moments. This is one of those times."

Obama compared the peaceful overthrow of Mubarak—the center-piece of US policy in the Arab world just three weeks earlier—to the fall of the Berlin Wall, Gandhi's civil disobedience against British colonialism, and student protests that brought down President Suharto in Indonesia. The nonviolent uprising at Liberation Square, he said, had "changed the world."

"The wheel of history turned at a blinding pace as the Egyptian people demanded their universal rights," he said. "Egyptians have inspired us . . . It was the moral force of nonviolence—not terrorism, not mindless killing—but nonviolence, moral force, that bent the arc of history toward justice once more."

FOR ALL THE initial giddiness about peaceful change in the world's most volatile region, the United States still struggled to find a policy formula that fit the unfolding history. The scope of change was greater than at any time since the Cold War's end a generation earlier. But American messages were mixed. Follow-through was awkward. And it was not evenhanded.

Libya's protests erupted in Benghazi on February 15, just four days after Mubarak resigned in neighboring Egypt. The flashpoint was the arrest of human rights lawyer Fathi Terbil, who was representing families of 1,200 men killed by security forces in a 1996 prison massacre.

The same day, Obama laid out common principles for a changing region. He warned leaders that they could no longer "maintain power through coercion . . . In any society, there has to be consent," he said. "The thing that will actually achieve stability in that region is if young people, if ordinary folks end up feeling that there are pathways for them to feed their families, get a decent job, get an education, aspire to a better life."

America's response differed from place to place, however. Each country certainly has its own dynamics and complexities, yet the inconsistency was also increasingly visible—carrying potential costs in credibility and cooperation down the road. When the United States initially backed Mubarak over Egypt's protesters, one of the signs at Cairo's Liberation Square declared, "USA: We hate your hypocrisy."

One month after Libya's uprising began, as Qaddafi's troops reached the outskirts of Benghazi, the United Nations passed a resolution calling for "all necessary measures" to protect civilians and imposing a no-fly zone over Libya. On March 19, the United States joined France, Britain, other NATO members, and two Arab countries in bombing Libyan military installations, aircraft, and air defenses. Obama also said, repeatedly, that Qaddafi had to surrender power.

The Obama administration was equally outspoken about new protests in Iran, which erupted at the same time. They were the first new demonstrations by the opposition Green Movement since the six-month uprising in 2009. Obama encouraged Iran's opposition to take to the streets.

"My hope and expectation," he said, "is that we're going to continue to see the people of Iran have the courage to be able to express their yearning for greater freedoms and a more representative government."

But the United States basically took a pass on democracy in Bahrain, despite its enormous influence in a country where the Fifth Fleet was headquartered. On February 14, Bahrainis rallied to demand long-promised reforms and the resignation of the prime minister, a member of the royal family who had been in the job since 1971. They set up a tent encampment around Pearl Square, a large traffic circle with a towering monument to the country's early pearl industry. The monument was a landmark synonymous with Bahrain, like France's Eiffel Tower.

Like Libya, the little sheikhdom responded with ruthless force. One month after the uprising began, it declared martial law. It invited Saudi Arabia and other Gulf neighbors to deploy troops. And on March 16, in the middle of the night, security forces stormed the tent encampment at Pearl Square to clear it out. Cell phone video captured security forces beating and firing on protesters. Several died; scores were wounded.

The army even tore down the pearl monument, a landmark engraved on the island nation's most valuable coin. "It was a bad memory," said the Bahrain foreign minister.[6]

Before the crackdown, the White House called on the sheikhdom to exercise restraint. After the deaths, however, it did not criticize the king nor question Saudi Arabia's troop deployment.

Even months into the rebellions, US policy seemed to be merely reacting to events across the region. The world's mightiest power did not appear to have a proactive strategy to foster, encourage, or take advantage of democratic movements, much less plan for the day after. Republicans were no wiser than Democrats. Their reactions often appeared to be based on crude partisan politics. Some who had endorsed the Iraq invasion to topple Saddam Hussein—which had no UN mandate—were critical of a comparatively modest American contribution to a UN-endorsed campaign against Moammar Qaddafi in Libya eight years later.

In reaction to Yemen's uprising, the United States initially charted a third and vaguer middle course. Protests demanding the resignation of President Ali Abdullah Saleh erupted in February, in the middle of Egypt's uprising. Saleh had ruled since 1978. And he was grooming his son as his successor.

Like Libya and Bahrain, Yemen cracked down cruelly on hundreds of thousands who turned out in peaceful throngs across the country for weeks on end. Protesters camped out in an area dubbed Change Square in Sanaa, the scenic capital of gingerbread houses and dagger-wielding tribesmen. The regime responded by deploying tanks. Snipers in civilian clothes fired on chanting crowds. On March 18 alone, more than fifty were killed.

As the rebellion grew, the embattled government suspended the constitution and imposed emergency rule. It outlawed all protests. The president seized new powers to detain without judicial process and to censor the media at his whim. In a public fury, he even blamed the United States and Israel for conspiring to destabilize the Arab world.

Yemen was complicated by many factors, including southern secessionists, northern rebels, tribal divisions, and an almost even sectarian split between Sunni and Shiite. None felt they got their fair share, politically or economically. Yemen also had the most active al Qaeda franchise. Al Qaeda in the Arabian Peninsula was linked to several plots against the United States, including the attempted Christmas Day bombing of a Northwest Airlines flight from Amsterdam to Detroit in 2009 and the printer-cartridge bombs planted on two US-bound cargo planes in 2010.

For weeks, the White House tasked its counterterrorism chief as the prime interlocutor with Yemen. On April 1, as massive protests spread to fourteen of Yemen's eighteen provinces, a State Department spokesman said that "counterterrorism efforts are foremost on our minds." He said the Yemeni leader had made concessions and urged protesters to "come together and forge a way forward" with the government.

Within days, however, US officials quietly conceded that Saleh was no longer a tenable leader. Once again, the United States was behind the curve.

The irony of Yemen was that both Democratic and Republican administrations had spent a decade talking up democracy as an antidote to militant ideologies. Washington also invested a good chunk of America's treasury to defeat militants and put democrats in their place, at great cost to the nation's long-term economic health. By the end of 2010, the United States had spent at least $750 billion in Iraq and $336 billion in Afghanistan.[7] But weeks passed, and no one had been bold enough to say publicly that an unpopular autocrat in an unstable country might actually fuel extremism—or commend the burgeoning call for democracy in Yemen.

Then there was Syria. The rebellion against President Bashar al Assad began on March 18 after more than a dozen children—most under the age of fourteen—were arrested for writing antigovernment graffiti on public walls in Daraa, a southern city.[8] Peaceful protests erupted to demand the children's release. Security forces killed three people the first day.

As throughout the Middle East, the protests spread. The crackdown widened. And deaths mounted.

The administration called on the Syrian leader to develop a "credible path" to "greater freedom, democracy, opportunity, and justice." Yet the administration also appeared to be betting on the Assad dynasty, which had ruled in Damascus for four decades. "There's a different leader in Syria now," Secretary of State Hillary Clinton said on March 27. "Many of the members of Congress of both parties who have gone to Syria in recent months have said they believe he's a reformer."[9]

Five days later, Syrians held a "Day of Martyrs" to commemorate the dozens who had died over the previous two weeks. At least four more were killed.

Four months into the rebellions, the American response still felt improvised—the very flaw Obama had criticized in his 2006 book *The Audacity of Hope*.

"The United States still lacks a coherent national security policy," he wrote. "Instead of guiding principles, we have what appear to be a series of ad hoc decisions, with dubious results.[10]

> Are we committed to use force wherever there's a despotic regime that's terrorizing its people—and if so, how long do we stay to ensure democracy takes root? ... Perhaps someone inside the White House has clear answers to these questions. But our allies—and for that matter our

enemies—certainly don't know what the answers are. More important, neither do the American people. Without a well-articulated strategy that the public supports and the world understands, America will lack the legitimacy—and ultimately the power—it needs to make the world safer than it is today.[11]

OVER THE NEXT decade, the United States faces a more basic challenge. The decade after 9/11 was shaped largely by fear of everything from a global clash of civilizations to a new neighborhood mosque. The fear bordered on panic. It was politically counterproductive. And it prevented recognition of conspicuous changes among Muslims, many produced by their own fears of extremism.

It also belied the reality in the Islamic world. During the defining decade after 9/11, extremists killed many more Muslims—in exponentially larger numbers—than Americans. And millions of Muslims have had their lives torn apart by brethren who turned to militancy. Political uncertainty deepened in every predominantly Muslim country where extremists gained a foothold, whether by political manipulation, force of arms, or terrorizing the public. Financial and property losses have been staggering, both for individuals and nations.

To move beyond 9/11, the United States faces three challenges in the decade ahead.

The most basic challenge is comprehending the post-jihadist phase. The battle cry across the Islamic world today is *selmiyya, selmiyya* or "peaceful, peaceful." For the first time in decades, the focus is on their own political life. At least in the opening round, it has not been about either the United States or the Arab-Israeli conflict.

"We no longer want to be subjects," said Abdelilah Ben Abdeslam of the Moroccan Association for Human Rights during peaceful protests held simultaneously in five Moroccan cities after Mubarak stepped down in Egypt. "We want to be citizens."[12]

Vastly different sectors of Muslim societies—from political protesters to playwrights and rappers—are proving that they share common values with the West in the twenty-first century. And they are actively tackling their extremist brethren, usually on their own initiatives and often imaginatively.

The Arab revolts were also not the first quests for freedom: the Islamic world has many young democracies, including some of its biggest members—Indonesia, Turkey, and Bangladesh. Other major players—Malaysia and Pakistan—are in the midst of difficult transitions. And despite the extraordinary challenges faced by Muslim females, five women have been elected president or prime minister in democratic polls since 1988—a better record than in the United States. In poor and teeming Bangladesh, one woman succeeded another.

The second challenge is recognizing that political change will be cacophonous, complicated, and sometimes uncomfortable. It may be as much of a wild ride for the outside world as for Muslim societies struggling with transformations.

The West may have to take some political risks along the way. New democracies in poor countries are always fragile. To foster the commonality of cultures, the West will need to invest economically and shift aid from security forces to human development—most notably in Egypt. To have credibility, it will have to acknowledge, if not enthusiastically embrace, any democratically elected leaders who renounce violence, play by international rules, and honor democracy's practices.

The reality is also that democracies are often harder to influence or control, as the United States has learned with even European allies. Popularly elected governments have their own opinions; they also have to be accountable first and foremost to their constituents. So there may well be many short-term flaps and even hard trade-offs ahead. But common values also create stronger bonds, cooperation, and alliances long-term.

The United States may have to engage in some damage control after decades of supporting autocrats. Several of Egypt's young protest leaders turned down an invitation to meet Secretary of State Hillary Clinton during her visit to Cairo after the uprising. Some cited her support for a slower transition of power and her acknowledged personal friendship with Mubarak and his wife. Others said they did not want to meet any foreign leaders as they chart their own future.[13]

Even cheerleading may have to be carefully calibrated. Because of past policies, too much American support may taint the very parties and politicians the United States would prefer to see come to power.

The United States will also have to use more carrot than stick in fostering democratic change, especially after the wars in Iraq and Afghanistan.

Military intervention in Libya was an exception, a one-time option, even a fluke. Qaddafi had little support among Arabs and Africans, the two worlds Libya straddled, even before his troops opened fire on protesters. His repression was so abhorrent, his behavior so erratic, and his sanity so uncertain that the United Nations, the Arab League, NATO, and a rapidly assembled military coalition set records in agreeing to impose sanctions and launch military action against his regime to save civilians.

The third challenge—for both individuals and nations—is moving beyond fear as the most influential factor in decisions. It may well be the toughest part. For some, it involves conquering instincts. For others, it means more exposure to Muslims or education about Islam.

I've experienced the same fear up close after the first suicide bombers struck American targets in Beirut in the 1980s. I lost friends, colleagues, and contacts in two US Embassy bombings and at the Marine peacekeepers' compound. I spent days finding injured Marines, including the battalion commander, who had been taken to clinics in Shiite neighborhoods where neither American diplomats nor military personnel could go. I've covered dozens of attacks in many countries since then, including the United States on 9/11.

Yet when I lecture about the region, I am often surprised by how many people do not know that Muslims embrace Judaism and Christianity as part of a single religious tradition. *Allah* is simply the Arabic word for the same God. Muslims recognize Abraham, Moses, Jesus, and others as their own. The Virgin Mary is the only woman mentioned by name in the Koran; many Muslim women consider her a role model. Many Old and New Testament prophets are revered in the Koran.

A decade after 9/11, the fear gap is still wide for Americans. My former research assistant, who is of mixed Christian and Jewish stock, wanted to understand what it is like to be a Muslim in America. She was a student at the University of Connecticut in Storrs, where she had also grown up. With help from an Egyptian student, she dressed in hejab and spent a day going to her regular haunts.

What surprised her the most, she later told me, was that no one would look her in the eyes. No one spoke to her, either on campus or in other parts of her hometown. It was as if she did not exist. The only place she was welcomed, even though she was a stranger, was the local mosque she visited as part of her experiment.

Neither blind hate nor blind fear makes for effective policy.

The rage and rebellions across the Islamic world have been most strik-ing because Muslims have shed many of their own fears—even in the face of greater uncertainty in their lives.

"I'm worried about our future. There are not enough signs that tell you liberalism will be achieved or freedom is guaranteed," said Dalia Ziada, the young Egyptian activist, shortly after she returned from a "Protect the Revolution" rally at Liberation Square six weeks after Mubarak's ouster.

"But I'm not afraid. I know now that I have power," she told me. "And I know what to do with it."

ACKNOWLEDGMENTS

When I started out, this book represented an intellectual risk in an environment not yet willing to embrace its counterintuitive themes. Yet from the beginning I had extraordinary help from hundreds of scholars, regional experts, officials, and ordinary people in dozens of countries. I feel exceptionally fortunate to have had their generous support.

First and foremost, I am enormously indebted to the Woodrow Wilson International Center for Scholars in Washington, DC, for supporting this book from its inception. Haleh Esfandiari and Mike Van Dusen pulled out all stops to provide a home and intellectual camaraderie as I developed the themes explored here. I tested many of the ideas for this book during daily exercise walks with Haleh and talks with Mike. Haleh generously and thoughtfully read the raw manuscript all the way through and offered great advice. No amount of thanks will ever be sufficient for two ever-modest scholars. Lee Hamilton, the Wilson Center president who helped define American foreign policy as chairman of the House Foreign Affairs Committee and codirector of the 9/11 Commission, was ever the sage in discussing ideas over the Wilson Center's legendary lunches. Jane Harman, the new Wilson Center president, offered great encouragement.

I then went on to write this book while a senior fellow at the United States Institute of Peace. I am deeply grateful for the enthusiastic support of Richard Solomon and my ever-energetic and thoughtful friend Tara Sonenshine, who can literally make anything happen. Chantal de Jonge Oudraat, Shira Lowinger, and Janene "Go blue" Sawers run a wonderfully collegial fellowship program. We had great fun together too.

Alice Mayhew, my editor at Simon & Schuster, deserves special thanks for her superb advice, timely questions, and insightful guidance, especially as history unfolded in the Middle East and the book quickly became much bigger in scope. I have been honored to work with her again. She has endless good ideas and enviable energy. Esther Newberg has now been my agent, mentor, and friend through five books. She is one of a kind in many ways. I've learned a great deal from both women, now dating back a quarter century.

Simon & Schuster Publisher Jonathan Karp was a wonderful shoulder during critical decisions and I'm especially grateful for his advice. Editor Roger Labrie provided important input and I'm fortunate to get to work with him for the first time. Art Director Michael Accordino designed this beautiful cover, which dramatically but simply captures so many different aspects of an historic transition. Renata Di Biase designed its lovely interior. Irene Kheradi, Gina DiMascia, John Wahler, Gypsy da Silva, and Peg Haller pulled out all stops to produce this book in record time. Brian Ulicky, Tracey Guest, and Rachelle Andujar helped launch "Rock" into the world. With great care, Elisa Rivlin ensured there were no legal issues. Rachel Bergmann assisted the editors. I'm tremendously grateful to them all.

Two friends have been wonderful advisers throughout this book and my life. Ellen Laipson, president of the Stimson Center in Washington, DC, has long been wonderful on all things worldly. Every Saturday morning for some two decades we've walked the Potomac River to discuss the latest twists in international crises and American foreign policy. Joanne Leedom Ackerman and I started our careers together as young reporters at the *Christian Science Monitor* in the 1970s. Our friendship has endured ever since. She read parts of the manuscript and, as with all things in life, offered extraordinary wisdom.

I was particularly fortunate in the specialists from dozens of countries willing to share their expertise. I have learned from them all.

I owe special thanks to several for their extra work on this book. Shaul Bakhash and Karim Sadjadpour have long been my very best guides on Iran. Shaul was particularly gracious in talking me through the final chapter. He knows more than I ever will. David Ottaway, a colleague of thirty years in both the Middle East and Africa, shared his expert insights on Saudi Arabia and read through my Saudi chapters.

On Turkey, Henri Barkey and Omer Taspinar provided thoughtful guidance on a country too little appreciated in the West for its transformative role in the Islamic world from the 1920s through today. I am hugely grateful to Ibrahim Kalin, the director-general of the SETA Foundation for Political, Economic and Social Research, for hosting me in Ankara. Taha Ozhan and Bekir Gur at SETA were exceptionally generous with their time in helping me reach a wide cross section of Turks, from the presidential palace in Ankara to the Islamist politicos in Istanbul. The German-Marshall Fund, particularly the late Ron Asmus and Iveta Kruma, also helped sponsor my research in Turkey and Azerbaijan.

In Egypt, Lina Attalah was an amazing assistant capable of making appointments on her cell phone as she simultaneously navigated through some of the world's most treacherous traffic in Cairo.

In Morocco, Amina Sbai, Kendra Salois, and Rod Solaimani were enormously helpful in navigating the world of rap and its intersection with politics. Josh Asen, director of *I Love Hip Hop in Morocco,* was also considerate in sharing his fascinating film.

Research assistant Brianna Rosen was my right arm through the first critical phase of the book. I still marvel at the scope of her knowledge, enthusiasm, and dedication, as well as the long hours she devoted to this book. I'll never forget the string of emails that arrived at 2:30 in the morning with some new nugget of information. In between competitive rowing races and before leaving for Iraq, researcher Matthew Trevithick, an adventurer at heart, spent a summer pulling together facts, figures, and chronologies essential to this book. He always did it with such good cheer. Tamara Qiblawi was incredibly agile at digging up background materials. And Avideh Mayville had the unenviable task of getting me through the final stages even as she finished her own thesis. She proved she could organize almost anything. Annie Killefer dropped everything to help with the final proofing. I am most grateful to them all.

I also owe special thanks to Dana Priest, John Burnham, and John Toerge. Their kindness was fuel for my soul. Jerry, June, and Nancy Libin have been a second family to me for more than two decades. They are very special people.

Robert Litwak of the Woodrow Wilson Center deserves full credit for coming up with the imaginative title for this book after many struggled for the right words to capture its essence. In his wonderfully gentle way, he was also extremely supportive in sharing his expertise on the world's most volatile region. I am indebted to him for both.

Last but not least, I owe a debt to The Clash, the British band that first sang "Rock the Casbah" in 1982. It was way ahead of its time.

NOTES

PROLOGUE: THE SANDSTORM

1. Street interview on *ABC World News* with Diane Sawyer, Jan. 31, 2011.

2. "Graffiti, Hip-Hop Sk8s: Tehran's Young Rebels Battle the Crackdown," *Time*, Aug. 7, 2009.

3. "Al Qaida No. 2 Issues Video after Egypt Upheaval." Associated Press, Feb. 18, 2011.

4. Ibid.

5. Laura Mansfield, *His Own Words: A Translation of the Writings of Dr. Ayman Al Zawahiri* (Old Tappan, NJ: TLG Publications, 2006), 225.

6. Peter L. Bergen, *The Osama bin Laden I Know: An Oral History of al-Qaeda's Leader* (New York: Free Press, 2006), 384.

7. Samuel Huntington, "The Clash of Civilizations," *Foreign Affairs* 72, no. 3 (1993): 22–49.

8. Ibid.

9. *Mapping the Global Muslim Population: A Report on the Size and Distribution of the World's Muslim Population*, Pew Forum on Religion & Public Life, Pew Research Center, Oct. 7, 2009.

10. Richard Cimino, "Islamic 'Revival' among Aboriginal Australians," OnIslam .net, Dec. 21, 2010, accessed Feb. 18, 2011, www.onislam.net/english/back-to -religion/covering-religion/450232-questioning-islamic-qrevivalq-among -aboriginal-aus.html.

11. *The Future of the Global Muslim Population: Projections for 2010–2030*, Pew Research Center Publications, Jan. 27, 2011.

12. Susan Schmidt, "Imam from Va. Mosque Now Thought to Have Aided Al-Qaeda," *Washington Post*, Feb. 27, 2008.

13. "Shaquille O'Neal Is a Muslim and Is Going to Hajj," www.youtube.com/ watch?v=4LvwLGC5PHs, retrieved Feb. 20, 2011.

14. Selena Roberts, "Enlightening the Clothes-Minded," *Sports Illustrated,* Mar. 5, 2009, http://sportsillustrated.cnn.com/2009/writers/selena_roberts/03/05/ clothesminded/index.html.

15. "University of Memphis' Abdul-Qaadir Receives Most Courageous Award," *Commercial Appeal,* Feb. 17, 2011, accessed Feb. 18, 2011, www .commercialappeal.com/news/2011/feb/17/university-memphis-abdul-qaadir -receives-most-cour/.

16. Interview on *Anderson Cooper 360°,* CNN, Feb. 18, 2011.

17. Borzou Daragahi, "Tens of Thousands March Peacefully in Morocco for Political Reform," *Los Angeles Times,* Feb. 20, 2011.

18. Russell Goldman, "Egyptian Names Baby 'Facebook' for Site's Role in Revolution," ABC News/Technology, Feb. 21, 2011, http://abcnews.go.com/ Technology/Egypt_Christiane_Amanpour/egyptian-names-baby-facebook -sites-role-revolution/story?id=12964978, retrieved Feb. 21, 2011.

19. Kareem Fahim, "Hopes of Egyptians, Poor and Wealthy, Converge in Fight for Cairo Bridge," *New York Times,* Jan. 28, 2011.

CHAPTER 1: THE SCENT OF JASMINE

1. Ellen Knickmeyer, "The Arab World's Youth Army," *Foreign Policy,* Jan. 27, 2011.

2. Kareem Fahim, "Slap to a Man's Pride Set Off Tumult in Tunisia," *New York Times,* Jan. 22, 2011; Kristen Chick, "How Revolt Sparked Life in Tunisia," *Christian Science Monitor,* Jan. 23, 2011; Rania Abouzeid, "Bouazizi: The Man Who Set Himself and Tunisia on Fire," *Time,* Jan. 21, 2011; Yasmine Ryan, "The Tragic Life of a Street Vendor," Aljazeera.net, Jan. 20, 2011; Yasmine Ryan, "How Tunisia's Revolution Began," Aljazeera.net, Jan. 26, 2011.

3. Ibid.

4. Ryan, "Tragic Life"; Ryan, "How Tunisia's Revolution Began."

5. Lin Noueihed, "Peddler's Martyrdom Launched Tunisia's Revolution," Reuters, Jan. 19, 2011.

6. Anita Elash, "Tracking the Assets of Tunisia's Ousted Leader," *PRI's The World,* Jan. 19, 2011, www.theworld.org/2011/01/19/tracking-the-assets-of -tunisias-ousted-leader/, retrieved Feb. 7, 2011.

7. Chick, "How Revolt Sparked Life."

8. "President Zine al Abidine Ben Ali Visits Young Man Mohamed Bouazizi," Tunisia Tour, Dec. 28, 2010, www.tunisia-tour.com/fr/tunisie/tunisia -news/1078-president-zine-el-abidine-ben-ali-visits-young-man-mohamed -bouazizi, retrieved Jan. 23, 2011.

9. David D. Fitzpatrick, "President of Tunisia Flees, Capitulating to Protests." *New York Times,* Jan. 15, 2011.

10. Jeffrey Fleishman, "Tunisia Nudges Arab World Out of Its Hopelessness," *Los Angeles Times,* Jan. 23, 2011.

11. "Self-immolation Spreads across the Mideast, Inspiring Protest, Controversy," The Media Line, www.themedialine.org/news/news_detail.asp?NewsID=31194, retrieved Feb. 8, 2011.

12. "Saudi Man Sets Himself Alight in Poor Border Region," Reuters, Jan. 22, 2011; "Saudi Man Dies after Setting Himself on Fire," Associated Press, Jan. 22, 2011.

13. "20,000 Take Over Qasr al-Nil Bridge," *Al Masry al Youm,* English edition, Jan. 29, 2011; Ahdaf Soueif, "An Eye-witness Account of the Egyptian Protests," *Guardian,* Jan. 28, 2011; Jenna Krajeski, "The Taking of Kasr al Nil," *The New Yorker Blog,* www.newyorker.com/online/blogs/newsdesk/2011/01/the-taking-of-kasr-al-nil.html#ixzz1CUgZW1ox, retrieved Jan. 29, 2011; Fahim, "Hopes of Egyptians"; Richard Spencer, "Battle of the Nile Balanced on a Knife Edge," *Daily Telegraph,* Jan. 29, 2011.

14. Ibid.

15. "20,000 Take Over," *Al Masry al Youm;* Krajeski, "The Taking of Kasr al Nil."

16. *ABC World News with Diane Sawyer,* Feb. 1, 2011.

17. Marjorie Olster and Sarah el Deeb, "At Cairo Square, Protesters Sow Seeds of New Egypt," Associated Press, Jan. 31, 2011.

18. Kareem Fahim and Anthony Shadid, "Quiet Acts of Protest on a Noisy Day," *New York Times,* Feb. 2, 2011.

19. Charles M. Blow, "The Kindling of Change," op-ed, *New York Times,* Feb. 5, 2011.

20. Jeremy Harding, "The Great Unleashing," *London Review of Books,* July 25, 2002.

21. "Young Egyptians Increasingly See Their Potential Untapped," Gallup poll in Egypt, Feb. 9, 2011.

22. Blow, "Kindling of Change."

23. Interview with Ivan Watson, CNN, Feb. 9, 2011.

24. Interview with Wolf Blitzer, *The Situation Room,* CNN, Feb. 9, 2011.

25. Ibid.

26. David Wolman, "Cairo Activists Use Facebook to Rattle Regime," *Wired,* July 23, 2008.

27. "Egypt," Open Net Initiative, Aug. 6, 2009, http://opennet.net/research/pro files/egypt, retrieved Feb. 10, 2011; "10 Worst Countries to Be a Blogger," Special Report, Committee to Protect Journalists, Apr. 30, 2009, http://cpj .org/reports/2009/04/10-worst-countries-to-be-a-blogger.php, retrieved Feb. 10, 2011.

28. Kristen Chick, "Beating Death of Egyptian Businessman Khalid Said Spotlights Police Brutality," *Christian Science Monitor*, June 18, 2010; Jennifer Preston, "Movement Began with Outrage and a Facebook Page That Gave It an Outlet," *New York Times*, Feb. 5, 2011.

29. "Egypt: Prosecute Police in Beating Death: Multiple Witnesses and Graphic Photos Belie Police Narrative," Human Rights Watch, June 24, 2010, www .hrw.org/en/news/2010/06/24/egypt=prosecute=police=beating=death.

30. YouTube, www.youtube.com/user/wolfinside1985#p/u/4/35t58GFfMbo, retrieved Feb. 11, 2011; Preston, "Movement Began with Outrage."

31. Interview on *John King, USA*, CNN, Feb. 2, 2011.

32. Souad Mekhennet and Nicholas Kulish, "2 Detained Reporters Saw Secret Police's Methods Firsthand," *New York Times*, Feb. 5, 2011.

33. David D. Kirkpatrick and David E. Sanger, "A Tunisian-Egyptian Link That Shook Arab History," *New York Times*, Feb. 13, 2011.

34. David D. Kirkpatrick and David E. Sanger, "Egypt Officials Seek to Nudge Mubarak Out," *New York Times*, Feb. 5, 2011.

35. Mike Giglio, "The Facebook Freedom Fighter," *Newsweek*, Feb. 13, 2011.

36. "Profile: Egypt's Wael Ghonim," BBC News, Feb. 8, 2011.

37. Sammy Ketz, "Iraq PM Pledges Not to Seek Third Term," Agence France-Presse, Feb. 5, 2011.

38. Lara Jakes, "Iraqi Premier Says He'll Cut His Salary by Half," Associated Press, Feb. 4, 2011.

39. Ibid.

40. Jay Solomon, "Interview with Syrian President Bashar al Assad," *Wall Street Journal*, Jan. 31, 2011.

41. Question from Wolf Blitzer in interview with Wael Ghonim on *Anderson Cooper 360°*, CNN, Feb. 11, 2011.

CHAPTER 2: THE COUNTER-JIHAD

1. Somini Sengupta, "Dossier Gives Details of Mumbai Attacks," *New York Times*, Jan. 6, 2009.

2. Robert F. Worth, "Muslims in India Put Aside Grievances to Repudiate Terrorism," *New York Times,* Dec. 8, 2008.

3. Thomas L. Friedman, "No Way, No How, Not Here," *New York Times,* Feb. 18, 2009.

4. "Attackers Buried Secretly," Reuters, Apr. 7, 2010.

5. Christian Caryl, "Sheikh to Terrorists: Go to Hell. Meet the Pakistani Sheikh Who Declared War on the Terrorists," *Foreign Policy,* Apr. 14, 2010.

6. Interview on Al Jazeera television news, aired several times between Jan. 30 and Feb. 2, 2009.

7. "30 Terrorists Plots Against the U.S. Failed since 9/11," http://s3.amazonaws .com/thf_media/2010/pdf/b2405_figure1_2.pdf; Samantha Gross, "Failed Terror Plots Leave NY Residents Wary," Associated Press, May 4, 2010.

8. www.revolutionmuslim.com/search?q=south+park.

9. Sadia Dehlvi, "The Threat of Political Islam," http://indianmuslims.in/the -threat-of-political-islam/, Mar. 29, 2009.

10. Pew Global Attitudes Project, "Mixed Views of Hamas and Hezbollah in Largely Muslim Nations," Feb. 4, 2010, and "Islamic Extremism: Common Concern for Muslim and Western Publics: Summary of Findings," July 14, 2005.

11. Pew Global Attitudes Project, "Mixed Views of Hamas and Hezbollah in Largely Muslim Nations," Feb. 4, 2010, 13.

12. Ibid.

13. "Phone Survey of Cairo and Alexandria," conducted by Pechter Middle East Polls for the Washington Institute for Near East Policy, Feb. 5–8, 2011.

14. Ethan Bronner, "Palestinians Try a Less Violent Path to Resistance," *New York Times,* Apr. 6, 2010.

15. Hossam Ezzedin, "Palestine," *Arab Reform Bulletin,* Carnegie Endowment for International Peace, Mar. 23, 2010.

16. Robert Mackey, " 'Avatar on the West Bank,' " The Lede Blog, *New York Times,* Feb. 16, 2010; "The Making of the West Bank's 'Avatar' Protest," *AOL News,* Feb. 12, 2010.

17. Mohammad Assadi, "Palestinian PM Ploughs Ahead with Future State," Reuters, Mar. 30, 2010; Bronner, "Palestinians Try."

18. Assadi, "Palestinian PM Ploughs Ahead."

19. Bronner, "Palestinians Try"; Ilene R. Prusher, "Palestinian Authority Steps Up Boycott of Goods Made in Israeli Settlements in West Bank," *Christian Science Monitor,* Feb. 25, 2010.

20. The bonfire coincided with a ruling from the European Union Court that goods produced in Israel's 120 settlements in the West Bank do not qualify for duty-free import. Only products made within Israel's pre-1967 borders qualified for duty-free status.

21. Bronner, "Palestinians Try."

22. "Hebron: 11 Tons of Settlement Watermelon Confiscated," Ma'an News Agency, Apr. 16, 2010; http://palestinenote.com/cs/blogs/news/archive/2010/04/15/settlement-watermelon-confiscated-in-west-bank.aspx.

23. Heather Sharp, "Palestinians Test Out Gandhi-style Protest," *BBC News*, Apr. 14, 2010; Bronner, "Palestinians Try."

24. Mohammed Mar'i, "Rajmohan Gandhi: Bil'in a Model for Nonviolent Resistance," *Arab News*, Apr. 5, 2010.

25. Susan Webb, "Palestinians and Israelis Call for Nonviolent People Power to End Occupation," *People's World*, Apr. 11, 2010; Mar'i, "Rajmohan Gandhi."

26. "Jordanian CIA Bomber Urges Muslims to Wage Jihad," Associated Press, Apr. 30, 2010.

27. Nic Robertson, and Paul Cruickshank, "In Bid to Thwart al Qaeda, Libya Frees Three Leaders of Jihadist Group," CNN, Mar. 23, 2010.

28. Michael Jacobson, "Learning from Dropouts," *Foreign Policy*, Feb. 2, 2010.

29. *9/11 Commission Report*, 2003, 62, 79, and 126.

30. Thomas Rid, "Cracks in al Qaeda," *Wilson Quarterly* (Winter 2010): 40–47.

31. Leah Farrall, "Hotline to Jihad," *The Australian*, Dec. 7, 2009.

32. John A. McCary, "The Anbar Awakening: An Alliance of Incentives," *Washington Quarterly* (Jan. 2009): 43–59.

33. Thomas E. Ricks, "Situation Called Dire in West Iraq," *Washington Post*, Sept. 11, 2006; "Anbar Picture Grows Clearer, and Bleaker," *Washington Post*, Nov. 28, 2006.

34. Sheikh Sattar was also known by his full tribal name Abdul Sattar Eftikhan al-Rishawi al-Dulaimi.

35. Joshua Partlow, Ann Scott Tyson, and Robin Wright, "Bomb Kills Key Sunni Ally of U.S.," *Washington Post*, Sept. 13, 2007.

36. McCary, "The Anbar Awakening."

37. "Obituary: Abdul Sattar Abu Risha," *BBC News*, Sept. 13, 2007.

38. Pamela Constable, "After Reaching Deal in North, Islamists Aim to Install Religious Law Nationwide," *Washington Post*, Apr. 20, 2009.

39. Saeed Shah, "Pakistani Taliban Turn Honeymoon Spot into Slaughterhouse," McClatchy Newspapers, Jan. 26, 2009.

40. Declan Walsh, "Taliban Hand Out 37 Lashes to Girl Seen with Married Man," *Guardian*, Apr. 2, 2009.

41. Pamela Constable, "Taliban-Style Justice Stirs Growing Anger," *Washington Post*, May 19, 2009.

42. Sabrina Tavernise, "Taliban Stir Rising Anger of Pakistanis," *New York Times*, June 5, 2009.

43. Constable, "Taliban-Style Justice."

44. Rania Abouzeid, "Taliban Ousted, Pakistan's Swat Valley Still Longs for Islamic Justice," *Time*, Apr. 25, 2010.

45. "Growing Concerns about Extremism, Continuing Discontent with U.S.," Pew Global Attitudes Project, Aug. 13, 2009, 1.

46. Ibid., 10–11.

47. Tavernise, "Taliban Stir Rising Anger."

CHAPTER 3: THE BIG CHILL

1. "Text of the Fatwa Declared against Osama Bin Laden by the Islamic Commission of Spain," March 17, 2005, http://webislam.com/?idn=537; original Spanish version: "La Comisión Islámica de España emite una fatua condenando el terrorismo y al grupo Al Qaida," March 10, 2005, www.webislam .com/?idn=399.

2. Fawaz A. Gerges, "Disowned by Mentor, Bin Laden Seeks New Pastures," *Yale Global Online Magazine*, http://yaleglobal.yale.edu; Khaled al-Awadh, "Oudah Denounces Bin Laden's Ideology," *Arab News*, Sept. 17, 2007. Other translations are available at www.muslimmatters.org and Special Dispatch no. 1717, Middle East Media Research Institute, Sept. 17, 2007.

3. CNN transcript of Osama bin Laden interview by Peter Arnett in eastern Afghanistan in late March 1997.

4. Bergen, *The Osama bin Laden I Know*, 149.

5. Jarret Brachman, *Global Jihadism: Theory and Practice* (New York: Routledge, 2009), 79.

6. CNN transcript of Osama bin Laden interview.

7. Stanley Reed, "Inside Saudi Arabia," Special Report no. 3759, *BusinessWeek International*, Nov. 26, 2001, 26.

8. "Awda, Salman al- (1955–), Personal History, Influences and Contributions, Biographical Highlights, Personal Chronology: Arrest and Imprisonment," http://encyclopedia.jrank.org/articles/pages/5548/Awda-Salman-al—1955 .html.

9. "Jordanian Authorities Expel Saudi Sheikh Salman al-Odeh," www.arabic news.com, Aug. 13, 2002.

10. Bernard Haykel, "The Enemy of My Enemy Is Still My Enemy," *New York Times*, July 26, 2006.

11. Sheikh Salman al-Oadah, "Violent Crimes in Islam's Name Are a Tragedy," Apr. 15, 2007, www.islamtoday.com.

12. Thomas Hegghammer, "The Failure of Jihad in Saudi Arabia," West Point Combating Terrorism Center Occasional Paper, Feb. 25, 2010, 12.

13. Ibid., 13.

14. Thomas Hegghammer, *Jihad in Saudi Arabia: Violence and Pan-Islamism since 1979* (Cambridge: Cambridge University Press, 2010), 204–5.

15. Thomas Hegghammer, "Failure of Jihad," 15–17.

16. Ibid., 4–10.

17. Ibid., 9.

18. Ibid.

19. Robert F. Worth, "Saudis Retool to Root Out Terrorist Risk," *New York Times*, March 22, 2009.

20. Rob Wagner, "Rehabilitation and Deradicalization: Saudi Arabia's Counterterrorism Successes and Failures," Peace and Conflict Special Report, Peace and Conflict Monitor, Aug. 1, 2010, www.monitor.upeace.org/inner pgcfm?id_article=735.

21. "Global Unease about Major Powers," Pew Global Attitudes Project, June 27, 2007; "Global Opinion Trends 2002–2007: A Rising Tide Lifts Mood in Developing World," Pew Global Attitudes Project, July 24, 2007, 55–59.

22. Phil Leggiere, "Is al Qaeda Imploding?" *HS Today: Homeland Security Insight and Analysis*, June 2, 2008.

23. Lawrence Wright, "The Rebellion Within," *New Yorker*, June 2, 2008.

24. Ibid.

25. Faiza Saleh Ambah, "In War on Terror, Saudis Try Amnesty," *Christian Science Monitor*, July 14, 2004.

26. Christopher Boucek. "Saudi Arabia's Soft Counterterrorism Strategy: Prevention, Rehabilitation, and Aftercare," Carnegie Papers no. 97, Carnegie Endowment for International Peace, September 2008, 7.

27. David Ottaway, "Saudi Effort Draws on Radical Clerics to Combat Lure of al-Qaeda," *Washington Post*, May 7, 2006.

28. Wagner, "Rehabilitation and Deradicalization."

29. Robert F. Worth, "Saudis' Help in Stopping Plot Is Part of Shift in Security Role," *New York Times*, Oct. 31, 2010.

30. Paul Handley, "20 Percent Failure Rate in Saudi Gitmo Rehab Program," Agence France-Presse, June 19, 2010; "Ex-Guantanamo inmates 'fail rehab,' " Aljazeera.net, June 20, 2010.

31. "Ex-Guantanamo Inmates 'Fail Rehab.' "

32. Abdullah al Oraifij, "Shihri's Father Damns Him for Returning to al Qaeda," *Saudi Gazette*, Jan. 26, 2009.

33. "A Glance at Saudi Government-Approved Fatwas," Associated Press, Oct. 9, 2010.

34. Boucek, "Saudi Arabia's Soft Counterterrorism Strategy," 21.

35. US Department of Justice Bureau of Justice Statistics on recidivism, http://bjs.ojp.usdoj.gov; "U.S. Prisons Overcrowded and Violent, Recidivism High," Infoplease.com, www.infoplease.com/ipa/A0933722.html#ixzz12vyHw4CY.

CHAPTER 4: A MIDSUMMER'S EVE

1. Borzou Daragahi, "Iran's Mousavi Calls for More Civil Disobedience," *Los Angeles Times*, Sept. 5, 2009.

2. *For Neda*, documentary produced by Antony Thomas, HBO, June 6, 2010.

3. Ibid.

4. Neil MacFarquhar, "Iran's New Ideal: Small Families," *International Herald Tribune*, Sept. 9, 1996.

5. Shaul Bakhash, "The Six Presidents," in *The Iran Primer: Power, Politics, and U.S. Policy*, edited by Robin Wright (Washington, DC: U.S. Institute of Peace and the Woodrow Wilson International Center for Scholars, 2010).

6. "Mousavi-Ahmadinejad June 3 Presidential Debate Transcript," www.iran tracker.org, retrieved Jan. 6, 2011.

7. Robert Tait, "Mahmoud Ahmadinejad in Bitter TV Clash with Iranian Poll Rival," *Guardian*, June 4, 2009.

8. "The FP Top 100 Global Thinkers," *Foreign Policy*, Dec. 2009.

9. Borzou Daragahi and Ramin Mostaghim, "Iran's President's Rivals Slam His Foreign Policy," *Los Angeles Times*, May 31, 2009.

10. Ibid.

11. Jason Keyser, "Speed of Iran Vote Count Called Suspicious," Associated Press, June 15, 2009; Roger Cohen, "My Name Is Iran," *New York Times*, June 18, 2009.

12. Many analysts had predicted the 2005 runoff would be between Rafsanjani and Karroubi—and that the little-known Ahmadinejad would not rank. Both Rafsanjani and Karroubi had hinted at fraud then too, although nothing close to the scale in 2009.

13. Robert F. Worth, "Results Spur Charge That Leaders Stole Presidential Vote," *New York Times*, June 14, 2009.

14. Bill Keller, "Wide Reverberations as Door Slams on Hope of Change," *New York Times*, June 14, 2009.

15. Nazila Fathi, "Iran's Top Leader Dashes Hopes for a Compromise," *New York Times*, June 19, 2009.

16. *For Neda.*

17. *A Death in Tehran*, produced by Monica Garnsey, *Frontline*, PBS, Nov. 17, 2009.

18. "Iran," Internet World Stats, www.internetworldstats.com/me/ir.htm, retrieved Mar. 17, 2011.

19. Nazila Fathi, "A Recount Offer Fails to Silence Protests in Iran," *New York Times*, June 17, 2009.

20. Ibid.

21. *A Death in Tehran.*

22. Fathi, "Iran's Top Leader"; Ali Akbar Dareini and Brian Murphy, "Iran's Leader: End Protests or Risk 'Bloodshed,' " Associated Press, June 19, 2009.

23. *A Death in Tehran.*

24. Ibid.

25. *For Neda.*

26. Damien McElroy, "Iranian Regime Targets Family of 'Angel of Freedom' Neda Agha Soltan," *Daily Telegraph*, June 23, 2009.

27. Martin Fletcher, "Doctor Who Tended Neda Soltan Breaks His Silence," *Times* (London), June 26, 2009.

28. *A Death in Tehran.*

29. Martin Fletcher, "The Face of Abbas Kargar Javid—Man Accused of Killing Neda Soltan," *Times* (London), Aug. 20, 2009; "Iran—Neda's Killer Confronted Video," YouTube.com, www.youtube.com/watch?v=01Ti-MnN3aY, Sept. 26, 2009, retrieved Jan. 11, 2011.

30. Andrew Malcolm, "Iran Ambassador Suggests CIA Could Have Killed Neda Agha-Soltan," *Los Angeles Times*, June 25, 2009.

31. *For Neda.*

32. *A Death in Tehran.*

33. *For Neda.*

34. Ibid.

35. "Neda's Grave: A Shrine to Anger at Iran's Regime," *Time*, Sept. 1, 2009.

36. Martin Fletcher, "Grave of Neda Soltan Desecrated by Supporters of Iranian Regime," *Times* (London), Nov. 16, 2009; *A Death in Tehran.*

37. Delphine Minoui, "A Téhéran, un étudiant ose critiquer Khamenei," *Le Figaro*, http://blog.lefigaro.fr/iran/2009/11/a-teheran-un-etudiant-critique .html, retrieved Jan. 11, 2011.

38. "Math student Mahmoud Vahidnia Stuns Iran by Criticizing Supreme Leader Ayatollah Ali Khamenei," Associated Press, Nov. 6, 2009; Robert Tait, "Iranian Student Dares to Criticize Ayatollah Ali Khamenei to His Face," *Guardian*, Nov. 6, 2009.

39. Ibid.

40. "Students Day Protests Sweep Campuses across Iran," Tehran Bureau, Dec. 8, 2009, www.pbs.org/wgbh/pages/frontline/tehranbureau/2009/12/student -protests-mark-16-azar-all-over-iran.html, retrieved March 21, 2011.

CHAPTER 5: HIP-HOP ISLAM

1. *Taqwacore: The Birth of Punk Islam*, documentary about Michael Muhammad Knight, 2009, www.philosufi.com/blog/2010/10/taqwacore-the-birth -of-punk-islam.html.

2. Vivienne Walt, "El Général and the Rap Anthem of the Mideast Revolution," *Time*, Feb. 15, 2011, www.time.com/time/printout/0,8816,2049456,00.html, retrieved Mar. 6, 2011.

3. Andy Morgan, "From Fear to Fury: How the Arab World Found Its Voice," *Guardian*, Feb. 27, 2011, www.guardian.co.uk/music/2011/feb/27/egypt -tunisia-music-protests, retrieved Mar. 6, 2011.

4. "President, Your People Are Dying—El General with Lyrics," YouTube.com, www.youtube.com/watch?v=9DpUo0cpiXM, retrieved Mar. 7, 2011; "El Général, the Voice of Tunisia, English Subtitles," www.youtube.com/watch?v =IeGlJ7OouR0&feature=related, retrieved Mar. 7, 2011.

5. "Tunisian Rapper Arrested after Online Protest Song," Reuters, Jan. 7, 2011.

6. Walt, "El Général and the Rap Anthem."

7. Ibid.

8. "Bombs Kill at Least 20 in Downtown Casablanca," CNN, May 16, 2003; Elaine Sciolino, "Officials Suspect Global Terror Tie in Morocco Blasts,"

New York Times, May 18, 2003; Elaine Sciolino, "Aftereffects: In Casablanca Neighborhood, Ruptured Calm," *New York Times,* May 19, 2003.

9. Barbara Surk, "MTV's New Arab Music Video Channel Looks to Use Hip Hop to Conquer Middle East Market," Associated Press, Nov. 18, 2007; Faiza Saleh Ambah, "Saudi Hip-Hop's Painful Birth," *Washington Post,* Feb. 22, 2008.

10. Ismail El-Mokadem, "Islamic Music Videos, All the Time," *Daily News* (Egypt), July 27, 2008.

11. " 'Islamic Idol' a Hit on World's First Muslim Pop Music Channel," Associated Press, Apr. 17, 2009.

12. Carla Power, "Muslim Punk Rock: A Mashup of Piety and Politics," *Time,* Dec. 3, 2009.

13. Ashraf Javed, "Huge Unemployment Can Push Youth to Militancy," *Nation,* Aug. 22, 2010; "Unemployment Doubles in a Space of a Year: Study," *Express Tribune,* Nov. 18, 2010.

14. Molly Kinder, "A Better Education for Pakistan's Youth: It Takes More than Money," in *Rethinking U.S. Foreign Assistance,* Center for Global Development, Oct. 1, 2010.

15. Omid Memarian and Tara Nesvaderani, "The Youth," in *The Iran Primer: Power, Politics, and U.S. Policy,* edited by Robin Wright (Washington, DC: U.S. Institute of Peace and the Woodrow Wilson International Center for Scholars, 2010).

16. "Jordan Queen: Arab Unemployment 'Time Bomb,' " Associated Press, Nov. 2, 2008; Mohammed bin Rashid al Maktoum, "More than Half of Arabs Are under 25 Years Old," *Wall Street Journal,* June 3, 2009.

17. Sherine el Madany, "Egypt's Youth on Political Sidelines—U.N. Report," Reuters, June 27, 2010.

18. Al Maktoum, "More than Half of Arabs."

19. "Jordan Queen: Arab Unemployment."

20. Tina Susman, "Iraq's Young Jobless Threaten Stability, Report Says," *Los Angeles Times,* Feb. 16, 2009.

21. Afshin Molavi, "Young and Restless," *Smithsonian,* Apr. 2006.

22. Roger Hardy, "Unemployment, the New Saudi Challenge," *BBC News,* Oct. 4, 2006.

23. Brigitta Burks, "Unemployment in Morocco," Institute for International Journalism, Mar. 15, 2010.

24. Amy Goodman, "Palestinian Rap Group DAM Use Hip-Hop to Convey the Frustrations, Hopes of a Dispossessed People," *Democracy Now,*

May 15, 2008, www.democracynow.org/2008/5/15/slingshot_hip_hop_pal estinian_rap_group.

25. Lisa Goldman, "Who's the Terrorist?" *Tablet*, Nov. 6, 2007.

26. Steven Erlanger, "Children of the Palestinian Intifada: The Lost Generation," *New York Times*, Mar. 11, 2007.

27. "The History of Israel: A Chronological Presentation 1977–1993," www .history-of-israel.org, accessed Nov. 29, 2010; "Fatalities in the First Intifada," B'Tselem: The Israeli Information Center for Human Rights in the Occupied Territories, www.btselem.org, accessed Nov. 29, 2010.

28. "Fatalities in the First Intifada."

29. Barton Gellman, "West Bank Families Wait for Their Daughters—Israel Hasn't Yet Kept Its Pact Promise," *Washington Post*, Oct. 3, 1995, www.ency clopedia.com/The+Washington+Post/publications.aspx?date=19951003&page Number=2.

30. "Victims of Palestinian Violence and Terrorism since September 2000," Israel Ministry of Foreign Affairs, accessed Nov. 29, 2010; "Fatalities since the Outbreak of the Second Intifada and until Operation 'Cast Lead,'" B'Tselem: The Israeli Information Center for Human Rights in the Occupied Territories, www.btselem.org/English/statistics/Casualties.asp?sD=29&sM=09&sY =2000&eD=26&eM=12&eY=2008&filterby=event&oferet_stat=before, accessed Nov. 29, 2010.

31. Matt Dearborn, "DAM Raps on Palestinian Nation," *Chronicle*, June 14, 2006, http://dukechronicle.com/article/DAM-raps-palestinian-nation.

32. Erlanger, "Children of the Palestinian Intifada."

33. "UN: 70% of Palestinian Youth Oppose Violence to Resolve Conflict with Israel," Deutsche Press Agency in *Haaretz*, Apr. 1, 2009.

34. Griffe Witte, "Gaza Children Recount Horror of War," *Washington Post*, Jan. 25, 2009.

35. "UN: 70% of Palestinian Youth Oppose Violence."

36. Ibid.

37. Goldman, "Who's the Terrorist?"

38. Ibid.

39. Ibid.

40. Sue Carter Flinn, "War & Beats: Somalian-Born Hip-Hop Artist K'naan Wants His Music to Have Purpose," *Coast*, Oct. 13, 2005.

41. Jim Welte, "K'Naan Breaks Out," MP3.com Live, Aug. 7, 2006.

42. Andrea Elliott, "The Jihadist Next Door," *New York Times Magazine,* Jan. 27, 2010.

43. By 2010, the United States had charged thirty Somali Americans from Minnesota and California with aiding or abetting al Shabab. Others were picked up before they could leave the United States.

44. "Al Qaeda Exporting Jihad with a Hip-hop Vibe," CNN, May 4, 2009.

45. "Somalia," www.atlapedia.com/online/countries/somalia.htm, retrieved Mar. 4, 2011.

46. "Somalia: Primary School Years," www.unicef.org/somalia/children_87 .html, retrieved Mar. 4, 2011.

47. "Education under Attack 2010—Somalia," Refworld, UN High Commission for Refugees, Feb. 10, 2010; Abdurrahman Warsameh, "Somalia: Fighting for an Education," IPS, July 1, 2008.

48. Jeffrey Gettleman, "Children Carry Guns for a U.S. Ally, Somalia," *New York Times,* June 13, 2010.

49. Jonathan Takiff, "Somali Singer K'Naan's Music Transforms Him into a Global Icon," *Philadelphia Daily News,* Apr. 5, 2010.

CHAPTER 6: THE NEW CHIC

1. Abigail Hauslohner, "Egypt Strengthens Ban on Female Genital Cutting," Reuters, June 28, 2007.

2. Maggie Michael, "Video Shows Egypt Prisoner's Humiliation," Associated Press, Jan. 21, 2007.

3. Riad Abu Awad, "Daring Egyptian Actress Dons Headscarf, Calls Iran 'Role Model,'" *Daily News Egypt,* June 17, 2006.

4. Ibid.

5. John L. Esposito and Dalia Mogahed. "What Do Muslim Women Want?" Excerpt from "Who Speaks for Islam?" Gallup poll, Mar. 20, 2008.

6. Ibid.

7. "Little Enthusiasm for Many Muslim Leaders: Mixed Views of Hamas and Hezbollah in Largely Muslim Nations," Pew Global Attitudes Survey, Feb. 4, 2010.

8. Isobel Coleman, *Paradise Beneath Her Feet: How Women Are Transforming the Middle East* (New York: Random House, 2010), xxv.

9. "Peacebuilder Profiles: A. Rashied Omar," interview July 2005, www.beyond intractability.org/reflections/peacebuilder_profiles/Rashied_Omar/Rashied_ Omar.jsp?nid=5300.

10. Amina Wadud, *Inside the Gender Jihad: Women's Reform in Islam* (Oxford: Oneworld Publications, 2006), 183.

11. Ibid., 172.

12. Ibid., 219.

13. Amina Wadud, *Qur'an and Woman: Rereading the Sacred Text from a Woman's Perspective* (New York: Oxford University Press, 1999), 9.

14. Ibid., 40.

15. Ibid.

16. Ibid., 80.

17. Sura 4:3.

18. Wadud, *Qur'an and Woman*, 77.

19. Ibid., 76–88.

20. Ibid., 86.

21. Wadud, *Inside the Gender Jihad*, 4.

22. Ibid., 9.

23. Ibid., 3.

24. Wiebke Walther, *Women in Islam: From Medieval to Modern Times* (Princeton, NJ: Markus Wiener, 1993), 111.

25. Marina Ottaway and Omayma Abdellatif, "Women in Islamist Movements: Toward an Islamist Model of Women's Activism," Carnegie Papers no. 2, Carnegie Endowment for International Peace, June 2007.

26. Ibid.

27. Robert F. Worth, "Challenging Sex Taboos, with Help from the Koran," *New York Times*, June 6, 2009.

28. Azza Karam, *Women, Islamism, and the State* (New York: St. Martin's Press, 1998), 222.

29. Yigal Schleifer, "In Turkey, Muslim Women Gain Expanded Religious Authority," *Christian Science Monitor*, Apr. 27, 2005.

30. "Turkey's 'Vaizes' Expedite Reform," *Washington Times*, May 2, 2006.

31. Yasmine Saleh, "Mufti's 'Hymen Fatwa' Causes Shock Waves Among Scholars," *Daily News Egypt*, Feb. 20, 2007.

32. Robin Shulman, "Morocco's New Guiding Force," *Washington Post*, May 30, 2009; Sally Williams, "Mourchidat—Morocco's Female Muslim Clerics," *Daily Telegraph*, Apr. 26, 2008.

33. Williams, "Mourchidat."

34. Aluma Dankowitz, "First Friday Prayers Led by a Woman: Muslim Reactions to an Historical Precedent," Middle East Meida Research Institute Inquiry and Analysis Series, no. 227, June 22, 2005.

35. Wadud, *Inside the Gender Jihad*, 222–23.

CHAPTER 7: THE LIVING POETS SOCIETY

1. Wadud, *Inside the Gender Jihad*, 10.

2. "Saudi Cleric Backs Gender Segregation with Fatwa," Reuters, Feb. 2, 2010. The fatwa was released on his website albarrak.islamlight.net.

3. "Bin Laden's Poetry of Terror," *Newsweek*, Mar. 26, 2001; "Bin Laden Reads Poem on Cole Bombing," *ABC News*, Mar. 1, 2000.

4. John Harlow, "Pray Silence for Bin Laden the Wedding Poet," *Sunday Times of London*, Sept. 21, 2008; Carolyn Kellogg, "Osama bin Laden, Poet," *Los Angeles Times*, Sept. 25, 2008.

5. David Rohde, "Verses from bin Laden's War," *New York Times*, Apr. 7, 2002.

6. "Million Poet's Finalist Defies Death Threats," *National*, Mar. 19, 2010.

7. Raid Qusti, "Coffee with Colleague Lands Woman in Trouble," *Arab News*, Feb. 5, 2008.

8. "Security, Religion Block Saudi Rights Progress: Amnesty," Agence France-Presse, May 26, 2010.

9. "Saudi Judge: It's OK to Slap Spendthrift Wives," CNN, May 10, 2010.

10. Alexandra Sandels, "Cleric Calls for Muslim-only Maids in Saudi Homes," Babylon & Beyond Blog, *Los Angeles Times*, July 27, 2010.

11. John L. Esposito and Dalia Mogahed, *Who Speaks for Islam? What a Billion Muslims Really Think* (New York: Gallup Press, 2007), 99–133.

12. Wajeha al Huwaider, "Why Don't We Read?" *Arab News*, Aug. 26, 2002.

13. William Dowell, "Saudi Arabia Life in the Slow Lane," *Time*, Nov. 26, 1990; Donna Abu-Nasr, "Stunning Saudi Car Ride Celebrated 18 Years Later," Associated Press, Nov. 14, 2008.

14. Abu-Nasr, "Stunning Saudi Car Ride."

15. Dowell, "Saudi Arabia Life in the Slow Lane"; Abu-Nasr, "Stunning Saudi Car Ride."

16. CNN interview with Peter Bergen, Mar. 1997.

17. Osama bin Laden. "Al Qaeda's Fatwa," Feb. 23, 1998, *PBS NewsHour*, www
.pbs.org/newshour/terrorism/international/fatwa_1998.html.

18. "Our Women Must Be Protected," *Economist*, Apr. 24, 2009.

19. "Saudi Woman Jailed for Not Using Male Guardian," Agence France-
Presse, Mar. 3, 2010; "Saudi Arabia: Free Woman Who Sought Court Aid,"
Human Rights Watch, Mar. 2, 2010, www.hrw.org/en/news/2010/03/02/
saudi-arabia-free-woman-who-sought-court-aid.

20. "Wajeha al Huwaider for Women's Day 2008," YouTube.com, www.youtube
.com/watch?v=q8GiTnb33wE, retrieved Mar. 8, 2011.

21. www.metransparent.com; A. Dankowitz, "Saudi Writer and Journalist
Wajeha al-Huwaider Fights for Women's Rights," Middle East Media Research Institute Inquiry and Analysis Series, no. 312, Dec. 28, 2006.

22. "New Arab-English Website on 'The Arab Rosa Parks,' " Middle East Media
Research Institute, Special Dispatch 1757, Nov. 2, 2007, www.memri.org/
report/en/0/0/0/0/0/220/2448.htm#_edn1, retrieved Mar. 9, 2011.

23. www.metransparent.com; Dankowitz, "Saudi Writer."

24. "Saudi Women's Rights Activist Wajiha Al-Huweidar Criticizes Middle
Eastern Men, Saudi Society," Middle East Media Research Institute, Report
1815, Jan. 18, 2008.

CHAPTER 8: SATELLITE SHEIKHS AND YOUTUBE IMAMS

1. Brian Murphy, "Moderate Muslims Using Quran to Wage Counter-Jihad
against Radicals' Interpretation of Islam," Associated Press, Mar. 27, 2005.

2. Robert F. Worth, "Generation Faithful: Preaching Moderate Islam and Becoming a TV Star," *New York Times*, Jan. 3, 2009.

3. Liz Gooch, "On This Reality Show, Islam Is the Biggest Star," *New York
Times*, July 29, 2010; "Malaysia Hit Show Picks Imam Muda," Aljzeera.net,
July 31, 2010.

4. "Water-Saving campaign Addresses Saudis on Daily Quotas," Al Arabiya,
Oct. 7, 2010.

5. Laura Bashraheel, "Aim for Stars! If You Miss, You Land on the Moon,"
Arab News, Nov. 29, 2009.

6. "The Rise of the Satellite Sheikhs," interview by Brooke Gladstone, *On the
Media* radio program, NPR, June 5, 2009.

7. "The Man behind 'Khawater' Offers Words of Wisdom," *Saudi Gazette*,
Aug. 10, 2010.

8. Ali Sharaya, "Islamic Satellite Channels' Popularity Booming," *Asharq Alawsat*, May 8, 2010

9. "A Social Foothold in Egypt," *Washington Post*, Feb. 3, 2011, www.washing
    tonpost.com/wp-dyn/content/article/2011/02/02/AR2011020206329.html,
    retrieved Mar. 5, 2011.

10. "Islamic TV preacher Amr Khaled Launches Reality TV Show for Muslims,"
    Middle East News and Discussion, *Huffington Post*, Jan. 19, 2010, www
    .huffingtonpost.com/meedan/islamic-tv-preacher-amr-k_b_427794.html, re-
    trieved Mar. 5, 2011.

11. Hassan Hassan, "At Last—A Worthwhile Reality Show," *National*, Mar. 21,
    2010; Safaa Abdoun, "Mujaddidun: Not Your Typical Reality Show," *Daily
    News Egypt*, Apr. 18, 2010, www.thedailynewsegypt.com/radio-a-television/
    mujaddidun-not-your-typical-reality-show-dp2.html, retrieved Mar. 5, 2011.

12. Ursula Lindsey, "The New Muslim TV: Media-Savvy, Modern and Moder-
    ate," *Christian Science Monitor*, May 2, 2006.

CHAPTER 9: THE AXIS OF EVIL COMEDY TOUR

1. Melik Kaylan, "Arab Humor . . . No Joke," *Wall Street Journal*, May 20,
    2009.

2. Meeting in Qom "broadcast by radio Iran from Qom on 20 August 1979,"
    quoted in Amir Taheri, *The Spirit of Allah* (London: Hutchinson, 1985), 259.

3. http://islamgreatreligion.wordpress.com/2009/01/19/prophet-muhammad
    -pbuh-sense-of-humor; www.scribd.com/doc/12266330/Humour-and-Our
    -Prophet; www.articlesbase.com/humor-articles/has-the-prophet-muham
    mad-sense-of-humor-1831380.html. The Koran also mentions laughter six-
    teen times and jokes three times, albeit in a different context.

4. James Poniewozik, "Stand-up Diplomacy," *Time*, Mar. 8, 2007.

5. Mandy Stadtmiller, "Original Sultans of Comedy," *New York Post*, Nov. 20,
    2006.

6. *Stand Up: Muslim American Comics Come of Age*, produced by Glenn
    Baker and Potomac Mediaworks, PBS, May 11, 2008.

7. Ibid.

8. Roya Heydarpour, "The Comic Is Palestinian, the Jokes Bawdy," *New York
    Times*, Nov. 21, 2006.

9. *Stand Up.*

10. Ibid.

11. Judy Valente, "Muslim Comedian," *Religion and Ethics Newsweekly,* PBS, Sept. 15, 2006, www.pbs.wnet/religionandethics/week1003/feature.html.

12. Wajahat Ali, "Allah Made Me Funny Comedy Tour," *Altmuslim,* Oct. 25, 2007, www.altmuslim.com/a/a/n/2615.

13. James Reinl, " 'Jerry Seinfeld of Saudi Arabia' Stands Up in New York," *National,* Apr. 30, 2010.

14. Steve Coll, "Letter from Jedda: Young Osama. How He Learned Radicalism and May Have Seen America," *New Yorker,* Dec. 12, 2005.

15. Ibid.

16. "The Religious Affiliation of Comic Book Characters," www.comicbookreligion.com.

17. Data available on www.adherents.com/lit/comics/comic_book_religion.html and www.comicbookreligion.com.

18. Faiza Saleh Ambah, "Author Looks to the Koran for 99 New Superheroes," *Washington Post,* June 11, 2008.

19. Carole Cadwalladr, "The 99: The Islamic Superheroes Fighting Side by Side with Batman," *Guardian,* Oct. 24, 2010, www.guardian.co.uk/books/2010/oct/24/99-islamic-heroes-batman-superman, retrieved Mar. 7, 2011.

20. "Twenty Trends Sweeping the Globe," www.forbes.com/2008/01/09/internet -culture-global-forbeslife-globalpop08-cx_ee_0109pop_slide_4.html?this Speed=30000.

CHAPTER 10: JIHAD JONES AND THE KALASHNIKOV BABES

1. Interview with author, Feb. 20, 2010.

2. Lee-Anne Goodman, "Lebanese Canadian Bank Accused of Links to Hezbollah, Global Narcotics Ring," *Star,* Feb. 11, 2011, www.thestar.com/news/world/article/936192--foreign-bank-with-canadian-ties-accused-as-money -launderer, retrieved Mar. 15, 2011; "Hezbollah Uses Mexican Drug Routes into U.S.," *Washington Times,* Mar. 27, 2009, www.washingtontimes.com/news/2009/mar/27/hezbollah-uses-mexican-drug-routes-into-us/, retrieved Mar. 15, 2011; William K. Rashbaum, "United States Attorney Plans Drug-Terrorism Unit," *New York Times,* Jan. 17, 2010.

3. H. Tavakoli, "New Dark Ages," *Letters,* www.theIranian.com, Sept. 20, 1999, www.iranian.com/Letters/1999/September/gay.html.

4. Ibid.

CHAPTER 11: THE BEGINNING OF THE BEGINNING

1. "Egyptians Protest to 'Protect Revolution,' " Reuters, Apr. 1, 2011.

2. Kareem Fahim, "In the Cradle of Libya's Uprising, the Rebels Learn to Govern Themselves," *New York Times*, Feb. 24, 2011; Alexander Dziadosz, "Benghazi Holds 'Mercenaries,' Readies Defense," Reuters, Feb. 24, 2011.

3. Ibid.

4. Tara Bahrampour, "Rebels' Ragtag Army Has Heart but Lacks Organization and Training," *Washington Post*, Mar. 27, 2011.

5. "US-Yemeni Cleric: Arab Unrest Chance for al-Qaida," Associated Press, Mar. 31, 2011; Erik Stier, "Arab Revolutions Will Boost Al Qaeda, Says Radical US Cleric Awlaki," *Christian Science Monitor*, Mar. 30, 2011; Scott Shane, "Islamists Are Elated by Revolts," *New York Times*, Mar. 30, 2011.

6. James Bell. "Will Enthusiasm for Democracy Endure in Egypt and Elsewhere?" Pew Research Center Publications, Mar. 8, 2011.

7. Mariam Isa, "South Africa Unemployment Rate Slips, but Still High," *Wall Street Journal*, Feb. 8, 2011.

8. Peter Navario, "HIV/AIDS in South Africa," Council on Foreign Relations, Feb. 22, 2010, www.cfr.org/foreign-aid/hivaids-south-africa-improved -prognosis/p21492, retrieved Mar. 26, 2011; "Jacob Zuma Cleared of Rape," *Guardian*, May 8, 2006, www.guardian.co.uk/world/2006/may/08/aids .southafrica, retrieved Mar. 26, 2011.

9. Ivan Watson and Jomana Karadsheh, "The Tunisia Fruit Seller Who Kickstarted Arab Uprising," CNN, Mar. 23, 2011.

10. Ibid.

11. "In Birthplace of Arab Uprising, Discontent Lingers," Associated Press, Mar. 12, 2011; Scott Sayare, "Now Feeling Free, but Still without Work, Tunisians Look toward Europe," *New York Times*, Mar. 24, 2011.

12. Brian Whitaker, "Tunisia Analysis: Old Guard, 'New' Government," *Guardian*, Jan. 17, 2011.

13. Steve Coll, "The Casbah Coalition," *New Yorker*, Apr. 4, 2011, 34–40; Antony Faiola, "Tunisia, Site of the First Arab Revolt, Seeks a Way Forward," *Washington Post*, Mar. 3, 2011.

14. Coll, "The Casbah Coalition."

15. Alessandra Rizzo, "UN: EU Must Help Italy Cope with Refugee Crisis," Associated Press, Mar. 22, 2011; "Berlusconi: Migrants to Leave Lampedusa in 48 Hours," *BBC News*, Mar. 30, 2011, www.bbc.co.uk/news/world -europe-12903771, retrieved Mar. 30, 2011.

16. "Egypt Population," Index Mundi, www.indexmundi.com/egypt/population .html, retrieved Mar. 26, 2011.

17. Deena Kamel Yousef, "Egypt's Tourism Suffers, but Recovery Likely to Be Quick," *Gulf News*, http://gulfnews.com/business/tourism/egypt-s-tour ism-suffers-but-recovery-likely-to-be-quick-1.757312, retrieved Mar. 27, 2011; Molly Hennessy-Fiske, "Egypt: More Than 160,000 Foreigners Have Evacuated," *Los Angeles Times*, Feb. 4, 2011.

18. "Egypt Stock Exchange Plummets on Reopening," Aljazeera.net, Mar. 23, 2011, http://english.aljazeera.net/news/middleeast/2011/03/201132394030 293459.html, retrieved Mar. 27, 2011.

19. "Egyptian Women Protesters Forced to Take 'Virginity Tests,' " Amnesty International, Mar. 23, 2011. www.amnesty.org/en/news-and-updates/ egyptian-women-protesters-forced-take-'virginity-tests'-2011-03-23.

20. Lina al Wardani, "Egypt Protests against Anti-protest Law," *Ahram On-line*, Mar. 24, 2011, http://english.ahram.org.eg/NewsContent/1/64/8484/ Egypt/Politics-/Egypt-to-protest-against-antiprotest-law-.aspx, retrieved Mar. 28, 2011; "Revoke Ban on Strikes, Demonstrations," Human Rights Watch, Mar. 25, 2011, www.hrw.org/en/news/2011/03/25/egypt-revoke-ban-strikes -demonstrations, retrieved Mar. 26, 2011.

21. "Mass Demonstrations in Egypt Today," *Ahram Online*, Mar. 25, 2011, http://english.ahram.org.eg/NewsContent/1/0/8543/Egypt/0/Mass-demon strations-in-Egypt-today.aspx, retrieved Mar. 28, 2011.

22. Amro Hassan, "Egypt: Protesters Call on Military to Try Hosni Mubarak and Cronies," Babylon & Beyond Blog, *Los Angeles Times*, Apr. 8, 2011; Mona el Naggar and Michael Slackman, "Hero of Egypt's Revolution, Military Now Faces Critics," *New York Times*, Apr. 8, 2011.

23. "Yemen Corruption Assessment," U.S. Agency for International Develop-ment, Sept. 25, 2006, 6–7.

24. "Yemen Revolt: Collapsing Economy 'Is Major Threat,' " *BBC News*, Apr. 5, 2011, www.bbc.co.uk/news/world-middle-east-12976946, retrieved Apr. 6, 2011.

25. Interview with Nadia Abdulaziz al Sakkaf, editor of *Yemen Times*, on *PBS NewsHour*, "Dignity, Justice among Goals of Yemeni Protesters Seeking President's Ouster," Mar. 24, 2011.

26. Abeer Allam, "Saudi King Unveils Raft of Welfare Measures," *Financial Times*, Feb. 23, 2011.

27. Ibid.

28. Caryle Murphy, "Saudi Arabia's King Abdullah Promises $36 Billion in Ben-efits," *Christian Science Monitor*, Feb. 23, 2011, www.csmonitor.com/World/

Middle-East/2011/0223/Saudi-Arabia-s-King-Abdullah-promises-36-billion
-in-benefits, retrieved Mar. 26, 2011.

29.   Donna Abu-Nasr, "Saudi Women Inspired by Fall of Mubarak Step Up Equality
      Demand," Bloomberg, Mar. 28, 2011, www.bloomberg.com/news/2011-03
      -28/saudi-women-inspired-by-revolt-against-mubarak-go-online-to-seek
      -equality.html, retrieved Mar. 28. 2011.

30.   Allam, "Saudi King Unveils Raft of Welfare Measures."

31.   Thomas Fuller, "Next Question for Tunisia: The Role of Islam in Politics,"
      New York Times, Feb. 20, 2011; "Troops Fire in Air at Tunis Protests," *Irish
      Times*, Feb. 20, 2011, www.irishtimes.com/newspaper/breaking/2011/0220/
      breaking19.html, retrieved Apr. 6, 2011.

32.   "Survey of Tunisian Public Opinion," International Republican Institute and
      Elka Consulting, Mar. 5–18, 2011.

33.   Richard Auxier, "Egypt, Democracy and Islam," Pew Global Attitudes Proj-
      ect, Jan. 31, 2011, http://pewresearch.org/pubs/1874/egypt-protests-democ
      racy-islam-influence-politics-islamic-extremism, retrieved Mar. 26, 2011.

34.   Charles Levinson, "Splits Emerge among Egypt's Young Activists," *Wall
      Street Journal*, Feb. 17, 2011.

35.   Ibid.

36.   Carrie Rosefsky Wickham, "The Muslim Brotherhood after Mubarak," *For-
      eign Affairs*, Feb. 3, 2011, www.foreignaffairs.com/articles/67348/carrie
      -rosefsky-wick ham/the-muslim-brotherhood-after-mubarak?page=show,
      retrieved Apr. 9, 2011.

37.   "Brotherhood Sticks to Ban on Christians and Women for Presidency," *Al
      Masry al Youm*, Mar. 14, 2011, www.almasryalyoum.com/en/node/352738,
      retrieved Apr. 6, 2011; Khalil al Anani, "Brother-tarianism," *Al Masry al
      Youm*, Apr. 6, 2011, www.almasryalyoum.com/en/node/388620, retrieved
      Apr. 6, 2011; Wickham, "Muslim Brotherhood after Mubarak."

38.   Ibid.

39.   Jeffrey Fleishman, "Islamists in Egypt Seek Change through Politics," *Los
      Angeles Times*, Apr. 3, 2011.

40.   Neil MacFarquhar, "Religious Radicals' Turn to Democracy Alarms Egypt,"
      New York Times, Apr. 1, 2011.

CHAPTER 12: THE DIPLOMATIC PAS DE DEUX

1.   White House statement after events in Tunisia, Jan. 14, 2011.

 2.   President Jimmy Carter's toast to the shah of Iran in Tehran, Dec. 31, 1977,
      www.presidency.ucsb.edu/ws/?pid=7080#axzz1HaHc24gV, retrieved Mar. 25,
      2011.

3. "Remarks by President George W. Bush at the 20th anniversary of the National Endowment for Democracy, Nov. 6, 2003, www.ned.org/george-w-bush/remarks-by-president-george-w-bush-at-the-20th-anniversary, retrieved Mar. 25, 2011.

4. Scott Shane, "Cables from American Diplomats Portray U.S. Ambivalence on Tunisia," *New York Times,* Jan. 15, 2011.

5. "Biden: Mubarak Is Not a Dictator, but People Have a Right to Protest," *PBS NewsHour,* Jan. 27, 2011.

6. "Bahrain Army Demolishes Monument at Pearl Square," Associated Press, Mar. 18, 2011.

7. Amy Belasco, "The Cost of Iraq, Afghanistan, and Other Global War on Terror Operations since 9/11," Congressional Research Service, Sept. 2, 2010.

8. "Thousands March to Protest Syria Killings," *New York Times,* Mar. 24, 2011.

9. *Face the Nation,"* CBS News, Mar. 27, 2011.

10. Barack Obama, *The Audacity of Hope: Thoughts on Reclaiming the American Dream* (New York: Crown, 2006), 302.

11. Ibid.

12. Daragahi, "Tens of Thousands March Peacefully" (see Prologue, n. 17).

13. Edward Cody, "Egypt Likely to Face More Difficult Relations with Israel, U.S.," *Washington Post,* Mar. 30, 2011.

BIBLIOGRAPHY

BOOKS

Abu Zayd, Nasr. *Reformation of Islamic Thought: A Critical Historical Analysis.* Amsterdam: Amsterdam University Press, 2006.

Afary, Janet. *Sexual Politics in Modern Iran.* New York: Cambridge University Press, 2009.

Ahmed, Salman. *Rock & Roll Jihad: A Muslim Rock Star's Revolution.* New York: Free Press, 2010.

Ajami, Fouad. *Crosswinds: The Way of Saudi Arabia.* Stanford, CA: Hoover Institution Press, 2011.

———. *Dream Palace of the Arabs: A Generation's Odyssey.* New York: Vintage, 1999.

Akhtar, Shabbir. *The Quran and the Secular Mind: A Philosophy of Islam.* New York: Routledge, 2007.

Alsanea, Rajaa. *Girls of Riyadh.* New York: Penguin Press, 2005.

Ayoob, Mohammed. *The Many Faces of Political Islam: Religion and Politics in the Muslim World.* Ann Arbor: University of Michigan Press, 2007.

Badran, Margot, and Miriam Cooke. *Opening the Gates: An Anthology of Arab Feminist Writing.* 2nd ed. Bloomington: Indiana University Press, 2004.

Barber, Benjamin R. *Jihad vs. McWorld: Terrorism's Challenge to Democracy.* New York: Ballantine Books, 1996.

Barlas, Asma. *"Believing Women" in Islam: Unreading Patriarchal Interpretations of the Qur'an.* Austin: University of Texas Press, 2002.

Bergen, Peter L. *Holy War, Inc.: Inside the Secret World of Osama bin Laden.* New York: Free Press, 2002.

———. *The Longest War: The Enduring Conflict between America and Al-Qaeda.* New York: Free Press, 2011.

———. *The Osama bin Laden I Know: An Oral History of al-Qaeda's Leader.* New York: Free Press, 2006.

Blank, Jonah. *Mullahs on the Mainframe: Islam and Modernity among the Daudi Bohras.* Chicago: University of Chicago Press, 2001.

Brachman, Jarret. *Global Jihadism: Theory and Practice.* New York: Routledge, 2009.

Bunt, Gary R. *Islam in the Digital Age: E-Jihad, Online Fatwas and Cyber Islamic Environments.* Sterling, VA: Pluto Press, 2003.

——. *Muslims: Rewiring the House of Islam.* Chapel Hill: University of North Carolina Press, 2009.

Cole, Juan. *Engaging the Muslim World.* New York: Palgrave Macmillan, 2010.

Coleman, Isobel. *Paradise beneath Her Feet: How Women Are Transforming the Middle East.* New York: Random House, 2010.

Cooke, Miriam. *Women Claim Islam: Creating Islamic Feminism through Literature.* New York: Routledge, 2001.

Cooke, Miriam, and Bruce B. Lawrence, editors. *Muslim Networks from Hajj to Hip Hop.* Chapel Hill: University of North Carolina Press, 2005.

Dhillon, Navtej, and Taqik Yousef, editors. *Generation in Waiting: The Unfulfilled Promise of Young People in the Middle East.* Washington, DC: Brookings Institution Press, 2009.

Eickelman, Dale F., and Jon W. Anderson, editors. *New Media in the Muslim World: The Emerging Public Sphere.* Bloomington: Indiana University Press, 2003.

Esposito, John L. *Islam: The Straight Path.* New York: Oxford University Press, 2010.

Esposito, John L., and Dalia Mogahed. *Who Speaks for Islam? What a Billion Muslims Really Think.* New York: Gallup Press, 2007.

Fandy, Mamoun. *Saudi Arabia and the Politics of Dissent.* New York: Palgrave, 1999.

Fisk, Robert. *The Great War for Civilisation: The Conquest of the Middle East.* New York: Vintage, 2007.

Fregosi, Paul. *Jihad in the West: Muslim Conquests from the 7th to the 21st centuries.* Amherst, NY: Prometheus Books, 1998.

Garrett, Greg. *Holy Superheroes: Exploring Faith and Spirituality in Comic Books.* Colorado Springs, CO: Navpress Publishing Group, 2005.

Green, Jerrold D., editor. *Understanding Iran.* Santa Monica, CA: Rand Corporation, National Security Research Division, 2009.

Hegghammer, Thomas. *Jihad in Saudi Arabia: Violence and Pan-Islamism since 1979.* Cambridge: Cambridge University Press, 2010

Ibrahim, Raymond, editor and translator. *The al Qaeda Reader.* New York: Broadway Books, 2007.

Karam, Azza. *Women, Islamism and the State.* New York: St. Martin's Press, 1998.

Kepel, Gilles. *Beyond Terror and Martyrdom: The Future of the Middle East.* Cambridge, MA: Belknap Press of Harvard University Press, 2010.

———. *The War for Muslim Minds.* Cambridge, MA: Belknap Press of Harvard University Press, 2006.

Kepel, Gilles, and Jean-Pierre Milelli. *Al Qaeda in Its Own Words.* Cambridge, MA: Harvard University Press, 2008.

Khomeini, Ayatollah Ruhollah. *The Position of Women from the Viewpoint of Imam Khomeini.* Translated by Juliana Shaw and Behrooz Arzoo. Tehran: Institute for Compilation and Publication of Imam Khomeini's Work, 2001.

Kraidy, Marwan M. *Reality Television and Arab Politics.* New York: Cambridge University Press, 2010.

Lawrence, Bruce, editor with introduction. *Messages to the World: The Statements of Osama bin Laden.* New York: Verso, 2005.

Levine, Mark. *Heavy Metal Islam: Rock, Resistance and the Struggle for the Soul of Islam.* New York: Random House, 2008.

Lewis, Bernard. *The Crisis of Islam: Holy War and Unholy Terror.* New York: Random House, 2004.

Lewis, Bernard, Ellis Lewis, and Buntzie Ellis Churchill. *Islam: The Religion and the People.* Upper Saddle River, NJ: Wharton School Publishing, 2008.

Litwak, Robert. *Regime Change: U.S. Strategy through the Prism of 9/11.* Washington, DC: Woodrow Wilson Center Press and The Johns Hopkins University Press, 2007.

———. *Rogue States and U.S. Foreign Policy: Containment after the Cold War.* Washington, DC: Woodrow Wilson Center Press and The Johns Hopkins University Press, 2000.

MacFarquhar, Neil. *The Media Relations Department of Hizbollah Wishes You a Happy Birthday: Unexpected Encounters in the Changing Middle East.* New York: PublicAffairs, 2009.

Mansfield, Laura. *His Own Words: A Translation of the Writings of Dr. Ayman Al Zawahiri.* Old Tappan, NJ: TLG Publications, 2006.

Mohagdam, Valentine M., editor. *From Patriarchy to Empowerment: Women's Participation, Movements, and Rights in the Middle East, North Africa, and South Asia.* Syracuse, NY: Syracuse University Press, 2007.

Muravchik, Joshua. *The Next Founders: Voices of Demcracy in the Middle East.* New York: Encounter Books, 2009.

Nasr, Vali. *Forces of Fortune: The Rise of the New Muslim Middle Class and What It Will Mean for Our World.* New York: Free Press, 2009.

Rabasa, Angel, and F. Stephen Larrabee. *The Rise of Political Islam in Turkey*. Santa Monica, CA: Rand Corporation, 2008.

Rabasa, Angel, and Alan Vick, editors. *The Muslim World after 9/11*. Santa Monica, CA: Rand Corporation, 2004.

Ramadan, Tariq. *Radical Reform: Islamic Ethics and Liberation*. New York: Oxford University Press, 2008.

Roberson, B. A. *Shaping the Current Islamic Reformation*. London: Routledge, 2003.

Roy, Olivier. *The Failure of Political Islam*. Cambridge, MA: Harvard University Press, 1994.

———. *Globalized Islam: The Search for a New Ummah*. New York: Columbia University Press, 2004.

———. *Holy Ignorance: When Religion and Culture Part Ways*. New York: Columbia University Press, 2010.

———. *The Politics of Chaos in the Middle East*. New York: Columbia University Press, 2008.

———. *Secularism Confronts Islam*. New York: Columbia University Press, 2007.

Stowasser, Barbara Freyer. *Women in the Qur'an, Traditions, and Interpretation*. Oxford: Oxford University Press, 1994.

Stratton, Allegra. *Muhajababes*. New York: Melville House, 2008.

Trofimov, Yaroslav. *The Siege of Mecca: The Forgotten Uprising in Islam's Holiest Shrine and the Birth of al Qaeda*. New York: Doubleday, 2007.

Wadud, Amina. *Inside the Gender Jihad: Women's Reform in Islam*. Oxford: Oneworld Publications, 2006.

———. *Qur'an and Woman: Rereading the Sacred Text from a Woman's Perspective*. New York: Oxford University Press, 1999.

Walther, Wiebke. *Women in Islam: From Medieval to Modern Times*. Princeton, NJ: Markus Wiener, 1993.

Wilcox, Lynn. *Women and the Holy Quran: A Sufi Perspective*. Volume 1. Riverside, CA: M.T.O. Shahmaghsoudi Printing and Publication Center, 1998.

Wright, Robin. *Dreams and Shadows: The Future of the Middle East*. New York: Penguin Press, 2008.

Wright, Robin, editor. *The Iran Primer: Power, Politics, and U.S. Policy*. Washington, DC: U.S. Institute of Peace and Woodrow Wilson Center, 2010.

ARTICLES

Abramowitz, Morton, and Henri J. Barkey. "Turkey's Transformers: The AKP Sees Big." *Foreign Affairs* 88, no. 6 (2009): 118–28.

Abu Bakr, Omaima. "Islamic Feminism: What Is in a Name?" *Middle East Women's Studies Review*, Winter–Spring 2001.

Anani, Khalil al. "Jihadi Revisionism: Will It Save the World?" Middle East Brief No. 35. Brandeis University Crown Center for Middle East Studies, April 2009.

———. "The Myth of Excluding Moderate Islamists in the Arab World." Working Paper. Saban Center for Middle East Policy at the Brookings Institution, March 4, 2010

Anderson, Perry. "After Kemal." *London Review of Books*, September 25, 2008.

Barkey, Henri J. "Turkey's Moment of Inflection." *Survival* 52, no. 3 (June–July 2010): 39–50.

Bayan, Zeyno. "Turkey Divided." *Journal of Democracy* 19, no. 1 (January 2008): 55–69.

Bergen, Peter. "Bin Laden's Lonely Crusade." *Vanity Fair*, January 2011.

Bergen, Peter, and Paul Cruickshank. "The Unraveling: al Qaeda's Revolt against Bin Laden." *New Republic*, June 11, 2008, www.tnr.com/print/article/the-unraveling.

Boucek, Christopher. "Saudi Arabia's Soft Counterterrorism Strategy: Prevention, Rehabilitation, and Aftercare." Carnegie Papers No. 97. Carnegie Endowment for International Peace, September 2008.

———. "Saudis Nip Extremism in the Bud." *Asia Times*, August 18, 2007.

Byman, Daniel. "Talking with Insurgents: A Guide for the Perplexed." *Washington Quarterly*, April 2009, 125–37.

Cilluffo, Frank J., and F. Jordan Evert. "Reflections on Jihad: A Former Leader's Perspective." Homeland Security Policy Institute, October 16, 2009.

Coll, Steve. "Letter from Jedda: Young Osama: How He Learned Radicalism, and May Have Seen America." *New Yorker*, December 12, 2005.

Dankowitz, A. "Saudi Writer and Journalist Wajeha al Huwaider Fights for Women's Rights." MEMRI Inquiry and Analysis Series, no. 312, December 28, 2006.

Demiralp, Seda, and Todd A. Eisenstadt. "Prisoner Erdogan's Dilemma and the Origins of Moderate Islam in Turkey." Department of Government, American University, August 31, 2006, www1.american.edu/ia/cdem/pdfs/case_study_2 .pdf. Retrieved February 23, 2011.

Doumato, Eleanor Abdella. "Gender, Islam and the Saudi State: Gulf War Perspectives." Chapter in *Continuity and Change: Women at the End of the Twentieth Century*. Columbia International Affairs Online, 16–24.

Eickelman, Dale F. "The Coming Transformation in the Muslim World." *Current History,* January 2000, 16–20.

Esfandiari, Haleh, and Margot Badran, editors. "Reformist Women Thinkers in the Islamic World." Woodrow Wilson International Center for Scholars Middle East Program Occasional Papers, Spring 2009.

Fernea, Elizabeth. "The Challenges for Middle Eastern Women in the 21st Century." *Middle East Journal* 54, no. 2 (Spring 2000): 185–93.

Hammond, Andrew. "Reading Lohaidan in Riyadh: Media and the Struggle for Judicial Power in Saudi Arabia." *Arab Media & Society* 7 (Winter 2009).

Hamzawy, Amr. "The Key to Arab Reform: Moderate Islamists." Policy Brief #40, Carnegie Endowment for International Peace, August 2005.

Hegghammer, Thomas. "The Failure of Jihad in Saudi Arabia." West Point Combating Terrorism Center Occasional Paper Series, February 25, 2010.

Huntington, Samuel. "The Clash of Civilizations." *Foreign Affairs* 72, no. 3 (Summer 1993): 22–49.

International Crisis Group. "Turkey and the Middle East: Ambitions and Constraints." Europe Report No. 203, April 7, 2010.

Jacobson, Michael. "Learning from Dropouts." *Foreign Policy,* February 2, 2010.

———. "Terrorism Drop-outs: One Way of Promoting a Counter-Narrative." *Perspectives on Terrorism* 3, issue 2 (August 2009): 12–27.

Jones, Toby Craig. "The Clerics, the Sahwa and the Saudi State." *Strategic Insights* 4, no. 3 (March 2005).

Keiswetter, Allen. "Political Islam: A Primer for the Perplexed." *Foreign Service Journal,* April 2008.

Knaus, Katharina. "Turkish Women: A Century of Change." *Turkish Policy Quarterly* 6, no. 5 (2007): 47–59.

Lewis, Bernard. "The Roots of Muslim Rage." *Atlantic Monthly* 266 (September 1990), www.theatlantic.com/magazine/archive/1990/09/the-roots-of-muslim-rage/4643/.

McCary, John A. "The Anbar Awakening: An alliance of Incentives." *Washington Quarterly,* January 2009, 43–59.

Mir-Hosseini, Ziba. "Muslim Women's Quest for Equality: Between Islamic Law and Feminism." *Critical Inquiry* 32, no. 4 (2006): 629–45.

Moll, Yasmin. "Islamic Televangelism: Religion, Media and Visuality in Contemporary Egypt." *Arab Media & Society* 10 (Spring 2010).

Ottaway, David. "The Arab Tomorrow." *Wilson Quarterly,* Winter 2010, 48–64.

Ottaway, Marina. "Women's Rights and Democracy in the Arab World." Carnegie

Endowment for International Peace Middle East Series, Democracy and Rule of Law Project, no. 42, February 2004.

Ottaway, Marina, and Omayma Abdellatif. "Women in Islamist Movements: Toward an Islamist Model of Women's Activism." Carnegie Endowment for International Peace, Carnegie Papers No. 2, June 2007.

Ozdalga, Elisabeth. "The Hidden Arab: A Critical Reading of the Notion of 'Turkish Islam.' " *Middle Eastern Studies* 42, no. 4 (July 2006): 551–70.

Rausch, Margaret J. "Women Spiritual Guides (Mourchidate) in Morocco: Agents of Change." Work in Progress 2010, www.yale.edu/macmillan/africadissent/rausch.pdf.

Rid, Thomas. "Cracks in al Qaeda." *Wilson Quarterly*, Winter 2010, 40–47.

Roy, Olivier. "This Is Not an Islamic Revolution." *New Statesman* 140, no. 5040 (February 14, 2011): 24.

Rubin, Judith Colp. "Lagging Far Behind: Women in the Middle East." *Middle East Review of International Affairs* 11, no. 2 (June 2007).

Sontag, Deborah. "The Erdogan Experiment." *New York Times Magazine*, May 11, 2003.

Swedenberg, Ted. "Islamic Hip-Hop versus Islamophobia: Aki Nawaz, Natacha Atlas, Akhenaton." In *Global Noise: Rap and Hip-hop outside the USA*. Tony Mitchell, editor. Middletown, CT: Wesleyan University Press, 2002.

Takeyh, Ray, and Nikolas K. Gvosdev. "Radical Islam: The Death of an Ideology?" *Middle East Policy* 11, no. 4 (Winter 2004).

Taspinar, Omar. "Turkey's Middle East Policies: Between Neo-Ottomanism and Kemalism." Carnegie Endowment for International Peace, Carnegie Papers No. 10, September 2008.

Thumann, Michael. "Turkey's Role Reversals." *Wilson Quarterly*, Summer 2010, 28–33.

Venhaus, John M. "Why Youth Join al Qaeda." Special Report No. 236, United States Institute of Peace, May 2010.

Wagner, Rob. "Rehabilitation and Deradicalization: Saudi Arabia's Counterterrorism Successes and Failures." Peace and Conflict Special Report, August 1, 2010.

Wilson, G. Willow. "The Show-Me Sheikh." *Atlantic*, July–August 2005.

Yaphe, Judith S., editor. "Nuclear Politics in Iran." *Middle East Security Perspectives Series, No. 1*, Center for Strategic Research, Institute for National Strategic Studies, National Defense University, Washington, DC, April 2010.

INDEX